STRATFORD-UPON-AVON STUDIES 9

General Editors

JOHN RUSSELL BROWN
& BERNARD HARRIS

171

Already published in this series:

STRATFORD-UPON-AVON STUDIES 9

ELIZABETHAN THEATRE

EDWARD ARNOLD (PUBLISHERS) LTD

41 Maddox Street, London W.1

Contents

Plates

Acknowledgements

THE editors and publisher wish to express their thanks to the Folger Shakespeare Library for permission to reproduce Plate I, and to the Honourable Society of Gray's Inn for permission to reproduce Plate II. Acknowledgement is also made to Professor Madeleine Doran for permission to reproduce a passage from *Endeavors of Art*.

Preface

TEN authors have collaborated for this latest volume of *Stratford-upon-Avon Studies* to investigate the theatre in which Shakespeare first worked. There are single chapters on Marlowe, Kyd, Lyly and Jonson, obvious landmarks in a difficult terrain of minor authors, anonymous plays, garbled or shortened texts, lost plays, uncertain authorship. But equal emphasis is upon lesser known works, general influences, and the prejudices and expectations of audiences. Some plays that were famous in their own day, like *Cambises* or *Mucedorus*, are not readily accorded a serious reading today, and never a professional performance; to these several chapters refer from varying points of view. The object is to lead the reader into the tangled, thriving world of the Elizabethan Theatre.

Despite important research in recent years, there are obstinate difficulties in this subject. A more precise chronology is needed, and better and more usable texts. The further a critic steps outside the Shakespearian pale, the more his judgement and knowledge will be challenged. No satisfactory general study of Thomas Kyd exists in English although his power to stimulate his contemporaries is as much beyond doubt as his ability to provoke spirited disagreement today. In his chapter on Marlowe in this present volume, Nicholas Brooke reports that the 'ways divide' for critics, 'not simply on how good a play Marlowe wrote, but on what *sort* of play.' The collaborative form of *Stratford-upon-Avon Studies* is therefore particularly suitable for this subject: each chapter uses a different approach, and each pursues its course as far as its factual basis and the author's experience can reach.

The volume starts with D. J. Palmer's account of tragic heroes and so opens a wide tract of time and a central concern of almost all Elizabethan dramatists. References to morality plays and interludes are taken further in the next chapter by T. W. Craik, who traces the enduring influence of these plays. Jonas A. Barish then develops a subsidiary theme of both earlier chapters, that of style; he writes of the dramatists' inheritance of rhetorical expertise and analyses closely the varieties of style within Kyd's *Spanish Tragedy*. Two further chapters are concerned with general influences: 'The Court and the Dramatists' by Marion Jones, and 'Plautus: the formal influence' by Richard Hosley. Both Brooke and Hosley are concerned with stagecraft, and this interest is followed by Jocelyn Powell in an account of the audience appeal of Lyly's fantastic and elaborate comedies. Dramatic structure is discussed by Patricia Russell with reference to the romantic narrative plays of the 1570's and 1580's, and by John Meagher in an account of the Huntingdon plays of Anthony Mundy—the dramatist who in 1598 was given the title of 'our best plotter'; in this chapter a new appraisal of literary and theatrical sources is used to reveal accepted dramatic principles. The volume concludes with Edward Partridge's account of the first years of Ben Jonson's career as a dramatist: a deliberate and sustained progress to set against many short-lived and some wild careers of earlier writers.

The theme of volume 3 of *Stratford-upon-Avon Studies* is *Early Shakespeare* and therefore while not ignoring Shakespeare—which would be impossible—our present contributors have been encouraged to present him in relation to general influences and rival dramatists, rather than for his own sake. The *Early Shakespeare* volume includes R. A. Foakes' account of 'the profession of playwright' and the conditions of his work, and Norman Sanders' comparison of Greene's romantic comedies with Shakespeare's; these topics are not re-considered, except by the way, in this volume of the series. Nor are some developments that look forward to the theatre of the next decade or two: such are the domestic tragedy of *Arden of Faversham* and *A Woman Killed with Kindness*, or the earliest works of Dekker. Necessarily some chapters do lead into the Jacobean period, but we wanted the book to be centred on the specifically Elizabethan elements of English theatre.

Each chapter has been provided with a prefatory note which gives factual information related to its subject, and a guide for further reading and study. The texts quoted in each chapter are specified here, and the titles of scholarly and critical works referred to later in shortened form, usually by author only. Texts used are the most responsible which are generally available; some have modernised and some 'old' spelling, but we have always used *u* and *v*, and *i* and *j*, in accordance with modern usage. Shakespeare is quoted from Peter Alexander's edition (1958). 'M.S.R.' stands for Malone Society Reprint and 'T.F.T.' for

Tudor Facsimile Text; titles of Shakespeare's plays are abbreviated as in C. T. Onion's *A Shakespeare Glossary* (ed. 1941).

The tenth volume of *Stratford-upon-Avon Studies* will be *American Theatre*, and further volumes are in preparation on *Victorian Poetry* and *Contemporary Criticism*.

JOHN RUSSELL BROWN
BERNARD HARRIS

Note

Scholarship and Criticism. W. Farnham's *The Medieval Heritage of Elizabethan Tragedy* (1936; second edition, 1956) is probably still the best general discussion of pre-Shakespearian tragedy and its antecedents. M. Doran in *Endeavors of Art* (1954; paperback ed., 1964) studies the basis of Elizabethan drama in Renaissance critical theory. W. Clemen's *English Tragedy before Shakespeare* (tr. 1961) is chiefly concerned with the set speech, but often illuminates the development of dramatic techniques before 1600. H. Baker's *Induction to Tragedy* (1939) seeks to qualify the usual estimate of Seneca's influence, and illustrates, with particular reference to *Gorboduc*, the complexity of literary influences which contributed to sixteenth-century tragic style. An account of the Renaissance interest in Seneca's plays is to be found in the Introduction to *The Poetical Works of Sir William Alexander*, ed. L. E. Kastner and H. B. Charlton (1921); and more recent material is contained in *Les Tragédies de Sénèque et le Théatre de la Renaissance*, ed. J. Jacquot (1964). Also relevant are M. C. Bradbrook's *Themes and Conventions of Elizabethan Tragedy* (1935; paperback ed., 1960); E. M. Waith's *The Herculean Hero* (1962); H. Craig's essay, 'The Shackling of Accidents', *Philological Quarterly* (1940), reprinted in *Elizabethan Drama: Modern Essays in Criticism*, ed. R. J. Kaufmann (1961); and two articles by S. F. Johnson, 'The Tragic Hero in Early Elizabethan Drama' (*Studies in English Renaissance Drama*, ed. J. W. Bennett, O. Cargill and V. Hall, 1959), and '*The Spanish Tragedy* or Babylon Revisited' (*Essays on Shakespeare and Elizabethan Drama in Honour of Hardin Craig*, ed. R. Hosley, 1963). Further references are contained in A. Brown's review of 'Studies in Elizabethan and Jacobean Drama since 1900', *Shakespeare Survey* (1961).

Texts. Seneca His Ten Tragedies, English translations edited by T. Newton (1581) is available in the Tudor Translations series (1927). *Early English Classical Tragedies* are edited by J. W. Cunliffe (1912). *Cambises* is printed in Vol. iv of *Dodsley's Old Plays*, ed. W. C. Hazlitt (1874) and in *Chief Pre-Shakespearean Dramas*, ed. J. Q. Adams (1924); it is quoted in this chapter from the Tudor Facsimile Text (1910). *The Interlude of Vice* [*Horestes*] is quoted from the M.S.R. (1962), and *The Tide Tarrieth for No Man* from the T.F.T. (1910).

(References to Kyd and Marlowe will be found preceding Chapters III and IV.)

I

Elizabethan Tragic Heroes

D. J. PALMER

★

THE blood which flows so copiously from the heroes of Elizabethan tragedy is as mixed as their complex descent from medieval and classical ancestry, yet they exemplify in their careers a consistent, universal pattern of divine and human justice. Tragedy was understood by the Elizabethans to teach, and its characteristic lesson was an affirmation of God's goodness and power in punishing the wicked and avenging the righteous. However heterogeneous was the literary grist which came to their mill, they leavened it with their own preconceptions and used it to enforce their tragic moralising. Yet this admonitory intent, more grossly palpable in the plays of the early part of the period, did not necessarily produce a simplified attitude to good and evil: much recent commentary upon Elizabethan tragedy, including the debate about *Tamburlaine*, is perhaps misled by the assumption that a dramatic plot can be reduced to one or other of the common places of sixteenth-century moral doctrine. All Elizabethan tragedies in fact try to illustrate several lessons at once, by incorporating within their actions a whole series of tragic catastrophes, each with its own significance. From this point of view, therefore, the most appropriate kind of tragic hero for the Elizabethan dramatist was the figure whose progress through the play would involve as many other characters as possible, so providing opportunities for emphasising a maximum number of moral lessons. The better playwrights, of course, managed to reconcile this taste for multiplicity with dramatic unity, but it did frequently produce inconsistent characterisation of the hero, and it certainly complicated the treatment of good and evil, since one man's crime was often another's just desert.

Even in the apparently exceptional case of Marlowe, who subordinates the moral issues of his plays to a somewhat metaphysical conception of motivation and conflict, the Elizabethan tragic hero is presented in terms of a scheme which accepts a rational and just basis for life. His plays, like those of his contemporaries, draw so much of their tragic authority from that profound awareness of humanity's mediate place between the angels and the beasts, and therefore of man's capacity for both transcendent glory and degradation. Marlowe does not contradict the more conventional teaching of other dramatists, that evil and catastrophe are explicable according to orthodox Christian belief; scepticism or a sense of an indifferent heaven may be permitted to heathens, villains, or those in despair, but such attitudes are never endorsed by the tragic scheme. It is the insistence upon tragedy as the working out of a just, ethical plan which ascribes to the Elizabethan hero a much greater scope in his control over his circumstances and in his exercise of free will than either Seneca or the medieval tragedies of Fortune afforded. The tragic conflict in Elizabethan drama is precipitated by human forces, and, particularly in the plays of Kyd, Marlowe and their successors, the situations are resolved at the level of character, often where the hero believes he is acting as the instrument of divine purpose. As a dramatic figure, he develops within a tradition in which to an increasing degree he is responsible for, and aware of, his destiny. While Chaucer and Lydgate had shown how pride, ambition, and other worldly sins greased the wheel of Fortune, the more typical Elizabethan emphasis upon moral responsibility is first reflected by the *Mirror for Magistrates* (1559). Here the world of the mighty is made insecure not by the blind operations of an external force, but by their own unrestrained lusts or neglect of true allegiance.

To the sixteenth century, Senecan tragedy also appeared to represent this moralised pattern of crime and punishment: one of the main difficulties in estimating Seneca's influence is their tendency to read him in the light of their own beliefs. The vindictive and arbitrary interventions of his deities, for instance, were grossly misrepresented in order to reconcile his teaching with the Christian scheme of heavenly justice, and Alexander Nevile, translating the *Oedipus* in 1563, attributed the fate of his hero to a divine judgement that is more biblical than stoic:

> Marke thou rather what is ment by the whole course of the History
> ... the right high and immortall God, will never leave such horrible
> and detestable crimes unpunished.

> ('Preface to the Reader.')

Seneca was revered first and foremost as a moralist; no other pagan writer, according to Thomas Newton in his dedication of the *Ten Tragedies* in 1581, 'more sensibly, pithily, and bytingly layeth doune the guerdon of filthy lust, cloaked dissimulation and odious treachery.' As far as the Elizabethans were concerned, Seneca showed wickedness bringing down destruction upon its own head, and he taught them to motivate this wickedness through passions like those that convulse his characters. Ambition, the lust for revenge, and sexual passion are the chief sources of Elizabethan tragic action, and the means for making character morally responsible in the dramatic scheme. From Seneca also came such rhetorical devices as the pithy *sententiae* and the speeches of lamentation and suffering which serve to heighten the sense of tragic loss and outrage. Seneca's concern with the ruler and his exercise of power naturally coincided with the Elizabethan interest in courts and princes, and with the traditional idea that the subject of tragedy ought to be a figure of high estate. Admired for his doctrine, therefore, Seneca also exerted his influence upon dramatic method.

The influence of Seneca was fertile where the ground was ready to receive him, but although seven of the ten plays then thought to be his were translated between 1559 and 1566, he was only one of the complex and disparate elements which converged in the development of the Elizabethan tragic hero. Medieval romance, the conventions of courtly pageants and the morality interludes, the Bible and Virgil, were also absorbed with that astonishing aptitude of the Elizabethans for harmonising the most alien and miscellaneous literary and philosophical models. The principal 'types' of tragic character were already established by the 1570's; the cunning villain, the cruel tyrant, the bereaved lover or parent, the conquering hero and the avenger, combined with each other in all possible ways, had made their appearances on the popular stage or in the academic drama. Yet the tragedies of the 1560's seem very remote as predecessors of Kyd and Marlowe, partly no doubt because so few plays have survived from the intervening years. The fact remains that the two later dramatists were received by their contemporaries as great originals, inaugurating a new phase of Elizabethan tragedy. They transformed the drama, to put it as briefly as possible, by their invention of the ironic method, and by their introduction of a plot-structure in which the final catastrophe is derived from the inner logic of character and situation, and comes as the dénouement to set the action in perspective. The plays of Kyd and

Marlowe express their judgements through irony, and their protagonists are distinguished from the earlier heroes by that greater measure of
awareness which endows them with spiritual grandeur. The later
dramatists greatly reduce the amount of undramatic exposition and
overt moralising which were features of primitive Elizabethan tragedy;
triumph and catastrophe are conceived in the particularised images of
the action, needing no reference to a larger world beyond the dramatised situation. Hieronimo and the Marlovian heroes are at the centre
of a situation which is not fixed and static, defining them immediately
as in the earlier tragedies, but which bears them forwards towards the
resolution that is needed to complete the judgement upon them. In
short, Kyd and Marlowe present a new conception of the hero, not
as a psychological or moral type, but as the dramatic embodiment of
the tragic vision.

*   *   *

The earliest Elizabethan tragedies, like their antecedents, are dramatic
homilies. Their plots are used as *exempla* to reinforce the admonitions
of the moralist, and this emphasis determines their formal characteristics
as much as their predilection for certain themes. In the Inns of Court
tragedies, the action is divided into a series of separate situations and
episodes; there is no central figure identified with the tragic issues,
which are often presented and resolved by direct commentary and
exposition. The moral scheme governing the action is not derived from
dramatic situation, and it exists independently of the characterisation.
Gorboduc (1561) is the first of these tragedies, and like its successors
Jocasta (1566) and *The Misfortunes of Arthur* (1588), its subject is civil
war. But if Gorboduc's division of his kingdom, and the subsequent
disorder, invite comparison with *King Lear*, this serves to stress that
Gorboduc is a political debate, not a play about human suffering. The
king is no more the protagonist than either of his sons, Ferrex or
Porrex, who gave their names to the title of the play in its second print-
ing. The play lacks a hero, possibly because like *Jocasta* it is conceived
on Senecan lines as the tragedy of a family; the theme of ambition
and the suddenness of the reversals recall Seneca, but the Senecan
interest in passion and suffering is subordinated to the oratory of debate
and the rhetoric of the council chamber. Good and evil counsellors
flanking the chief characters resemble allegorical figures in a morality
play more closely than the confidants of Seneca. Consequently the

tragic figures are presented separately, each holding the stage in turn, and each has only a partial view of the total action, determined by his particular situation. Later Elizabethan tragedy was to exploit such limited awareness with dramatic irony, but there is no real tragic inevitability in *Gorboduc*, since the moral and political lesson is precisely that this tragedy need never have happened at all. The dramatic action is set in a wider perspective to show that wisdom and foresight can avert disaster: its contemporary application to the succession issue strictly qualifies its value as drama.

Such a conception of tragedy is unpropitious for the creation of a tragic hero. But, as Sir Philip Sidney recognised, *Gorboduc* claims our respect, if not our affection, for establishing a dignified and solemn rhetoric as the medium of tragic speech. The fourteener used by the translators of Seneca, and surviving on the popular stage after *Gorboduc*, is too awkward a unit to control, and it usually breaks down into a jingle of six and eight, contorting the syntax and depending too heavily upon alliteration to bind it together. The ten-syllable line of *Gorboduc*, probably suggested by the heroical and sententious pieces in the same metre from Tottel's Miscellany (1557), is a more articulate vehicle than anything previously heard in English drama, and later dramatists stood indebted to Norton and Sackville for the basic sobriety and decorum which they gave to tragic poetry. As Sackville's 'Induction' shows in the 1563 edition of the *Mirror for Magistrates*, it was the imitation of Virgil's epic style as much as the admiration of Seneca's impassioned rhetoric which contributed towards the evolution of that sombre gravity and stately eloquence considered by the Elizabethans appropriate for tragedy.

Some of the more spectacular dramas performed at Court in the 1560's do present the central figure of a hero, but he remains the puppet of the moralist illustrating the judgements of providence upon the wicked. Thomas Preston's *Cambises* (*c.* 1561), correctly described on its title page as a 'lamentable tragedy', displays a cruel tyrant in a series of loosely-connected *exempla*, until his career is abruptly terminated by what is held to be a miraculous intervention of divine justice in human affairs. Cambises is a near cousin of the tyrants in *Appius and Virginia* and *Damon and Pythias*, and a descendant of the Herod in the mystery cycles: if he bears a slight resemblance to that other oriental despot, Tamburlaine, it only serves to contrast the limited awareness of the early character with the magnificent vision and insight of Marlowe's hero, confronting his destiny. So swift and unexpected is the punishment which overtakes Cambises that the play produces no tragic crisis; crime and punishment are not directly related to each other as they were to become for later villains. Though he falls upon his own sword, he is not hoist with his own petard. The very looseness of the dramatic structure, however, reveals the emergence of tragedy from the form of the morality. *Cambises* illustrates the gradual eman-cipation of the interlude hero from the Vice: the tyrant is wicked enough himself to dispense with the professional attentions of personified evil. The Vice Ambidexter therefore has to keep company with Huff, Ruff and Snuff for most of the time, much to the play's detriment.

A similar intermediate stage in the development from morality play to tragedy in the 1560's is represented by John Pickering's *Interlude of Vice* or *Horestes* (1567). This classical revenge story is taken from Caxton's medievalised version of the Trojan legends, and the play is coloured by the romantic traditions of courtly love, knightly honour, and spectacular battles:

> Go make your lively battel and let it be longe eare you can win ye
> Citie and when you have won it let Horestes bringe out his mother
> by the arme and let ye droum cease playing and the trumpet, also
> when she is taken let her knele downe and speake.

Such diversions do not suffice to make it a good play, but Horestes is of considerable interest as one of the earliest revenge heroes in Eliza-bethan tragedy. He first appears with a speech that poses his moral dilemma: he must avenge his father, but recoils from killing his mother. The problem is immediately resolved for him in the same scene by the assurance of the Vice, disguised as Courage, who claims to have been sent by the gods to give Horestes their command to exact vengeance. Horestes thus overcomes his scruples, and with commendable piety and the aid of Idumeus, he defeats Egistus and Clytemnestra in battle, dispatches them to a speedy execution, and ascends the throne himself. The tragic lesson in the retribution overtaking Egistus and Clytemnestra is obvious, but Pickering has added considerable confusion to his story by deliberately departing from the source to suggest that Horestes is deceived in his belief that he is the instrument of heavenly justice. In adapting Caxton for the stage, he has given the Vice his traditional rôle in misleading the hero, and possibly he wished to show thereby that private vengeance is a crime. But after the Vice has been allowed to trick Horestes in such a vital issue, the play seems nevertheless to endorse the hero's sense of righteousness, and indeed almost goes out of its way to uphold his honourable motivation, as in Caxton. Horestes' debate with Nature serves to reaffirm that the will of the gods must overrule natural law, and at his subsequent trial he defends himself by successfully convincing his accusers:

> I never went, revengment for to do
> On fathers fose tyll by the godes, I was commaund there to,
> Whose heaste no man dare once refuse, but wyllingly obaye.
> (l. 1154)

The play ends triumphantly with Horestes' marriage to the daughter of Menelaus and his coronation by Truth and Duty.

There is no ironic exploitation of Horestes' deception by the Vice, and the episode is not referred to in the subsequent action. His goodness itself, and his faith in the gods, are the very means which the Vice uses under false pretences. Horestes is no villain, but clearly the pattern of dutiful and heroic knighthood. This method of initiating the revenge action simply allows the presentation of Horestes as the just and pious hero, without committing the play to sharing his belief in divine sanction. A parallel might be found in *The Misfortunes of Arthur*, where Arthur is idealised as a just king, although his death is a retribution brought about by the embodiment of his own sin in his wicked son Mordred. Urging Horestes to revenge by supernatural soliciting of an ambiguous kind, the Vice corresponds to the ghost of Hamlet's father in his function; but Hamlet's scepticism served him well, and, like Hieronimo receiving Bel-imperia's letter, he sought grounds more relative than the zealous Horestes evidently supposed necessary. It is, however, the contrast in structure between *Horestes* and *The Spanish Tragedy* which reveals their different conceptions of the tragic hero. The ambiguity which in the earlier play is little more than a morally evasive stage-device for precipitating the action becomes in Kyd the basic situation and the source of tragic conflict. Both heroes are good men, unable to act without the belief that they are performing the will of heaven; but whereas the dilemma of Horestes is resolved in a moment by a device which leaves his characterisation unaffected, Hieronimo undergoes a prolonged and terrible agony in his search for divine judgement. This contrast in awareness, in the use of character as the medium of tragic vision, and in the potential effectiveness of

B

ironic situations, epitomises the difference between the tragic heroes of Kyd and Marlowe and their predecessors.

*   *   *

Hieronimo plays only a secondary part in the first Act of *The Spanish Tragedy*, and indeed his situation resembles that of a minor character in Seneca, extended to heroic proportions. The figure of the bereaved father is paralleled in other tragedies by those witnesses of calamity who appear briefly but lament at length the victims of human wickedness or divine wrath. But Hieronimo's grief is not used to heighten Lorenzo's villainy or Horatio's untimely death, and as he emerges in the course of the action as the tragic hero himself, it becomes apparent Hieronimo's antecedents are more biblical than Senecan in character. He is the just and upright servant of God, suddenly overtaken by a catastrophe which leaves him so utterly destitute of redress that he almost despairs of God's justice. The play is about Hieronimo's quest for justice, and his tragic sufferings recall those of Job. Biblical echoes reverberate through the tragedy: Hieronimo's impassioned appeals to heaven are not merely rhetorical gestures of affliction and outrage; they are prayers, and they derive more from the lamentations of the psalmist than from the Senecan set speech. At times indeed, the authority of the Bible seems to be used in deliberate contradiction of Seneca: Hieronimo's *'Vindicta mihi'* ('Vengeance is mine, I will repay, saith the Lord') is as brilliant a substitution in context as the much-praised *'O lente, lente currite, noctis equi'* from Ovid in the last speech of Marlowe's Faustus.

Biblical ideas and imagery, particularly from the Old Testament, are encountered throughout Elizabethan tragedy frequently enough, since the Bible is the record of God's judgements and of the way providence works through human affairs. Usually, however, Biblical authority provides the simple scheme of absolutes according to which wickedness is overthrown and justice reasserted. But *The Spanish Tragedy* takes from the Bible itself a situation in which divine justice seems to neglect its office: like that of Job, Hieronimo's very trust in the ways of heaven is made the grounds for his agony, since he presumes too far in his faith that heaven will act according to his prayers. The wisdom and justice of God cannot be measured by human wisdom and law. The play does not directly deal with God's punishment of murder: its subject is Hieronimo, and we see him first claiming the help of God, then giving way to despair in his impatience, and determining to take matters into his own hands, though finally he accomplishes his vengeance in the belief that he is an agent of God's judgement. He ends not as a villain, therefore, turning away from God, but as the righteous man, trusting that he is accomplishing the will of heaven.

The progressive movement of the action makes Kyd's intentions clear enough. Hieronimo first vows vengeance as he takes up Horatio's bloody handkerchief. There is no need to assume that he means more than a determination to bring the murderers to justice, but he must first discover the identity of the villains, and when he next appears, it is to heaven that he looks for help:

> O sacred heavens! if this unhallow'd deed,
> If this inhuman and barbarous attempt,
> If this incomparable murder thus
> Of mine, but now no more my son,
> Shall unreveal'd and unrevenged pass,
> How should we term your dealings to be just,
> If you unjustly deal with those that in your justice trust?
>
> (III. ii. 5)

He is plagued by evil thoughts which he knows to be the temptations of hell:

> The ugly fiends do sally forth of hell,
> And frame my steps to unfrequented paths,
> And fear my heart with fierce inflamed thoughts.
>
> (III. ii. 16)

But at the end of this speech, as if in answer to his appeal for 'some man, some mean', the letter from Bel-imperia mysteriously falls at his feet, and he reads that Lorenzo is the murderer. Instead of taking this as a sign of heavenly aid, however, he suspects a trap, and determines to seek confirmation of Bel-imperia's testimony. At the trial of Pedringano, it is still 'by justice of the heavens' that he awaits 'To know the cause that may my cares allay', yet in the following scene he verges upon despair, since his prayers, that

> Beat at the windows of the brightest heavens,
> Soliciting for justice and revenge,
>
> (III. vii. 13)

have seemingly gone unanswered. Immediately he ceases speaking, the

Hangman brings him the letter from Pedringano to Lorenzo, which contains the confirmation of Bel-imperia's note. He also recognises that now God has already punished one of Horatio's murderers through the execution of his own judgement upon Pedringano:

> I ne'er could find
> Till now, and now I feelingly perceive,
> They did what heaven unpunish'd would not leave.
>   (III. vii. 54)

The scene ends as he decides to bring his case before the king, having now secured sufficient proof to condemn Lorenzo. But at his next appearance, with poniard and rope, he contemplates suicide, fearing that his enemies at Court will prevent him from approaching the King. Realising that with his death, Horatio's murder will go unavenged, he resolves once again to see the King, who enters with his retinue and the Portuguese ambassador. The ransom for Balthazar has been brought for Horatio, which, despite Lorenzo's attempts to silence him, gives Hieronimo his cue to pantomime with savage irony his search for Horatio beneath the ground ('He diggeth with his dagger'). He turns to Hell as he leaves the bewildered courtiers:

> For I'll go marshal up the fiends in hell,
> To be avenged on you all for this.
>   (III. xii. 77)

Thwarted in his attempt to obtain justice by due process of law, Hieronimo opens the next scene with the crucial soliloquy in which he determines to take matters into his own hands, by feigning a calm indifference that will enable him to await a suitable opportunity: 'Till to revenge thou know, when, where, and how'. The soliloquy is sometimes obscure, because Hieronimo is given to speaking in hints and cryptic threats; but as the last line suggests, although he has now chosen not to leave all to providence, he has as yet no plan of murder, and he is still dependent upon the advent of propitious circumstances. He has learned a new and terrible patience, which nevertheless collapses temporarily when he confronts Don Bazulto, the old man whose son has also been murdered. Finally, Bel-imperia is released to join forces with Hieronimo at the beginning of the fourth Act, and as he learns for the first time that she too desires revenge, her support seems to him a sign that heaven is taking a hand in their plans:

> But may it be that Bel-imperia
> Vows such revenge as she hath deign'd to say?
> Why then, I see that heaven applies our drift,
> And all the saints do sit soliciting
> For vengeance on those cursed murderers.
>
> (IV. i. 30)

The scheme of divine justice which governs the action is not abstracted and presented in general terms as in earlier Elizabethan tragedy, but is enacted through the concrete situations of the play. It is revealed by the timely appearance of the letters, by the ironies of the plot, and even by Hieronimo's tormented impatience, as a providence which moves mysteriously and circuitously to encompass its designs. Hieronimo's eventual assumption of a cunning pretence of indifference mirrors the indirect methods of providential justice itself. Hieronimo's revenge is also the instrument of Don Andrea's revenge, and the concept which underlies these supernatural subterfuges is expressed in the dialogue between Andrea's ghost and the Spirit of Revenge at the close of the third Act: Andrea is alarmed that his own vengeance will be frustrated by Hieronimo's show of friendship with Lorenzo in the scene which has just concluded:

> ANDREA.   Awake, Revenge, or we are woe-begone!
> REVENGE.   Thus worldlings ground, what they have dream'd, upon.
> Content thyself, Andrea; though I sleep,
> Yet is my mood soliciting their souls:
> Sufficeth thee that poor Hieronimo
> Cannot forget his son Horatio.
> Nor dies Revenge although he sleep awhile,
> For in unquiet, quietness is feign'd,
> And slumb'ring is a common worldly wile.
>
> (III. xv. 17)

Perhaps Andrea himself has been dozing, since he fails to recognise Hieronimo's stratagem; but our knowledge of the truth enables us to corroborate the assurance of Revenge. The origin of this brief episode is biblical, and it illuminates the whole play: 'Awake, why sleepest thou, O Lord? Arise, cast us not off forever' (Psalm 44, v. 23). The spirit of Revenge shares the eternal watchfulness of divine justice. It is a favourite theme of Calvin's,[1] and there are many parallels in

---

[1] For an illustration from Calvin, see S. F. Johnson, 'The Spanish Tragedy, or Babylon Revisited', p. 28. Johnson's essay does more justice to the play's

Elizabethan writing, such as these lines from the morality, *The Tide Tarrieth No Man* (1576):

> But God is not dead, neyther is he a sleepe,
> Although for a time his hand he doth hold:
> Yet doth he remember his little sheepe,
> And will revenge the wrong done to his folde.
>
> (F3)

Similarly, a passage from Thomas Beard's *Theatre of God's Judgements* (1597) reads like a commentary on Hieronimo's frantic appeals to heaven:

> For though it may seem for a time that God sleepeth, and regardeth not the wrongs and oppressions of his servants, yet he never faileth to carry a watchfull eie upon them, and in his fittest time to revenge himself upon their enemies.   (p. 56)

Turning this concept into drama, Kyd gave to his tragic hero an awareness which extends far beyond the immediate response to Horatio's death. Hieronimo's situation is not static, it releases a wave of passion that carries him forward through the play. He is the hero of a quest, which lends shape and movement to the dramatic plot, as the secret purposes of heaven are revealed to him step by step. The action is composed of a sequence of ironies, appropriate to its theme. Hieronimo, for instance, has a judicial function at the court which serves to emphasise his powerlessness to redress his own wrongs, yet also his duty to do so:

> Thus must we toil in other men's extremes,
> That know not how to remedy our own.
>
> (III. vi. 1)

His relations with the court are used to heighten this isolation, for Kyd's sense of dramatic contrast and irony is the principal source of many of his brilliant theatrical effects. There is a skilful exploitation of contrasting moods and feelings that appears to be a new development in Elizabethan dramatic technique. Too many of the earlier tragedies sustained a uniform and monotonous emotional tone; Kyd discovered the secret of varying pitch and emotional

---

unity and tragic meaning than most other criticism since the days of his name-sake Benjamin.

tension from scene to scene. Thus, at the opening of *The Spanish Tragedy*, from the vehement clamour of Andrea's ghost we move into the chivalrous world of the Spanish court, from the darkness into the light, as the victorious warriors are welcomed home, and their noble prisoner Balthazar received with courteous ceremony. Even here contrast and tension are felt, for just beneath the surface plays the hostility of Lorenzo and Horatio, anticipating the much greater irony later in the play when Lorenzo and Hieronimo cross each other's path, while before the king apparently observing the decorum of courtly behaviour.

Kyd develops the character of Hieronimo from these contrasts: during the first Act he has only a minor part, as presenter of the masque, though again this anticipates a much more sinister occasion in a subsequent scene. Hieronimo comes to the centre of dramatic interest with his discovery of Horatio's body, and the swift transition from the dutiful court official to the grief-stricken father intensifies the dramatic impact of his overwhelming loss. Hieronimo is snatched from the secure unsuspecting world of normality, visualised at that moment by his arrival on the scene clad in no more tragic dignity than his nightgown: he is roused from sleep, and plunged into horror and insupportable suffering. Thereafter his isolation is emphasised by a persistent contrast between the normality which he must seem to assume in the outward forms of the court, and the private nightmare in which he really lives. His solitary grief becomes in time the totally enclosed world of his madness, which transforms all around him into his vision of injustice and despair.

Hieronimo's search for justice is rendered desperate by his grief and by his sense of utter helplessness. Since he can only give vent to his passion in words, all other relief in action being denied him, his speeches acquire an urgency and immediacy which release tremendous dramatic energy. Characters in earlier tragedies used the rhetoric of lamentation to describe their feelings: Kyd achieves a more direct representation of passion by making the emotional disturbance itself seem to control the language. If Hieronimo's complaints are contrasted with Videna's lament at the beginning of the fourth Act of *Gorboduc*, for instance, it is evidence that whereas Videna paints a picture of herself as a 'most wofull wight', Hieronimo's speeches do not personify himself at all, but seem wrung from him by a pressure of feeling within, a passion embodying itself not in an image of the speaker but in a climactic series of conceits that bring the whole world within the compass of his grief:

> O eyes, no eyes, but fountains fraught with tears;
> O life, no life, but lively form of death;
> O world, no world, but mass of public wrongs,
> Confus'd and fill'd with murder and misdeeds.
>
> (III. ii. 1)

If the ridicule of Jonson and of others has not finally put these lines beyond the reach of criticism, it might be possbile to see that the difference between them and the lamentations of Videna, Jocasta, Antigone, Gismond, Tancred and other woeful characters of the earlier drama, is that Hieronimo must act his speech, while the descriptive and narrative methods of the older plays leave nothing to be supplied beyond the words themselves. The notorious opening figure of this soliloquy is in fact borrowed from Petrarchan poetry: another reminder that Seneca had no monopoly over the language of suffering developed in Elizabethan poetry.

Hieronimo's verse is powerful because he speaks under the compulsion of his profound distress. Whether his speeches are meant to arouse and spur on the heavens to vengeance, or whether at other times he resorts to declamation as a substitute for action, from the sheer necessity of unburdening his frustrated spirit in gesture, his passion expresses a primitive, almost ritualistic sense that words have a shaping power over reality; as though in prayer or mimic enactment he can turn the tables on his enemies. Ben Jonson's contempt for *The Spanish Tragedy* was not wholly due to his hypocritical embarrassment at the thought of his part in the additions of 1602; as an admirer of Bacon, he shared a radically different conception of the relationship between words and things. His similar distaste for the rhetoric of *Tamburlaine* classes the two plays together in their use of poetry to body forth the shape of things unknown.

Kyd's most discerning pupil was Shakespeare, and the spirit of Hieronimo survives not only in the revenge heroes, but as a creative influence on the development of all those tragic figures who believe themselves more sinned against than sinning. The very derivative characterisation of Titus Andronicus reveals Shakespeare attempting to surpass Kyd in presenting a hero driven to the utmost extremes of suffering by his sheer helplessness, acting out the intolerable frustration of his agony in pantomime. His elaboration of Kyd's methods produces a grotesque effect which robs Titus of tragic dignity, as though Shakespeare was too engrossed by the theatrical and rhetorical problems of articulating a response to such overwhelming injustice. Richard II is a more coherent and sympathetic representative of this kind of hero. He has that capacity for a depth of suffering which extends the tragic vision of the play, and that eloquence and self-awareness, which, like Hieronimo's, serve to heighten his powerlessness and dependence on the support of heaven. Hamlet of course is a far more complex creation than Hieronimo: there is a paralysis of will as well as a suspension of situation, but his lineal connection with Kyd's hero is obvious. Like Hieronimo, he is isolated from the court at which he lives, and he inherits something of the instability, the vacillation between resolve and despair, and the alternation of trust and doubt, through which is dramatised a sense of the devious and mysterious providence governing both tragedies. Shakespeare's ultimate development of Kyd's prototype, however, is seen in King Lear, whose tragic progress raises to prodigiously greater intensity that terrible question asked of heaven by Hieronimo:

> How should we term your dealings to be just
> If you unjustly deal with those that in your justice trust?
> (III. ii. 10)

Lear's identification of the whole world with his torment, his confrontation with Mad Tom, 'the thing itself' on the heath, his mock trial of his pelican daughters, his meeting with the blind Gloucester on the way to Dover, and his waking vision of Cordelia as 'a soul in bliss', are anticipated as devices of characterisation by the transfiguring vision of Hieronimo, who saw in the old man who came to him for justice a projection of his own case:

> Ay, now I know thee, now thou nam'st thy son,
> Thou art the lively image of my grief:
> Within thy face, my sorrows I may see.
> (III. xiii. 161)

The pantomime of madness, in this scene as in *King Lear*, becomes a means of dramatising tragic recognition: it was Kyd who first turned the conventions of lamentation and distracted passion into a tragedy of spiritual revelation, embodied in the suffering of his protagonist.

*　　*　　*

Tamburlaine and Faustus inhabit a vaster, more spacious world than Elizabethan drama had previously known, for not only do they have it more to themselves, but their passions convulse the whole universe, soaring beyond that limited sphere of action which circumscribes the lives of tyrants, revengers, and lovers. Marlowe's drama is more intellectual and metaphysical than moral in its conception of human will and action: he brings to the stage a diversity of speculative interests, notably in theology, political theory and astronomy. But his learning is not bookish adornment or scholarly affectation: it is vital to his presentation of character and tragic conflict. No other Elizabethan dramatist is both as philosophical and as exciting; what earlier hero, for instance, could have justified his ambition with the ideas which Marlowe has given to Tamburlaine?

> Nature, that fram'd us of four elements
> Warring within our breasts for regiment,
> Doth teach us all to have aspiring minds:
> Our souls, whose faculties can comprehend
> The wondrous architecture of the world,
> And measure every wandering planet's course,
> Still climbing after knowledge infinite,
> And always moving as the restless spheres,
> Wills us to wear ourselves and never rest,
> Until we reach the ripest fruit of all,
> That perfect bliss and sole felicity,
> The sweet fruition of an earthly crown.
> (I, *Tam.*, II. vii. 18)

The motives which drive Tamburlaine and Faustus do not arise from a particular situation, from an interaction between character and circumstance: their passions are self-generated. It is the essential nature of these heroes which Marlowe dramatises; there needs no Vice or any external mechanism to propel them along the course they choose. They are not creatures of deed or occasion, they themselves create the situations in which they exist. This intellectual temper of Marlowe's tragedy, his singleness of vision in liberating character from every thing but will-power, produce that sense of power and magnificence which his heroes convey. As Tamburlaine's speech explains, they are conceived dynamically, moving in an action which encompasses the whole creation.

In order to present Tamburlaine and Faustus in these terms, Marlowe establishes a new relationship between character and speech. The impassioned poetry in which they express themselves can sometimes be a response to a localised situation, as when each finally confronts suffering and death, but their eloquence has a function beyond the articulation of feeling. It establishes the stage on which these heroes play their parts, since the physical stage can only be an emblematic representation of the spiritual dimensions of their grandeur. In these two plays, like Kyd but for different reasons, Marlowe gives to the word a much greater creative force, a power over reality which it did not possess in earlier Elizabethan tragedy. Marlowe's rhetoric not only persuades or terrifies; it summons into imaginative existence the world of dazzling splendour and unlimited possibility:

> Forsake thy king and do but join with me,
> And we will triumph over all the world.
> I hold the Fates bound fast in iron chains,
> And with my hand turn Fortune's wheel about;
> And sooner shall the sun fall from his sphere
> Than Tamburlaine be slain or overcome.
> Draw forth thy sword, thou mighty man at arms,
> Intending but to raze my charmed skin,
> And Jove himself will stretch his hand from heaven
> To ward the blow, and shield me safe from harm.
> See how he rains down heaps of gold in showers,
> As if he meant to give my soldiers pay,
> And as a sure and founded argument
> That I shall be the monarch of the East,
> He sends this Soldan's daughter rich and brave,
> To be my queen and portly emperess.
>
> (I, *Tam.*, I. ii. 171)

Marlowe's mighty line is clearly epic in style, but it is not a medium for narrative; the iterative future tense is characteristic of both Tamburlaine and Faustus in their speech, and as well as dramatising their aspirations, 'always moving as the restless spheres', it transforms an idealised vision into a dramatic presence:

> I will be Paris, and for love of thee,
> Instead of Troy, shall Wittenberg be sack'd;

And I will combat with weak Menelaus,
And wear thy colours on my plumed crest:
Yea, I will wound Achilles in the heel,
And then return to Helen for a kiss.

(V. i. 114)

The theatrical power and immediacy of this poetry rests not so much in its definition of passion as in its capacity to take hold of the auditor's imagination, to make him enter the world of illusion it presents. Significantly, the eloquence of Tamburlaine and Faustus is built into their characters. As Hieronimo is a judge, himself pleading at the bar of divine justice, so Tamburlaine is a most persuasive orator and leader of men, and Faustus a conjurer believing in the force of words to raise spirits.

Both these Marlovian heroes arouse wonder and astonishment, not in place of the tragic emotions of pity and fear, but as the means of heightening pity and fear. Tamburlaine does not achieve full tragic status until the second part of the play, when he confronts for the first time the meaning of suffering and death. Even here, however, death comes not as a punishment of his ambition, but as the natural end which even he must accept. The scene in which the dying hero spreads out a map of the world, and contemplates with dismay all the unconquered territories that remain, displays the very essence of the character, for his ambition is infinite, and as Shakespeare wrote for a rather different occasion, 'the desire is boundless, and the act a slave to limit'. This in the end is the tragedy of Tamburlaine, an irony visited upon him not by any divine retribution, but by the Nature to whom he appealed at the outset in justifying his aspiring mind. Despite the hero's aware- ness of a 'God who sits on high and never sleeps', the play shows no sign of miraculous intervention in his rise and fall, even though Tamburlaine literally tempts providence in his boasts and blas- phemies.

Whether or not Marlowe originally conceived the two parts to- gether (and the fact that he almost exhausts his historical sources in Part I does not prove anything), the sequel becomes in effect a moral commentary on the apparently unconfined optimism of the first part. This earlier Tamburlaine resembles most of all the fabulous champions of romance, with a love of adventure that takes them from one challenge to the next; the demented hero of Part II recalls Seneca's *Hercules Furens* in his rage and anguished defiance of the gods, though Tamburlaine is much more the victim of his delusions than Hercules. Tamburlaine, however, is not a lone hero of single-handed exploits, and his heroic stature derives as much from his inspiring leadership as from his personal prowess. By the skilful use of decorum in presenting Tamburlaine as a pagan, Marlowe balances our admiration for his rhetorical visions of mythological splendour with our condemnation of his ruthless inhumanity. He brings about the tragedies of established rulers as though he were indeed the Scourge of God, yet we recognise too the justice of their commentary upon his insatiate ambition. If he displays a *virtù* which is Machiavellian, his motives are much more idealised than the immediate, practical aims of the Machiavellian or Senecan tyrant: he enjoys the winning of power, not its use, and is exhilarated most by the thought of what is yet to be achieved. Of course, as a Scythian shepherd, Tamburlaine does not always behave with the manners of a Christian gentleman, and as a man of action he may strike the academic as rather vulgar in his conception of achievement; but even in his most barbaric cruelties he shows no awareness of wrongdoing, as a true Elizabethan villain would. On the other hand, he is capable of great tenderness and generosity, he has courage and a sense of honour, and he inspires the loyalty of his followers. At the risk of seeming to patronise him, he must be regarded as a kind of noble savage.

Tamburlaine's world is controlled by Nature: we see nothing of the direct influence of providence, and consequently Tamburlaine seems marvellously free in the exercise of his will. *Dr. Faustus* deals directly with the will of God, and the hero's attempts to defy it: the story has an explicitly theological frame of reference. Nevertheless the main interest is focussed here too upon the human will. Faustus brings about his own tragedy; to the very end, it is within his power to seek God's mercy, but he chooses damnation and persists in his choice. It is finally a tragedy of despair, as Faustus commits this one sin which puts him beyond God's grace.

In a precise theological sense, Faustus' career runs through the whole gamut of sins, from pride to despair. The torments of hell, as Mephistophilis warns him, are not located in one place, and Faustus suffers damnation in the despair of his last speech. There is a dreadful irony pervading the play, which amounts to its controlling method of presentation, and this irony, unlike that in *Tamburlaine*, operates at the verbal level. When Faustus first summons Mephistophilis, it is to discover that his words have no compelling power, that the devil came of his own accord:

> For, when we hear one rack the name of God,
> Abjure the Scriptures and his Saviour Christ,
> We fly, in hope to get his glorious soul.
>
> (I. iii. 49)

Later, when Faustus calls upon Christ, it is Lucifer and Beelzebub who answer him. The invocation of Helen, that superb piece of lyric poetry, is shot through with ironic meanings not intended by Faustus, reminding us that this vision is an evil spirit, an illusion in more than the theatrical sense. The action and words constantly serve to divorce the soaring imaginative visions of Faustus' poetry from the realities of his self-elected situation; his desires inhabit a splendid, open world of infinite possibilities, but his choice commits him to an enclosed, inescapable destiny. The last soliloquy seems to concentrate and epitomise all that the play has already shown; expressed with a powerful urgency which arises from its context, Faustus' desperation is embodied in imagery which both contracts and extends the dimensions of time and space. The acceleration of clock-time, and his almost claustrophobic sense of being trapped in his study, are sensations ironically intensified by the imminence of eternity and infinity. This speech is a form of prayer, or a magic spell to suspend the inevitable pace of time, to open up the furthest recesses of heaven and earth. Even the line from Ovid's love poem, *O lente, lente currite, noctis equi*, assumes in its new context the solemnity of an incantation. But here as before Faustus' words are impotent: they cannot command the elements: they transform nothing. The poetry does create a theatrical illusion; its only power is over the imagination, and its imagery summons the whole universe to witness Faustus' end. Unlike *Tamburlaine*, however, the visionary stage of the hero's imagination cannot contain the whole drama. It is encompassed by a much vaster theatre than man himself can create.

Barabbas and Edward II dwell in a diminished world. Here Marlowe shifted the centre of dramatic interest from the titanic hero and his eloquence to the tensions of intrigue and character conflict. His heroes in these two plays do not rise above their fellow-men, though Marlowe's interest in the egoistic, aggressive nature persists. The character relationships in *The Jew of Malta* and *Edward II* are therefore wholly limited to hatred and conflict. The world is atomised: each man is at odds with his neighbour, friendships are unstable and temporary, and the passions at play are unheroic, though fierce and uncompromising.

The setting of the *Jew of Malta* is not established through poetic imagery, and Marlowe furnishes Barabbas with a source of action which is not self-generated, in the manner of Tamburlaine and Faustus, but precipitated by a situation in which his initial role is passive. Like Hieronimo, therefore, Barabbas first suffers wrong, and begins his career as a revenge hero; but once the action has been launched, Barabbas is no longer confined by the terms of his original motivation. He is unleashed upon the world of the play, but this is a world given over entirely to wickedness and double-dealing, and governed by the spirit of Machiavelli, who acted as Prologue. Barabbas triumphs only for as long as he outstrips the others in cunning and treachery. This conception of a universal and thoroughgoing villainy gives to the play a curious logic. It is like an elaborate game, played by Barabbas with consummate skill against others who either do not know the rules, or cannot exploit them so well. The plot of intrigue, very different from that in *The Spanish Tragedy*, is composed of a series of masquerades, or macabre jests; since there is no moral distinction between the characters, except Abigail (and even she, it seems to Barabbas, is a cunning traitress), the villainy of Barabbas has a harsh intellectual appeal, described in T. S. Eliot's famous phrase as 'the terribly serious, even savage comic humour' of farce.

Barabbas is brought to his end by the very logic of the game; he so far forgets himself that he trusts his original enemy, Ferneze. The plot therefore needs no providential direction, though in a world so totally depraved the Jew is used to expose Christian hypocrisy and fraud. Such trenchant ironies in situation are reflected in the sardonic humour of the verse: Barabbas displays a zest for wickedness and self-congratulation reminiscent of the morality Vice, and like the Vice he uses others to accomplish his wicked purposes. But there is in his speech a tone of contempt and hatred that finds expression in a new kind of dramatic verse:

> I learn'd in Florence how to kiss my hand,
> Heave up my shoulders when they call me dog,
> And duck as low as any bare-foot friar;
> Hoping to see them starve upon a stall,

> Or else be gather'd for in our synagogue,
> That, when the offering-basin comes to me,
> Even for charity I may spit into't.
>
> (II. iii. 23)

In the unheroic world of the Jew, this low prosaic diction is the perfect vehicle for his malicious scorn. Barabbas, like Faustus and Tamburlaine, is animated by a single dominating passion: he has none of the complex humanity which Shakespeare gives to Shylock. But the very intensity of his malevolence distinguishes him from the Vice, and even invests him with a kind of grim integrity.

The fall of Edward II fulfils no grand design, or providential purpose: it is a tragedy of character in the sense that the issues signify only the victory or defeat of those involved. Edward, Gaveston and Mortimer are engaged in a struggle for power in which their aspirations cannot be justified by any values other than self-interest. The play presents no absolutes outside the will of the characters themselves; their determination to have their own way is an end in itself. It is once again a Machiavellian world, and Edward is characterised in the cut and thrust of his conflicts with his enemies. The vicissitudes of this struggle are dramatised in scenes of passionate quarrelling, and there are few set speeches: such a sustained use of dialogue to generate dramatic tension is unusual in Elizabethan tragedy. As a result Edward is seen as a part of the savage, brutal world he tries to command; he is not detached from the conflict which circumscribes his sovereignty until finally he is defeated and imprisoned. Edward's character does not change: he repents nothing of his pride and folly, and learns no wisdom, but his shifting fortunes are mirrored by our attitudes to him. As the balance of power moves between Edward and Mortimer, it is almost axiomatic in the play that we should side with the defeated. Such is the contrast with Tamburlaine:

> And there in mire and puddle have I stood
> This ten days' space; and, lest that I should sleep,
> One plays continually upon a drum.
> They give me bread and water, being a king;
> So that, for want of sleep and sustenance,
> My mind's distempered, and my body's numb'd,
> And whether I have limbs or no I know not.
> O, would my blood dropp'd out from every vein,
> As doth this water from my tattered robes.

> Tell Isabel, the queen, I look'd not thus,
> When for her sake I ran at tilt in France,
> And there unhors'd the Duke of Cleremont.
>
> (V. v. 58)

This compassionate treatment of Edward's fall draws no moral, but, in its plainness and simplicity, the speech translates into particularised images of humiliation and loss the traditional complaint of *De Casibus* tragedy. Tragic meaning lies in the fact of suffering itself, and the ironic contrasts give Edward an awareness and sense of perspective that dignify him in the face of death.

Nevertheless death in Marlovian tragedy is the final victor, whether it comes with sudden terror and violence, or whether, as in *Tamburlaine*, the hero is at last vanquished by Nature alone. The sense of mortality is felt with peculiar intensity, as the power which ultimately extinguishes all heroic pride and aspiration, the inevitable end which irreconcilably contradicts man's unlimited will and infinite desires: 'What art thou, Faustus, but a man condemn'd to die?' Quite alien to Marlowe's conception of the tragic hero is the Shakespearian implication of values which transcend mortality, where the death of the protagonist becomes his victory rather than his defeat.

*   *   *

The development of the ironic method by Kyd and Marlowe enabled them to define and resolve the tragic issues through the inner logic of character and situation. Although Marlowe's rather metaphysical conception of dramatic conflict left little room for a sense of mystery or religious awe in his plays, he was a much greater poet than Kyd, and the sheer impact of his rhetoric made him the dominant influence of the early 1590's. To *Tamburlaine* probably belongs the dubious honour of being the most imitated of all Elizabethan plays. Oriental conquerors crowded the stages, and the 'mighty line' became the established vehicle for tragic bombast. The *Tamburlaine* idiom was of course highly distinctive, and its mannerisms were easily reproduced and debased, while Marlowe's philosophical spirit was less readily appropriated. Plays such as *Selimus* and *Locrine*, in fact, suggest that Marlowe's influence was often disastrous for the minor playwright.

Shakespeare does not seem to have been as strongly attracted by the Tamburlaine figure as by Barabbas, and Aaron the Moor in *Titus Andronicus* is the first of a long line of Shakespearian villains, who like

c

Barabbas play it cool, revel in their outrageous strategems, and speak with the blunt pugnacity of the low style. Richard III adds charm and brilliance to the part, and with profounder psychological insight Shakespeare derives from Richard's deformity a strain of self-mockery which borders upon self-disgust. Though Shakespeare was not a great innovator in dramatic technique, he was highly resourceful and ready to adapt to his own purposes the prevailing fashions of his day. He was an acute critic of style, and while he used the available rhetorical models of Kyd and Marlowe, he did so with a certain detachment. Richard III, and the Bastard Faulconbridge in *King John*, are both character-ised as heroes who parody the heavy tragic style of other characters, and consequently they possess an extra dimension of awareness. Simi-larly, Romeo is first presented as the conventional romantic lover before he meets Juliet, and thereafter the contrast helps to individualise him. Romeo in fact is transformed from a hero of comedy into a tragic hero, and Shakespeare's fondness for using and simultaneously abusing conventional style is a feature of his comedies as well, from *Love's Labour's Lost* to *As You Like It*. The satire directed towards Pistol and Hotspur in *Henry IV* suggests that by about 1598 the Marlovian rhetoric had had its day, for Shakespeare at least. What Shakespeare learned from Plutarch in composing *Julius Caesar* is reflected in the greater subtlety and detail with which character and motive are there presented. Shakespeare was following a master of psychological analysis, and the result was a development in the complexity of his art which left his earlier models far behind in its depth and realism. This richer apprehension of the tragic hero is fully developed in *Hamlet*, a play which also reflects the new vogue of tragical satire.

The rise of satire in the final years of the sixteenth century had as great an impact upon tragedy as upon comedy, and it quickly superannuated Kyd and Marlowe as creative models. The chief innovator of tragical satire was John Marston, and in the figure of the malcontent he in-troduced a new type of tragic hero to the stage. The malcontent is the honest villain, the satirical commentator who is both detached from and involved in the evil and corruption he sees around him. The bitterness and melancholy of his vision establish in the tragedies of the early seventeenth century that mood which is sometimes character-ised as 'Jacobean', though whether in Marston himself, or in Shake-speare, Tourneur or Webster, it has more to do with the formal properties of satire, as they were understood, than with what some modern critics have described as the spirit of the age. The simplified approach to literature as social criticism has produced many false antitheses between 'Elizabethan optimism' and 'Jacobean pessimism'. But while the malcontent often represented an attitude of profound scepticism which undermined the old tragic scheme of providential justice, at the same time he revived that homiletic spirit which was never far beneath the surface of Elizabethan tragedy.

Note

Texts. No satisfactory large collection of Tudor interludes exists. The most useful is still *Dodsley's Old English Plays* (fourth edition by W. C. Hazlitt, 15 volumes, 1874): the modernised text is well printed, though it is not to be relied upon. J. S. Farmer published several small collections (1905-7), also in a modernised text, with notes: *Anonymous Plays* (first, second and third series); '*Lost*' *Tudor Plays; The Dramatic Writings of John Bale; The Dramatic Writings of Richard Wever and Thomas Ingelend.* J. Q. Adams, *Chief Pre-Shakespearean Dramas* (1924), contains a small number of interludes; these include the most accessible text of *Mankind*, in a bowdlerized form. The bibliography of T. W. Craik's *The Tudor Interlude* (1958) lists the modern editions of each interlude. *Fulgens and Lucrece* is available in *Five Pre-Shakespearean Comedies* (World's Classics), ed. F. S. Boas. For faithful facsimile texts, the Tudor Facsimile Texts (J. S. Farmer, 143 volumes, 1907-14) and the Malone Society Reprints (various editors: since 1907) should be consulted. Interludes are quoted in this chapter from Dodsley or M.S.R. or T.F.T. editions and as follows: *Fulgens and Lucrece,* (H. Medwall), ed. F. S. Boas and A. W. Reed (1926); *The Longer Thou Livest, the More Fool Thou Art* (W. Wager), ed. A. Brandl in *Shakespeare Jahrbuch* (1900); *The Play of the Weather* (J. Heywood), ed. J. Q. Adams; *A Satire of the Three Estates* (D. Lindsay), ed. D. Hamer, *Works of Sir David Lindsay,* Scottish Text Society (1931); Lyly's *Endimion* is quoted from the collected edition of R. W. Bond (1902); Green's *Friar Bacon and Friar Bungay* from that of J. C. Collins (1905); Marlowe's *Dr. Faustus* from the 1616 text in W. W. Greg's parallel-texts edition (1950), and his *Jew of Malta* from the Arden edition of H. S. Bennett (1931); Jonson's plays from the edition of C. H. Herford and P. and E. Simpson (1925-52); Tourneur's *Atheist's Tragedy* from I. Ribner's edition of the play in the Revels Plays series (1964); Massinger's *A New Way to Pay Old Debts* from A. H. Cruickshank's edition (1926).

Scholarship and Criticism. C. F. Tucker Brooke's *The Tudor Drama* (1912) is still a good survey of the period, though some important interludes have been discovered since its publication, notably *Fulgens and Lucrece* and *Enough is as Good as a Feast.* A. W. Reed's *Early Tudor Drama* (1926) deals with Heywood, Rastell and Medwall. Dramatic techniques and conventions are discussed in T. W. Craik's *The Tudor Interlude: Stage, Costume and Acting* (1958). Books by W. Farnham, M. Doran and M. C. Bradbrook cited in the note preceding Chapter I are relevant, together with A. P. Rossiter's *English Drama from Early Times to the Elizabethans* (1950), D. M. Bevington's *From 'Mankind' to Marlowe* (1962) and M. C. Bradbrook's *The Growth and Structure of Elizabethan Comedy* (1955). On staging, E. K. Chambers's *The Elizabethan Stage* (1923) is fundamental; it may be supplemented by G. Wickham's *Early English Stages, 1300 to*

II

The Tudor Interlude and Later
Elizabethan Drama

T. W. CRAIK

*

THIS chapter will be much concerned with the interludes, as well as with the plays written for public and private theatres. Though it will suggest how the drama of Medwall, Heywood and their successors is related to that of Shakespeare and his contemporaries, it will also dwell on the characteristics of the interlude itself. The interlude should not be dismissed as a drab grub from which emerged a glorious dragon-fly. It was an achievement, not merely a transitional process, and its interest is artistic as well as historical.

Its historical importance is very plain. English secular drama virtually begins with the interludes performed at royal palaces and great houses at the end of the fifteenth century, the beginning of the Tudor period. It is from this time that dramatic texts survive, though a reference to 'layking [playing] of enterludes' at Christmas in *Sir Gawain and the Green Knight* (late fourteenth century) implies a tradition, the existence of which we might deduce from the assured accomplishment of Medwall's *Fulgens and Lucrece* (1497?). For practical purposes, then, the interlude may be considered a Tudor dramatic form; and it was a dramatic form capable of handling the various matter which the sixteenth century thrust upon it: scientific instruction in Rastell's *Four Elements* (1517?); political controversy in Skelton's *Magnificence* (1516?),

---

1660 (1959, 1963: in progress). R. Southern writes on 'The Contribution of the Interludes to Elizabethan Staging', in *Essays on Shakespeare and Elizabethan Drama in Honour of Hardin Craig*, ed. R. Hosley (1963).

Craik and Bevington have articles in the first issue of *Renaissance Drama* in its new form (1964), both on Heywood's plays; this journal promises to be a welcome vehicle for presenting studies on early Elizabethan drama.

37

Lindsay's *Satire of the Three Estates* (1540; expanded 1552, 1554), and the anonymous *Respublica* (1553); theological controversy, with a strong political bias, in the plays of Bale; treatments of prodigal children in *Nice Wanton* (1550?) and Ingelend's *Disobedient Child* (1560?); social morality in Lupton's *All for Money* (1560?) and William Wager's *Enough is as Good as a Feast* (1564?). This list of topics is by no means exhaustive, and any reader acquainted with these interludes themselves will recognise that the classification, though convenient, is superficial, because it cannot show the essentially mingled character of the material, nor the variety of manner with which the material is treated. No mention has yet been made, for instance, of the morality structure of temptation, sin and repentance (the common pattern of three fifteenth-century plays as diverse as *The Castle of Perseverance*, *Wisdom* and *Mankind*), which, found at its simplest and most direct in *Youth* (1520?), underlies many of the interludes already named. Nothing has been said, either, of the growing interest in sheer story-telling on stage, which produces Phillip's *Patient Grissell* (1559?), Preston's *Cambises* (1569?) and Garter's *Susanna* (1569?), each stating its moral lessons and including allegorical characters (among them the vice, his rôle somewhat detached from the main action of these self-contained narratives) among the *dramatis personae*. The discovery of Plautine and Terentian plotting (another aspect of dramatic narration) is another factor in the development of the interlude. *Roister Doister* and *Gammer Gurton's Needle* (both 1553?) can thus be classified as academic importations, yet both draw, too, upon traditional European vernacular farce of the kind represented by Heywood's *Johan Johan* (1529?: adapted from a French original) and the Cupar Banns to Lindsay's *Satire of the Three Estates*: we may, for example, consider the assault on Custance's house in *Roister Doister* (IV. viii), where all Merrygreek's blows light on his master, or the ceremonial use of Hodge's breech in the dénouement of *Gammer Gurton's Needle* (V. ii: compare, in Lindsay's play, the Pardoner's divorce of the Sowtar and his wife, l. 2171: 'Ilk ane of yow uthers arsse kis').

This flexibility—which can descend into formlessness: the success of the interludes varies according to their authors' ability—continues into the drama of the Shakespearean age. 'Their great problem', writes Madeline Doran of the Elizabethan dramatists:

> was the achievement of unity out of diversity . . . Achievement of minor stylistic form came easy, achievement of major structural

form came hard. Success in structural form was never very uniformly achieved in English renaissance drama; when it was, it was never at the sacrifice of variety. Elizabethan and Jacobean drama is always a teeming drama. (pp. 19–20)

It was the existence of a robust tradition of secular drama, robust but not rigid, that made the later richness possible.

*   *   *

The special dramatic virtues of the best Tudor interludes, as I have argued elsewhere, are intimacy and spontaneity. The characters, from their first entrance, put themselves on familiar terms with the spectators, and will turn aside to address them during the action; the action itself seems unpremeditated, developing from a casual encounter between disputants holding opposed principles. It is worth remembering that there is nothing essentially undramatic about didactic intention and allegorical method (nobody uses the argument to allege that Defoe is necessarily a more interesting narrator than Bunyan or Swift). In fact, reading the interludes, one sees how the didactic purpose lends itself to direct address, and how the allegorical characterisation does away with any feeling that the play is a re-telling of something that happened in the past: how, in short, there is a fitness of matter and method in the plays.

It must, of course, be allowed that such dramatic virtues, at their most elementary, are very easily come by, as they belong to the most elementary form of play-making. The entering 'boast' of the miracle-play character, and the 'in comes I' formula of the folk-play, spring to mind. The opening speech of *Hickscorner* (1513?) illustrates the convention at its simplest:

> Now Jesu the gentle, that bought Adam fro hell,
> Save you all, sovereigns, and solace you send:
> And, or this matter that I begin to tell,
> I pray you of audience, till I have made an end;
> For I say to you, my name is Pity,
> That ever yet hath been man's friend.
> In the bosom of the second person in Trinity
> I sprang as a plant, man's miss to amend;
> You for to help I put to my hand:
> Record I take of Mary that wept tears of blood;
> I Pity within her heart did stand,

When she saw her son on the rood;
The sword of sorrow gave that lady wound,
When a spear clave her son's heart asunder;
She cried out, and fell to the ground;
Though she was woe, it was little wonder.
This delicate colour, [sic:? flower] that goodly lady,
Full pale and wan, she saw her son all dead,
Splayed on a cross with the five wells of pity,
Of purple velvet powdered with roses red.
Lo, I Pity thus made your errand to be sped,
Or else man for ever should have been forlore.
A maiden so laid his life to wed,
Crowned as a king the thorns pricked him sore.
Charity and I of true love leads the double rein;
Whoso me loveth damned never shall be.
Of some virtuous company I would be fain;
For all that will to heaven needs must come by me;
Chief porter I am in that heavenly city.
And now here will I rest me a little space,
Till it please Jesu of his grace
Some virtuous fellowship for to send.
(Dodsley, i, 147–8, corrected from T.F.T.)

This is a straightforward statement about the divine nature of pity,
giving a clear theological context to all that follows. The opening is
formal, alliterative, able to claim the spectators' attention. The conclusion is an artless cue for Contemplation's entrance; he introduces
himself to the spectators just as Pity has done, and then, with Pity's
'God speed, good brother', enters into dialogue, after a dozen lines of
which we have

PITY. I thank God that we be met together.
CONTEMPLATION. Sir, I trust that Perseverance shortly will come
hither.

—and two lines later Perseverance appears (Contemplation has mentioned him already, so his introduction is not quite as bald as it looks),
with the same kind of introductory speech. They briefly discuss the
wickedness of the times, poverty, selfishness, lawlessness and ignorance.
Then Contemplation says,

Now God, that ever hath been man's friend,
Some better tidings soon us send!
For now I must be gone.
Farewell, good brethren here;
A great errand I have elsewhere,
That must needs be done:
I trust I will not long tarry;
Thither will I hie me shortly,
And come again, when I have done.
(Dodsley, i. 154)

No one asks him what his errand is, and it has no bearing on the future action. It is simply a means of his leaving the stage. Perseverance also goes out, and perhaps Pity does so too, or he may remain through the rogues' dialogue which follows; certainly he interrupts it when it grows to a quarrel, but on the other hand the author has not given him any asides to keep his attentive presence before the audience. Enough has now been said to show the simplicity of the dramatic technique, almost the absence of it. In structure the play is equally elementary. It turns on the reclaiming of evildoers. The first crisis is their fettering of Pity when he interposes between them, the second their conversion. Even this pattern is not completed, because Hickscorner never returns to be converted. As for the conversions of his fellows, they are as conventionally abrupt as any in Elizabethan drama. The dramatic interest of the play lies chiefly in the evildoers' self-exhibition. Here is Freewill, bursting in after the opening dialogue of the virtues:

Aware, fellows, and stand a-room:
How say you? am not I a goodly person?
I trow, you know not such a guest:
What, sirs, I tell you, my name is Freewill;
I may choose whether I do good or ill;
But for all that I will do as me list:
My conditions ye know not, perdè,
I can fight, chide, and be merry;
Full soon of my company ye would be weary,
And you knew all.
What, fill the cup, and make good cheer!
I trow I have a noble here:
Who lent it me? By Christ, a frere;
And I gave him a fall.

> Where be ye, sir? be ye at home?
> Cock's passion, my noble is turned to a stone.
> Where lay I last? Beshrew your heart, Joan;
> Now, by these bones, she hath beguiled me.
>
>   (Dodsley, i. 154–5)

This is vigorous, and lets Freewill act with his hands and face, but it is rude and unsophisticated. When the effects of intimacy and spontaneity are nicely calculated, and the author's contrivance is concealed, then his art is substantial.

Dramatic experiment during the present century has helped us to appreciate plays showing an equivocal attitude towards 'dramatic illusion', and to react against the strict assumption that a play is a play and an audience an audience, and that the stage action must be supposed capable of proceeding without the spectators' presence. This assumption springs from rigorous theory: a practising dramatist will seize his dramatic opportunities where he may. In *L'Avare*, Molière's characters do not acknowledge the audience's presence, but when Harpagon misses his treasure he suddenly perceives the spectators in the midst of his soliloquy:

> Sortons. Je veux aller quérir la justice, et faire donner la question à toute la maison: à servantes, à valets, à fils, à fille, et à moi aussi. Que de gens assemblés! Je ne jette mes regards sur personne qui ne me donne des soupçons, et tout me semble mon voleur. Eh! de quoi est-ce qu'on parle là? De celui qui m'a dérobé? Quel bruit fait-on là-haut? Est-ce mon voleur qui y est? De grâce, si l'on sait des nouvelles de mon voleur, je supplie que l'on m'en dise. N'est-il point caché là parmi vous? Ils me regardent tous, et se mettent à rire. Vous verrez qu'ils ont part sans doute au vol que l'on m'a fait.
>
>   (IV. vii)

Here it is the very breach of a convention which produces the comic effect. The authors of the Tudor interludes had no such convention to defy, and their comic tone comes from the free-and-easy commerce between reality and makebelieve. An illustration from *Fulgens and Lucrece* will make the point conveniently. This interlude is divided into two parts, the second part containing the disputation between Lucrece's two suitors, the one pre-eminent in birth and the other in virtue, with which the play is principally concerned. There are two actors who serve as commentators, and one tells the other that the forthcoming interval is to allow the disputants to prepare their arguments. He then adds,

> An other thing must be considred withall,
> These folke that sitt here in the halle
> May not attende theretoo.
> Whe may not with oure long play
> Lett them fro theyre dyner all day,
> Thay have not fully dyned;
> For and this play where ones overe past
> Some of them wolde falle to fedyng as fast
> As thay had bene almost pyned;
> But no forse hardely and they do,
> Ussher gete them goode wyne therto,
> Fyll them of the best;
> Let it be do or ye wyll be shent,
> For it is the wyll and commaundement
> Of the master of the fest.
> And therfore we shall the matter forbere,
> And make a poynt evyn here
> Lest we excede a mesure;
> And we shall do oure labour & trewe entent
> For to play the remenant
> At my lordis pleasure.
>
> (Part I, l. 1412)

The double reason for the interval is typical of Medwall's attitude to theatrical illusion: the suitors' convenience is considered, and so is the convenience of the banqueting spectators, which latter is of course recognized by all as the real reason for the interval. The very actor who gives this double explanation has at the beginning of the play, with his fellow, pretended to join the dramatic action from the audience, as does Merry Report, Jupiter's crier in Heywood's *Play of the Weather* (1527?). Each is given a message to Lucrece from his employer; one forgets it, and the other well-meaningly converts it to indecency, and both these mismanaged messages give the audience the comic satisfaction of seeing pre-arranged things going wrong between master and servant, while the mistakes are themselves pre-arranged between author and actor. In Lindsay's *Satire of the Three Estates* the interval itself is the occasion for an apparently unrehearsed incident. After the player king's messenger Diligence has announced the interval, and the spectators have begun to eat their food, 'the Kings, Bischops and principall players being out of their seats' (it is a play-field performance, with a stream, a pavilion, and scaffolds for the chief characters),

Heir sall entir the peur man

PAUPER, THE PURE MAN.
    Of your almis gude folks for Gods luife of heavin,
    For I have motherles bairns either sax or seavin:
    Gif ye'ill gif me na gude for the luife of Jesus,
    Wische me the richt way till Sanct-Androes.
DILIGENCE. Quhair have wee gottin this gudly companyeoun?
    Swyith out of the feild fals raggit loun.
    God wait gif heir be ane weill keipit place,
    Quhen sic ane vilde begger Carle may get entres.

Diligence rebukes the officers of the town for not managing affairs better: he threatens,

    Without ye cum and chase this Carle away
    The Devill a word ye'is get mair of our play.
             (l. 1926)

After this the stage directions tell their own story: 'Heir sall the Carle clim up and sit in the Kings tchyre'; 'Heir Diligence castis away the ledder'; 'Heir sall the Carle loup aff the scaffald'. Pauper informs Diligence that he does not care if he does spoil the play,

    For thair is richt lytill play at my hungrie hart,

and recounts how the vicar has taken his three cows as his mortuary right, leaving him destitute. Then he lies down to rest, while Diligence, who now leaves the action, presumably retires to the pavilion in disgust. During Pauper's sleep a Pardoner comes in, displays his relics ('Heir sall he lay doun his geir upon ane buird'), and divorces the Sowtar and his wife (see page 38 above). Pauper wakes, stretches himself, and trades his last groat for a pardon, but, learning with dissatisfaction that he will not benefit from it until he is in purgatory (and the Pardoner in hell), demands his groat again: 'Heir sal thay fecht with silence and Pauper sal cast doun the buird, and cast the relicts in the water.'

DILIGENCE. Quhat kind of daffing is this al day?
    Suyith smaiks out of the feild, away.
    Into ane presoun put them sone,
    Syne hang them quhen the play is done.
             (l. 2290)

Having got rid of the intruders by a sudden reappearance, Diligence can now introduce the second part of the play.

The Tudor interludes show other aspects of this deliberate creation of apparent spontaneity: for example, the structure of John Heywood's interludes. The lying contest in *The Four PP* (1529?) evolves out of a very indirectly connected dispute about sending men quickly and surely to heaven. The petitioners in *The Play of the Weather* appear, like Chaucer's pilgrims telling their tales, in no formal order; and, again like Chaucer's pilgrims, some of them quarrel in pairs. In *The Play of the Weather*, too, we find Heywood exploiting the comedy of boy actors (the play can be assigned to a boys' company, probably the Chapel Children, on internal evidence). Little Dick asks for frost and snow for his winter games, and Merry Report thinks him too trivial a suitor: 'Geve boyes wether, quoth a!' Now Little Dick is a small boy ('the least that can playe') acting a boy; and Merry Report is a bigger boy acting a man. This sophisticated recognition of the reality underlying the fiction runs from the interludes to Lyly and Shakespeare. It develops alongside the courtly taste for childish pertness (on the stage at least). Thus the second Act of the anonymous *The Marriage of Wit and Science* (1567?) belongs to Will, Wit's page and his envoy to Science. Wit tells him,

> Thou must commend me to be rich, lusty pleasaunt
> and wyse;

Will retorts,

> I can not commend you, but I must make twentie lies
> Rich quoth you, that appeareth by the port that you kepe,
> Even as rich as a newe shorne sheepe . . .
> Wyse as a woodcocke: as brage as a bodylouse,
> A man of your handes, to matche wyth a mouse.
>   (M.S.R., l. 248)

These 'mad toyes', as Wit calls them, are clearly inspired by the dialogues of Roister Doister and Matthew Merrygreek (Udall's play also was written for boys). Will delivers his message, and delivers it well. Probably he ended his twenty-line speech with a flourishing bow and won a round of applause from the spectators; certainly he gets his tribute from Science and her parents:

EXPERIENCE.   I have not harde a meyssage more trymlee done,

SCI[E]NCE. Nor I, what age art thou of my good sonne,
WILL. Betwene eleven and xii, Madame more or lesse.
REASON. He hath bene instructed this errand as I gesse.
SCIENCE. How old is the gentilman thy maister canst thou tell?
WILL. Seventene or there about I wote not verye well.

(M.S.R., l. 460)

These statements would be close enough to the truth to make the
spectators smile. Will and his master are both boys; and so is Science,
which adds a touch of comedy to her exit. She agrees to receive Wit's
visit, and adds,

> Tyll then adew both hee and thou myne owne swete
> little Will.

Will, almost overcome with female charm against his boyish better
knowledge, looks after her retreating figure.

> Ah flattering Queene, how neatly she can talke
> How minionly she tryps, how sadly she can walke.

(l. 506)

Lyly, writing for the Chapel Children within twenty years of this
interlude, is drawing on the same comic tradition when a waiting-maid
weeps after a quarrel and a page comments, 'Excellent, and right like
a woman' (Endimion, II. ii. 51).

For the subtler comedy of the disguised girl who is played by a boy,
we have to wait till Lyly. The interludes do not handle such romantic
narrative, whether invented, like his Gallathea, or based upon existing
stories, like Shakespeare's As You Like It and Twelfth Night. In Lyly,
and above all in Shakespeare, dramatic irony becomes the essence of
the comic situation—

OLIVIA. Are you a comedian?
VIOLA. No, my profound heart; and yet, by the very fangs of
malice I swear, I am not that I play.

(Twelfth Night, I. v. 171)

—but it is combined with the comedy of the half-dispelled, half-
preserved illusion (a comedian is playing Viola: Viola is playing
Cesario), of which Shakespeare shows himself well aware:

FABIAN. If this were play'd upon a stage now, I could condemn
it as an improbable fiction.

(III. iv. 121)

Norman Sanders has recently discussed those scenes in Greene and
Shakespeare in which characters are observed and commented upon
by other characters, and their use of the play-within-the-play: the
Oberon-Bohan framework of *James the Fourth*, for example, whereby
'the audience are simultaneously distanced from and brought closer
to the world of the play'.[1] In this instance, Oberon actually intervenes
in the action which he is 'presenting' (it is as though Don Andrea's
ghost in *The Spanish Tragedy* were to speak to Horatio and Bellimperia
as well as to Revenge), an unusual freedom even upon the Elizabethan
stage, and a technical indecorum of which Greene must have been
conscious. Whether Greene's device is in fact aesthetically satisfying
is debatable: the present point is that without the interludes' dramatic
tradition it would not have been available to him. As it was, that
tradition had to fight for its life in the middle years of the century,
when regularity became a much-prized literary virtue, manifesting
itself in versification (Tottel's Miscellany appeared in 1557) and in
dramatic structure (*Gorboduc*, where each of the king's two sons has
one good and one bad counsellor, points towards the remorseless
symmetry of *Mother Bombie's* opening scenes).

The informal tradition survived because household drama was well
established. The familiar use of plays-within-plays on the public stage,
from the fatal play-acting in *The Spanish Tragedy* (*c.* 1589) to the boisterous farce which concludes *A Mad World My Masters* (1604-6), shows
how well established it was, and the travelling players' company in
Hamlet shows that the rise of the public theatres did not put an end to
it. The sophisticated but uninhibited comedy of the early Tudor interlude depends on the relationship between the author, the actors and
the spectators. Plays written for patrons display a mingled familiarity
and courtesy, and a sense of the occasion, sometimes a banquet, at
which the entertainment is given. The mood is convivial and relaxed.
Little Dick's statement in *The Play of the Weather* that Jupiter has come
down 'this night to suppe here with my lord' expresses exactly this
mood.

*   *   *

[1] 'The Comedy of Greene and Shakespeare': *Stratford-upon-Avon Studies*, 3:
Early Shakespeare (1961), p. 51.

The word 'interlude', derived probably from the giving of plays in the intervals of banquets (as *Fulgens and Lucrece* was given), comes to be virtually synonymous with 'pastime' and hence with 'play'. But the best pastime was profitable pastime: Honest Recreation, in Redford's *Wit and Science* (1539?), is a virtuous woman, whereas Idleness is a harlot. At the beginning of *Fulgens and Lucrece*, one of the two by-standers who later become servants tells the other,

> I love to beholde suche myrthes alway
> For y have sene byfore this day
> Of suche maner thingis in many a gode place
> Both gode examples and right honest solace;
> (Part I, l. 150)

and at its end he sums up the moral lesson:

> Thow toldest me that other day
> That all the substaunce of this play
> Was done specially therfor
> Not onely to make folke myrth and game,
> But that suche as be gentilmen of name
> May be somwhat movyd
> By this example for to eschew
> The wey of vyce and favour vertue,
> For syn is to be reprovyd
> More in them, for the degre,
> Than in other parsons such as be
> Of pour kyn and birth.
> This was the cause principall,
> And also for to do withall
> This company some myrth.
> (Part II, l. 887)

The subject of *Fulgens and Lucrece*, that virtue is the true nobility, was older than Chaucer (who treats it in *The Wife of Bath's Tale*), but it had an obvious relevance a dozen years after the Tudors came to the throne and the new dynasty began to bring forth new gentlemen: it recurs throughout the Tudor period. Most interludes combined the universal and the topical in this way, and one great reason for their appeal was their contemporary and immediate nature. J. Dover Wilson (*The Fortunes of Falstaff*, 1943) has detected a morality pattern beneath Shakespeare's *Henry IV* plays, and we may notice at present that Youth and Riot, wearing the dress and speaking the idiom of the day, were as actual to an audience of Henry VII'.s time as Prince Hal and Falstaff were to an audience at the Globe. When personal attacks were introduced (as upon Wolsey n *Magnificence*), and bitter controversies were broached (as in the plays of Bale), the interlude's power of moral criticism was considerable.

The impact of militant protestantism is heavy in Bale's attacks on Rome and in the social morality of William Wager's interludes. There is a sombre pleasure, sometimes a ;leeful violence, in the exposure and destruction of falsehoods and abuses. A change in substance accompanies this change in mood. The typical morality plot has hitherto been one of temptation, si and repentance: from the middle of the century we find plays in which the unrepentant evildoer is overtaken in his wickedness and damned.

> Cum forth of thy folly to receive thy hyre,
> Confusion, povertye, sickenes, and punishment,
> And after this life eternall fyre,
> Due for fooles that be impenitent.
>
> (l. 1836)

Thus Confusion addresses Moros, the wicked fool who is the central character of Wager's *The Longer Thou Livest, The More Fool Thou Art* (1564?); and the fate of Worldly Man in his *Enough is as Good as a Feast*, or of Lust in *The Trial of Treasure* (1565?; probably also Wager's), is depicted with equally pitiless relish. These plays may be considered alongside *Nice Wanton*, in which Ismael is hanged for highway robbery, Dalila dies of the pox, and their too-indulgent mother is saved from a remorseful and desperate suicide only by the intervention of her one virtuous child Barnabas. The author of *Nice Wanton* does not shrink from the consequences of violence and prostitution, but he allows Barnabas to reclaim his sister's soul as well as his mother's, and Ismael's trial and sentence are presented in a matter-of-fact way (only the exposure of Iniquity, the Vice and the children's tempter, has its comic aspect in this scene: he fights, but the Judge orders him to be taken away). In *The Longer Thou Livest, the More Fool Thou Art*, on the other hand, the whole treatment of Moros is broadly comic, from his first entrance 'counterfaiting a vaine gesture and a foolish countenance'. A few other directions indicate the style in which the part is to be played: 'Betweene whiles let Moros put in his head'; 'reade as fondely as you

D

can devise'; 'Make curtsie backward'; 'Florish with your sworde';
'Looke upward to see the fether. Stumble and fall.' At the same time,
the moral commentary is severely critical: Moros is a wilful fool who
refuses to learn, and when Fortune capriciously gives him power he
oppresses the commons and persecutes Protestants. His damnation is
meant to be taken seriously, but his stage presence defies seriousness:
to Confusion's stern invitation (quoted above) he replies,

> Go with thee ill fa oured knave,
> I had lever thou w rt hanged by the necke;
> If it please the Devill me to have,
> Let him carry me away on his ba e.
>
> CONFUSION. I will carry thee to the Devill in d de,
> The world shalbe well ridde of a foole.
>
> MOROS. A dew to the Devill God send us good speede,
> An other while with the Devill I must go to schole.
>
> GOD'S JUDGME[N]T.
>
> For sinne though God suffreth Impietie,
> Greatly to the dishonour of his name,
> Yet at length he throweth downe Iniquitie,
> And putteth the Authours therof to shame.
>
> (l. 1840)

The comments of God's Judgement are expanded by Discipline,
Piety and Exercitation, and the play ends.

This juxtaposition of the grotesque with the sententious is characteristic of the Elizabethan interlude. Moros's exit resembles the wholly
frivolous one of Nichol Newfangle, the Vice of *Like Will to Like*
(1568?):

> Now if I had my nag, to see the world wag,
> I would straight ride about:
> Ginks, do fill the bag: I would not pass a rag
> To hit you on the snout.
>
> *Here entereth the* DEVIL.
>
> LUCIFER. Ho, ho, ho! mine own boy, make no more delay,
> But leap upon my back straightway.
>
> NEWFANGLE. Then who shall hold my stirrup, while I go to horse?
>
> LUCIFER. Tush, for that do thou not force!
> Leap up, I say, leap up quickly.
>
> NEWFANGLE. Woh, Ball, woh! and I will come by and by.
> Now for a pair of spurs I would give a good groat!

> To try whether the jade doth amble or trot.
> Farewell, my masters, till I come again,
> For now I must make a journey into Spain.
>> *He rideth away on the* DEVIL's *back. Here entereth*
>> VIRTUOUS LIFE *and* HONOUR.
>>> (Dodsley, iii. 356, corrected from T.F.T.)

And Nichol Newfangle's exit, in due time, inspired that of Miles in Greene's *Friar Bacon and Friar Bungay*, where similar jests are made about ambling and trotting and spurs. Friar Bacon has commissioned the devil to carry Miles away, 'for careles watching of his Brasen head', but this is merely a removal, not a damnation: if Miles goes to hell, he goes to a comic hell wherein is all manner of delight:

> Faith, tis a place I have desired long to see: have you not good tipling houses there? may not a man have a lustie fier there, a pot of good ale, a paire of cardes, a swinging peece of chalke, and a browne toast that will clap a white wastcoat on a cup of good drinke?
>
> DEVIL.   All this you may have there.
>
> MILES.   You are for me, freinde, and I am for you. But I pray you, may I not have an office there?
>
> DEVIL.   Yes, a thousand: what wouldst thou be?
>
> MILES.   By my troth, sir, in a place where I may profit my selfe. I know hel is a hot place, and men are mervailous drie, and much drinke is spent there; I would be a tapster.
>>> (V. ii; l. 1996)

In Jonson's *The Devil is an Ass*, the minor devil Pug makes the same exit, at the command of Satan, but this time the devil rides on the vice:

> INIQUITY.   Mount, dearling of darkenesse, my shoulders are broad:
> He that caries the fiend, is sure of his load.
> The *Divell* was wont to carry away the evill;
> But, now, the Evill out-carries the *Divell*.
>>> (V. vi. 74)

This is a typically Jonsonian reversal of convention, in a play that has used the moral interlude as a basis on which to build a satiric attack on the ingenious viciousness of the present time (1616), viciousness which makes Pug a novice by comparison (this is the inner meaning of Iniquity's final line). Greene's incident is a straightforwardly humorous application of a piece of stage business which the presence of devils in his play suggested to him. Jonson's is a sophisticated revival, for his own ends, of archaic machinery.

*   *   *

By the end of the Elizabethan period, when the drama had firmly cast in its lot with intrigue, the tradition of the moral interludes was beginning to look archaic; and dramatists allude to it either for special artistic purposes implicit in their material or for purposes of burlesque and ridicule. An example of the former reason is in *Dr. Faustus*, where Faustus's inner tensions, shown in soliloquy, are formalised in his dialogues with the Good and Evil Angels:

EVIL ANGEL.   Go forward *Faustus* in that famous Art.
GOOD ANGEL.   Sweete *Faustus* leave that execrable Art.
(text of 1616, l. 403: II. i)

Marlowe here looks back to the conflict between vices and virtues, but he adapts it to his needs. In the moral interludes, vice and virtue do not plead together: they take different occasions, so that man's backsliding can give structure to the play, and sometimes also for the practical reason that the actors may thereby double their parts. By bringing on his Good and Evil Angels together, Marlowe presents good and evil in objective and visually interesting form, and their stichomythia (still fashionable on the stage) makes a good contrast with Faustus's soliloquies. In *The Merchant of Venice*, Launcelot Gobbo makes his first entrance in soliloquy, uncertain whether to leave Shylock's service, and his soliloquy is a comic record of the rival appeals of his conscience and the devil:

> . . . well, my conscience says 'Launcelot, budge not'. 'Budge' says the fiend. 'Budge not' says my conscience. 'Conscience,' say I 'you counsel well.' 'Fiend,' say I 'you counsel well.'
(II. ii. 22)

Shakespeare frequently suggests his familiarity with the moral interlude and its theatrical tradition: another passage from *The Merchant of Venice*,

> There is no vice so simple but assumes
> Some mark of virtue on his outward parts
(III. ii. 81)

recalls the vices' self-disguising; Kent calls Goneril 'Vanity' (*King Lear*, II. ii. 33), and in the same scene is put in the stocks like the sage virtues in *Hickscorner*, *Youth* and the *Satire of the Three Estates*; Angelo talks of writing good angel on the devil's horn (*Measure for Measure*, II. iv. 16); Hamlet calls Claudius 'a vice of kings' (*Hamlet*, III. iv. 98); almost every play would yield examples, either in action or allusion. Falstaff, besides having something of the old vice in him, has something of the young prodigal too, and of this he is conscious. His highway robbery gains a dimension if set beside the comparable episodes in *Nice Wanton* and *Liberality and Prodigality* (1567?): 'They hate us youth'; 'Young men must live' (1 *Henry IV*, II. ii. 82, 88). Gadshill's curious phrase, 'I am joined with ... nobility and tranquillity' (II. i. 73), catches up a rhyme from the final speech of *Nice Wanton*:

> Let us pray for the honourable council and nobility,
> That they may always counsel in wisdom with tranquillity.
>   (Dodsley, ii. 183, corrected from T.F.T.)

Shakespeare's interest in interlude style was mainly, as this reminiscence suggests,[2] a parodist's interest, though what he preferred parodying was fustian blank verse ('King Cambyses' vein', 1 *Henry IV*, II. iv. 376, is not the style of the interlude *Cambises*) and the excessively regular fourteener (Costard's speech as Pompey in *Love's Labour's Lost*, V. ii. 546; the death-scene in Bottom's Pyramus play, *Midsummer Night's Dream*, V. i. 268: both these have alliteration and internal rhyme to emphasise their coarse artificiality). Likewise Jonson, in *Volpone* (I. ii; III. iii), uses irregular doggerel for Mosca's entertainments given by the dwarf, eunuch and hermaphrodite; and in *The Devil is an Ass*, whereas Satan and Pug speak ordinary Jonsonian blank verse, rhymed couplets in triple rhythm are reserved for Iniquity (I. i; V. vi), because, as Satan points out, he is an old-fashioned vice, a survival from less sophisticated and less wicked times.

Blank verse had almost, but not entirely, driven out the irregular rhymed verse of most interludes. There are outcrops of the old style in Shakespeare:

> She that's a maid now, and laughs at my departure,
> Shall not be a maid long, unless things be cut shorter,

[2] R. P. Cowl (*T.L.S.*, 26 March, 1925; quoted in Furness Variorum edition) thinks that the reminiscence is of a couplet (ll. 1915–16) of Phillip's *Patient Grissell*, where the same rhyme occurs.

says Lear's Fool (I. v. 48). The style belongs to comedy, or, as here, to the comic fragments in plays which are not comic. It is found in the more boisterous scenes of *The Comedy of Errors* (such as III. i), and in IV. iii of *Love's Labour's Lost*, when Costard produces Berowne's sonnet, to Berowne's mortification:

KING.	How now! What is in you? Why dost thou tear it?
BEROWNE.	A toy, my liege, a toy! Your Grace needs not fear it.
LONGAVILLE.	It did move him to passion, and therefore let's hear it.
DUMAIN.	It is Berowne's writing, and here is his name.
BEROWNE.	Ah, you whoreson loggerhead, you were born to do me shame.
	Guilty, my lord, guilty! I confess, I confess.
KING.	What?
BEROWNE.	That you three fools lack'd me fool to make up the mess;
	He, he, and you—and you, my liege!—and I
	Are pick-purses in love, and we deserve to die.

(IV. iii. 196)

The characteristics of this verse are rhyme (often feminine, sometimes internal) and a tendency towards triple rhythm; but the metre is not regular, even though *Love's Labour's Lost* is a sophisticated comedy and these are its most sophisticated characters. The passage may be compared with this from *Jacob and Esau* (1550?):

> And Ragau my man, is not that a fine knave?
> Have any mo maisters suche a man as I have?
> So idle, so loytring, so trifling, so toying?
> So pratling, so tratling, so chiding, so boying? . . .
> In play or in pastime, so jocunde, so mery?
> In worke or in labour so dead or so weary?
> Oh that I had his eare betwene my teeth now,
> I should shake him even as a dog that lulleth a sow.
>
> (M.S.R., l. 552)

The freedom with which Shakespeare falls into various metres in various parts of his comedies, though far surpassing the interludes in variety, was inherited from them, as was his freedom in construction and in the use of theatrical illusion. It is a long way from *Fulgens and Lucrece* and *The Four PP* to *A Midsummer Night's Dream*, both in structure and style, to say nothing of the imaginative scope of Shakespeare's play, but a line of descent is traceable.

It is comedy, the more informal dramatic mode, which is the most evident descendant of the interludes. Their sententious rhyme-royal stanza utterly disappeared:

> Mine apparel is not like unto thine,
> Disguised and jagged, of sundry fashion;
> Howbeit, it is not gold always that doth shine,
> But corrupting copper of small valuation;
> Too horrible besides is thy operation,
> Nothing more odious unto the just,
> Than the beastly desires of inordinate lust.
>   (Dodsley, iii. 264)

These lines come from a dialogue (admittedly a formal first confrontation) between Lust and Just in *The Trial of Treasure*. Elizabethan tragedy employed quite different versification and diction. In theme and dramatic technique, moreover, the visible debts are few, apart of course from the ever-present tendency to comic episode, and the occasional introduction of allegorical figures, like Lust, Chastity and Murder in *A Warning for Fair Women* (1599?), a domestic tragedy. How much the gusto of such Elizabethan villains as Marlowe's Barabbas and Shakespeare's Richard III may owe to that of the vice of the interludes is hard to decide. The vice, where he has a conspicuous part in the action (as distinct from a vivacious commentary on it, as in *Cambises*),[3] is a tempter and a deceiver, but he is not an intriguer: tragedy needed a complicated plot before the Elizabethan villain could assume his full character and boast his allegiance to Machiavelli's supposed principles.

The importance of complex plotting in Elizabethan tragedy is fundamental, and must be borne in mind when comparison is made with the interludes. Retributive justice, for example, marks the end of the sinners in *Enough is as Good as a Feast*, *The Trial of Treasure* and *The Longer Thou Livest, the More Fool Thou Art*, but it is different from the retribution in *The Jew of Malta* and *Volpone*. In these plays the evildoers reap as they have sown, but furthermore they suffer a neat poetic justice directly related to their own scheming: the engineer is hoist with his own petard, and by human, not divine, agency (the concluding

[3] See Chapters IV and V, pp. 94–5 and 109–10 below.

couplet of *The Jew of Malta*, ascribing Barabbas's downfall 'neither to Fate nor Fortune, but to Heaven', merely underlines the irony and can hardly be taken literally). By contrast, Tourneur's *Atheist's Tragedy* invokes the obvious hand of heaven, in the coincident deaths of D'Amville's two sons (V. i) and in the extraordinary manner of his own death:

> EXECUTIONER. In lifting up the axe, I think h'has knock'd
> His brains out—
>
> (V. ii. 242)

which is rightly ascribed to

> The power of that eternal providence
> Which overthrew his projects in their pride.
>
> (V. ii. 271)

Here we have both extreme poetic justice (D'Amville is killed by the axe with which he is trying to behead his nephew) and stern divine intervention.[4] The end of a comedy, Massinger's *A New Way to Pay Old Debts*, similarly introduces these two factors. Sir Giles Overreach is foiled, by ingenious devices needless to particularize, of his revengeful and ambitious hopes. His rage at his deserved and self-induced discomfiture is so violent that he goes mad, and in his ravings he recognises that divine justice has struck him:

> Ha! I am feeble:
> Some undone widdow sitts upon mine arme,
> And takes away the use of 't; and my sword
> Glew'd to my scabberd, with wrong'd orphans teares
> Will not be drawne.
>
> (V. i. 362)

The comment of a bystander underlines the moral lesson:

> Here is a president [*i.e.* precedent] to teach wicked men,
> That when they leave Religion, and turne Atheists,
> Their owne abilities leave 'em.
>
> (V. i. 380)

The drama of the later Elizabethan and Jacobean stage was mingled

---

[4] D'Amville's fatal accident recalls that of Cambises, who falls on his own sword when mounting his horse, and moralises, 'A just reward for my misdeeds my death doth plain declare' (Dodsley, IV. 245).

of many elements; and an important element was the Tudor interlude, itself an essentially mingled type of drama. Study of the interludes, therefore, though it can hardly define their precise contribution to the later plays, will help towards the appreciation of those plays, and will also provide the reader with some (perhaps unexpected) enjoyment.

Note

Biography. Thomas Kyd's father was a London scrivener; Kyd himself was born in 1558. He was entered at the Merchant Taylors' School in 1565, but records do not indicate how long he studied there. He did not, so far as is known, attend either university. He probably wrote for the theatre, especially for the troupe of Philip Henslowe, from about 1585 until within a year or two of his death. In the last year of his life, Kyd became embroiled in a charge of libel against the state, and, through his association with Marlowe, in the more serious charge of atheism. After his release from imprisonment and (apparently) torture, he wrote to the Lord Keeper exculpating himself and incriminating Marlowe. He died intestate in 1594.

Works. *The Spanish Tragedy*, first printed in 1592, may have been written during the later 1580's. No early edition of the play bears Kyd's name, and attribution of it to him depends on a reference in Thomas Heywood's *Apology for Actors* (1612), but is questioned by no modern authority. Kyd translated a pamphlet by Torquato Tasso under the title of *The Householder's Philosophy* (1588), adapted Robert Garnier's Senecan tragedy *Cornélie* into English as *Cornelia* (1594), and was the probable author of a sensational tract based on a recent notorious crime, *The Murder of John Brewen* (1592).

Kyd's name continues to be linked to two further plays. One, the tragedy of *Soliman and Perseda*, dramatises (with some variations) the tale that forms the basis of the play-within-the-play in Act V of *The Spanish Tragedy*, and is most likely Kyd's. The other no longer survives—the presumptive *Ur-Hamlet*.

Modern Editions. The standard edition of Kyd's *Works* is by F. S. Boas (1901). *The Spanish Tragedy* has been excellently edited for the Revels Plays by P. Edwards (1959); citations in the present chapter are to this text.

Scholarship and Criticism. No satisfactory general study of Kyd (or even of *The Spanish Tragedy*) exists in English. The best comprehensive treatment of Kyd, though now out of date, is Boas' Introduction; a useful critical survey of *The Spanish Tragedy* is Peter Wilhelm Biesterfeldt's *Die Dramatische Technik Thomas Kyds* (1936). The nature of the revenge ethic in the play was treated by F. Bowers, *Elizabethan Revenge Tragedy 1587–1642* (1940), pp. 62–100, and has been debated inconclusively since, in numerous articles. Three books on tragic drama contain excellent discussions of the language of *The Spanish Tragedy*: Howard Baker, *Induction to Tragedy* (1939), Moody E. Prior, *The Language of Tragedy* (1947) and Wolfgang Clemen, *English Tragedy before Shakespeare*, tr., 1961). G. Lambrechts' article in *Études Anglaises* (1963) argues that *Edward III* is by Kyd. Three books of rhetoric have been newly edited, Sir Thomas Wilson's *Art of Rhetoric* (1560), by G. H. Mair (1909), G. Puttenham's *Art of English Poesy* (1589) by Gladys D. Willcock and Alice Walker (1936) and A. Fraunce's *Arcadian Rhetoric* (1588) by Ethel Seaton (1950).

III

The Spanish Tragedy, *or The Pleasures and Perils of Rhetoric*

JONAS A. BARISH

*

The Spanish Tragedy is, as has long been recognised, a repository of 'patterned' speech. What has perhaps been less well recognised is that this speech derives, for the most part, not so much from the dramatic as from the nondramatic verse of Kyd's predecessors and contemporaries among the poets. Specifically, it seems to represent Kyd's adaptation of the rhetoric of the 'middle style', the rhetoric of the schemes, tropes and figures, as enshrined in the poetical miscellanies of the later sixteenth century and codified in the manuals of style. The figures had as their purpose simply to please, 'to avoyd sacietie [sic], and cause delight: to refresh with pleasure, and quicken with grace the dulnesse of mans braine' (Wilson's *Art of Rhetoric*, p. 180), and thus to assist the poet in his aim of persuasion. Doubtless it was the acknowledged delightfulness of the figures that led Kyd to employ them so bountifully in *The Spanish Tragedy* that the play might almost have served, like Sidney's *Arcadia*, as a text on which to base a rhetorical lexicon, but it was wholly a consequence of his feeling for the connection between language and gesture that he was able to take devices that had often proved intractable in the hands of other playwrights, and turn them into vital constructive elements. Unlike his predecessors, Kyd used the figures of rhetoric not simply to decorate the action but to articulate it.

By 1550, when Richard Sherry first tabulated them in English as an aid to readers of the Bible, the figures had long since lost their original strict connection with oratory, and had become part of a technique of rhetorical analysis applicable to any kind of writing. By the time of Fraunce's *Arcadian Rhetoric* (1588) and Puttenham's *Art of English Poesy* (1589) a generation later, they could be discussed in complete isolation from oratory, and viewed simply as part of the rhetorical equipment necessary to poetry. The very delightfulness that made them a boon to poets, indeed, rendered them suspect as adjuncts to public pleading. The judges of the Areopagus, declares Puttenham, acted wisely in forbidding 'all manner of figurative speaches to be used before them in their consistorie of Justice, as meere illusions to the minde, and wresters of upright judgement', since 'to allow such manner of forraine & coulored talke to make the judges affectioned, were all one as if the carpenter before he began to square his timber would make his squire crooked'. But the poet's aim being precisely to make his judges—his gentle readers—'affectioned', the use of the figures was in his case to be recommended rather than discouraged, the more so since, again unlike the professional orator, he tended to plead 'pleasant & lovely causes and nothing perillous', and since his audience characteristically consisted not of severe magistrates but 'princely dames, yong ladies, gentlewomen and courtiers'. The burden of his text was love, for which purpose it was fitting that he 'dispose the hearers to mirth and sollace by pleasant conveyance and efficacy of speach' (Puttenham, pp. 154–5) —i.e., by adopting the schemes and tropes that beautified discourse.

The figures, that is, lent themselves well to love poetry; love poetry itself still maintained its close associations with music. *The Paradise of Dainty Devices*, compiled in 1576 by Richard Edwards, 'sometimes of her Majesties Chappel', was *'aptly made to be set to any song in .5. partes, or song to instrument'*.[1] The poets thus continued to regard their art as, in principle at least, an auditory one, and the schemes and tropes were above all, in Puttenham's term, 'auricular' devices, enabling writers to enchant and delight with harmonious sounds. Even the so-called 'figures rhetoricall', for Puttenham,

doe also conteine a certaine sweet and melodious manner of speech, in which respect, they may, after a sort, be said *auricular*; because the eare is no lesse ravished with their currant tune, than the mind is with their sententiousnes. For the eare is properly but an instrument of conveyance for the minde, to apprehend the sence by the sound. And our speech is made melodious or harmonicall, not onely by strayned tunes, as those of *Musick*, but also by choise of smoothe words: and . . . marshalling them in their comeliest construction and order . . . (pp. 196–7)

[1] *The Paradise of Dainty Devises* (1576–1606), ed. H. E. Rollins (1927), p. 4.

The figures, thus, were designed to enable lyric verse to cultivate its natural bent for song, so that it could better fulfil its 'sententious' purpose. One might expect dramatic verse to have had an even stronger claim on 'auricular' helps. But in fact Puttenham, though he acknowledges its identity of aim with politer poetry, speaks snubbingly of its limitations. Both the 'artificiall' poets, who write for learned readers, and 'popular' versifiers, who scribble for the stage, address themselves to the ear. The ear, however, in one case is a highly trained and responsive organ; in the other case it is ill-trained, inattentive, and debauched by competition with the eye. Heavy, thumping effects of prosody, such as rhymes between polysyllabic inkhorn terms, or between words of foreign derivation, 'smatch more the schoole of common players than of any delicate Poet *Lyricke* or *Elegiacke*' (p. 127). And the crudity of 'common players' may be laid directly at the door of their crude audiences,

> the common people, who rejoyse much to be at playes and enterludes, and besides their naturall ignoraunce, have at all such times their eares so attentive to the matter, and their eyes upon the shewes of the stage, that they take little heede to the cunning of the rime, and therefore be as well satisfied with that which is grosse, as with any other finer and more delicate.
>
> (p. 82)

Puttenham, it is plain, regards dramatic verse as an intrinsically inferior species, and the circumstances of theatrical production as an obstacle to subtlety. In the theatre poetry must reach a public distracted by visual spectacles and 'attentive to the matter'—i.e., indifferent to the manner, unconcerned with the 'finer and more delicate' effects, the niceties. But the niceties spring precisely from skilful use of the figures, which exist to heighten and refine ordinary language. So that Kyd's wholesale importation of them into the drama may be thought of as the translation into a grosser environment of effects associated originally with nuance and delicacy.

That his success with them should not be taken as a matter of course we may infer from the ineptitude of most earlier attempts to use them on the stage. The cardinal exception would be Lyly, who into his court comedies of the 1580's reworked most of the devices with which he had already dazzled his contemporaries in his two prose fictions. But

Lyly cultivated verbal elegance in his comedies for a special purpose, to transmute all pangs and all passions to brightness and transparency, to turn them into precious stuffs from which the element of pain was either missing altogether, or present only as another glittering golden thread in an iridescent texture. Kyd would use the figures not to lighten and brighten but to darken and weigh down, to project feelings of disruptive intensity and make us feel them as disruptive.

Other playwrights of the 1580's, Marlowe aside, were still struggling to learn to manage narrative, define character, and articulate plot in the theatre. When they attempted to transfer into their plays the figurative rhetoric of the miscellanies and the pedagogues, they often ran afoul of their own more strictly theatrical purposes. Mundy's *Fidele and Fortunio*, for example, contains a good deal of neo-Petrarchan rhetoric in the love scenes between the two protagonists and their mistresses. Early in the play, one of the mistresses, Victoria, sits at her window, picks out a doleful strain on her lute, sings a song to it, and then launches into a lament over her hopeless passion for Fortunio. Below on the stage, her swain Fidele overhears, and breaks out into a lament of his own over Victoria's fickleness:

> I serve a Mistres whiter then the snowe,
> Straighter then Cedar, brighter then the Glasse:
> Finer in trip and swifter then the Roe,
> More pleasant then the Feeld of flowring Grasse.
>   More gladsome to my withering Joyes that fade:
>   Then Winters Sun, or Sommers cooling shade,
> Sweeter then swelling grape of ripest wine,
> Softer then feathers of the fairest Swan:
> Smoother then Jet, more stately then the Pine,
> Fresher then Poplar, smaller then my span.
>   Clearer then Beauties fiery pointed beam:
>   Or Ysie cruste of Christalles frozen stream.
> Yet is shee curster then the Beare by kinde,
> And harder harted then the aged Oke:
> More glib then Oyle, more fickle then the winde,
> Stiffer then Steele, no sooner bent but broke.
>   Loe thus my service is a lasting sore:
>   Yet will I serve although I dye therfore.
>   (M.S.R., l. 224)

Here we have a competent, though quite undistinguished amatory 'sonnet' of 18 lines, which uses as its central figure a trope termed by Puttenham the '*Icon*, or Resemblance by imagerie', wherein 'lively creatures' are likened to each other, or to 'any other naturall thing, bearing a proportion of similitude' (pp. 241, 244). The various likenesses between Victoria and 'naturall things' turn suddenly against her in the final stanza, when she is charged with being as much like them in sharpness and hardness as she resembled them before in freshness and beauty. Nearly everything in the poem is stereotype, but what would have constituted a creditable, if uninteresting lyric in one of the miscellanies proves quite discreditable and incompetent as dramatic verse. As an independent poem, the sonnet would not have had to refer to anything beyond itself. The lady addressed would not have to be measured against any impression of her acquired elsewhere, nor would the lover. But dramatic characters have a history, and a speech in a play forms a moment in that history. As a description of Victoria, of whom they are ostensibly spoken, Fidele's lines are nothing to the purpose. By loading her down with run-of-the-mill similitudes, they obliterate all sense of an individual presence. As an expression of Fidele's own sentiments the lines are similarly defective, especially in the vapid cliché of the last stanza, where Victoria turns suddenly into the obdurate goddess, and Fidele himself into the eternally hopeless adorer. It is only a moment ago that Fidele, and we, first learned of Victoria's infatuation with Fortunio. Nothing justifies the attribution to her of persistent hardness of heart, or Fidele's assumption to himself of the role of the forever despairing votary. The sonnet is a mere *recitation*, clumsily thrust in to serve the function of lyric (somewhat like Victoria's song), but too cluttered with detail to sound much like music, and the detail too irrelevant to convey useful dramatic information. Doubtless there is some distinction to be drawn between Mundy's inept use of the figure itself and the inappropriate Petrarchism he falls back on, but the two vices are closely related: the figures offer an indefinitely expansible formal arrangement, which calls for a certain quantity of detail to fill up its pattern, and Petrarchan convention supplies a ready stock of formulaic particulars. Elsewhere in *Fidele and Fortunio*, at other moments of figured rhetoric, we find the same habit, of pinning onto the dramatic character inappropriate trappings hastily filched from the wardrobe of the courtly lover—the habit, that is, of substituting prefabricated rhetorical propositions for concrete dramatic observation.

Analogous considerations apply in other plays, for example to the scenes concerning the hermit Bomelio in the anonymous masque-comedy *The Rare Triumphs of Love and Fortune*. The playwright fashions Bomelio's soliloquies as formal speeches, adopting rhetorical machinery on a lavish scale, and extending his ruminations endlessly, in apparent obedience to the law of the day that 'Among all the figures of *Rhetorique*, there is no one that so much helpeth forward an Oration, and beautifieth the same with such delightfull ornaments, as doth amplification' (Wilson, p. 116). Bomelio's soliloquies display defects like those of Fidele's sonnet; they bear too tenuous a relation to the speaker's own situation, and they are weighed down almost to the point of stasis by conventional generalities. When we meet him first, emerging from a cave and clad as a hermit, Bomelio addresses us thus:

> He that hath lost his hope and yet desires to live,
> He that is overwhelmde with woe, and yet would counsell give,
> He that delightes to sigh to walke abroad alone,
> To drive away the weary time with his lamenting mone,
> He that in his distresse dispaireth of releefe,
> Let him begin to tell his tale to rip up all his greefe.
>
> (M.S.R., l. 572)

Let him begin indeed! we fervently concur—noting, however, that the leisurely amplitude of the exordium forebodes a lengthy discourse. Bomelio continues,

> And if that wretched man can more then I recite,
> Of fickle Fortunes froward checke and her continuall spite,
> Of her unconstant change, of her discurtesie,
> I will be partner with that man to live in miserie.
>
> (l. 578)

So far, nothing distinguishes the speaker from any other man cast low by Fortune. We have no clue yet to his former eminence, or to the nature of his dethronement. We await further particulars. Bomelio recommences:

> When first my flowring yeeres began to bud their prime,
> Even in the Aprill of mine age, and May month of my time [,]

When like the tender Kid new weaned from the teat:
In every plesant springing Mead, I took my choice of meat,
When simple youth devis'd to lengthen his delight: . . .

(l. 582)

But by this time we have stopped listening. For this will outlast a night in Russia, when nights are longest there. Worse, this is not dramatic poetry at all, but a nondramatic rehearsal of a few well-worn topoi. Nothing we have heard in the patterned exposition relates it to the speaker's individual plight; nothing links it to the action of which it forms part. Only toward the end of what proves to be a forty line monologue does Bomelio let fall a few general facts concerning his misfortunes. The rest lurches along in the deep ruts of platitude, reiterating commonplaces on the instability of life in a gnomic deluge similar to those found often in the miscellanies. One feels that the patterning in such cases works to inhibit particularity. It seems to encourage the playwright to substitute strips of presynthesised abstraction for dramatic realities, and so to reinforce a habit, common to much English drama of the period and doubtless traceable to the influence of the moralities, of seeing characters nearly entirely as exemplary, as illustrative of certain constants in human nature, and not as individuals undergoing unique experiences.

Undeniably, it is only by a modern definition of the dramatic that we protest the tenuous relations between plot and language in Bomelio's monologue. The public for whom such scenes were written enjoyed them, no doubt, as they enjoyed the rhetoric of the miscellanies, and with small concern for dramatic congruence. It was playwrights like Kyd who helped bring into being our present sense of the dramatic. What Kyd does is to make functional the schemes and tropes of the figured style. He pares away the fatty amplification that writers like Mundy did not even recognize as encumbering, and what remains he remanages so as to fit it for its new context. When he borrows directly, he improves. Lorenzo's notorious echoing of a sonnet by Thomas Watson represents, simply on the level of versification, a distinct advance:

My lord, though Bel-imperia seem thus coy,
Let reason hold you in your wonted joy:
In time the savage bull sustains the yoke,
In time all haggard hawks will stoop to lure,
In time small wedges cleave the hardest oak,

E

> In time the flint is pierc'd with softest shower,
> And she in time will fall from her disdain,
> And rue the sufferance of your friendly pain.

BALTHAZAR.   No, she is wilder, and more hard withal,
> Than beast, or bird, or tree, or stony wall.

(II. i. 1)

Watson's version ran thus:

> In time the Bull is brought to weare the yoake;
> In time all haggred Haukes will stoope the Lures;
> In time small wedge will cleave the sturdiest Oake;
> In time the Marble weares with weakest shewres:
>   'More fierce is my sweet *love*, more hard withall,
>   Then Beast, or Birde, then Tree, or Stony wall.[2]

'The oftener it is read of him that is no great clarke', declares Watson
patronisingly in his headnote to the sonnet, 'the more pleasure he shall
have in it', thus emphasising the auricular drubbing to which he will
subject his vulgar readers. Kyd provides dramatic context for the lines,
and uses them to score a dramatic point. The familiar conflict in the
mind of the Petrarchan lover, between the spectacle of his mistress'
cruelty and the hope that she may relent, turns into a lively inter-
change between the confident Lorenzo, unimpressed by the genuine-
ness of his sister's indifference toward Balthazar, and the despairing
Balthazar, already daunted by the conviction of his own worthlessness.
Kyd resists the temptation to shovel a complete poem, with its own
beginning, middle and end, into his play; where Munday, following
Watson, would have spun twelve lines more of schematic parallels
on the properties of bulls, hawks, oaks and flints, Kyd cuts short the
amplification, makes the quatrain a vivid moment of persuasion in
Lorenzo's speech and allots only the despondent rejoinder to Balthazar.
In addition, he confers a new compactness and energy on the familiar
images by curbing the stream of monosyllables, reducing the shower of
sibillants and practising other small but significant metrical improve-
ments.

When, in short, we turn from the sporadic and halting attempts of
earlier playwrights to *The Spanish Tragedy*, we find that the figures

---

[2] *The Hekatompathia, or Passionate Century of Love* (1582), facs. ed. S. K.
Heninger, Jr. (1964), p. 61.

have ceased being mere aimless embroidery. They no longer represent self-indulgence on the playwright's part, nor do they suggest a flagging imagination. They now work actively to order the materials of the play. In addition to being 'auricular' and 'rhetorical', they have conceptual force. They help articulate the relationships among the characters; they aid the plot to incarnate itself as a physical event on a physical stage. At the same time, they gradually serve the playwright to turn a critical eye on language itself. Words come to oppose physical events as well as to buttress them, and in the tension between speech and act lies much of the tragic force of the plot.

The tendency for most of the schemes of antithesis, parallel, and balance to carve experience into dualities, triads, tetrads, and the like— in short, to impose a symmetrical patterning on phenomena—pervades the language of *The Spanish Tragedy* from the start, long before the figures, as figures, begin to press themselves on our notice. The solemn periphrasis with which the ghost of Don Andrea makes his entry lodges us at once in a realm of precise distinctions and complementary rejunctions:

> When this eternal substance of my *soul*
> Did live imprison'd in my wanton *flesh*,
> *Each* in their function *serving other's* need, . . .
> (I. i. 1, my italics)

Andrea elaborates the body-soul dualism in two successive lines, and then in a third reunites the separated halves into a mutually co-operative union. The use of the word 'flesh' rather than 'body', in contrast to 'soul', slightly mutes the rhetorical emphasis of the opposition, without affecting its conceptual import. Death is next viewed as a divisive power that cleaves in sunder not the body and soul, as we might expect, but the speaker and his mistress:

> But in the harvest of my summer joys
> Death's winter nipp'd the blossoms of my bliss,
> Forcing divorce betwixt my love and me.
> (I. i. 12)

Here a new series of antitheses—between summer and winter, harvest and frost, life and death—runs obliquely against the earlier opposition of flesh and soul and the splintered unity of the lovers arrived at in the final line. The mode of thinking is continuously antithetical and disjunctive, but the disjunctions at this moment remain slightly out of phase with one another, so that they do not crystallise into obvious patterns.

Andrea's description of his visit to the underworld, based on the voyage in Book VI of the *Aeneid*, condenses and abridges Virgil's account; it also regularises and patterns it. At the threshold of Hades, Aeneas meets only Minos among the infernal judges; Rhadamanth appears further on, in Tartarus; and Aeacus is not mentioned at all. Kyd makes Andrea's arrival in Hades the occasion of a ceremonious debate in which all three judges, sitting as a high tribunal, ponder the fate of their new charge. They comprise a perfect trinity of thesis, antithesis and synthesis. Aeacus recommends that Andrea, a lover, be sent to the fields of love; Rhadamanth proposes to send him, as a soldier, to dwell with martialists; Minos, finally, arbitrates the difference by referring the question to Pluto. The journey toward Pluto deals in a like manner with infernal geography; on the right, the path leading to the fields of lovers and warriors; on the left, the steep descent to hell; in between, the entrance to the Elysian fields, where Pluto holds court. The arrangement revises Virgil's plan of the region so as to satisfy Kyd's liking for symmetrical patterns and the reconciliation of opposites.

The epic narrative of the victory of Spain over Portugal is conducted along similar lines. When, in the account of the Spanish general, the opposing armies set forth, they confront each other in a six-fold sequence of identical gestures:

> Both furnish'd well, both full of hope and fear,
> Both menacing alike with daring shows,
> Both vaunting sundry colours of device, . . . [etc.]
> (I. ii. 25)

The battle itself proceeds like a tournament. Each aggressive move made by one side is countered by an equivalent defensive manœuvre from the other:

> I brought a squadron of our readiest shot
> From out our rearward to begin the fight:
> They brought another wing to encounter us.

> Meanwhile our ordnance play'd on either side,
> And captains strove to have their valours tried.
>   (I. ii. 35)

First the assault from the rear of one army, then the riposte from the
flank of the other. First the challenge and answer of the ordnance, then
the striving of the anonymous captains. When the smoke clears enough
to enable us to discern and identify individual combatants, the same
arrangement prevails. First,

> Don Pedro, their chief horseman's colonel,
> Did with his cornet bravely make attempt
> To break the order of our battle ranks.
> But Don Rogero, worthy man of war,
> March'd forth against him with our musketeers,
> And stopp'd the malice of his fell approach.
>   (I. ii. 40)

So, Don Pedro with his cavalry must oppose Don Rogero with his
musketry; the first launches an attack which is repulsed by the energy
of the second. Kyd allots three lines to each opponent: the first gives
the identity of the officer, the second indicates the nature of the troops
in his command, the third specifies the purpose of his mission.

And so with the rest of the description; group is pitted against group
in symmetrical antagonism. Kyd has done more than 'straighten out'
Grimald's contorted lines in 'The Death of Zoroas' on which he may
have based his narrative (H. Baker, p. 77); he has nearly reimagined
the scene. Instead of an impenetrable confusion, he visualises a battle
of nearly heraldic formality. Even the description of a field strewn with
the dead acquires an ordered clarity:

> On every side drop captains to the ground,
> And soldiers, some ill-maim'd, some slain outright:
> Here falls a body scinder'd from his head,
> There legs and arms lie bleeding on the grass,
> Mingled with weapons and unbowell'd steeds,
> That scattering overspread the purple plain.
>   (I. ii. 57)

There is no gainsaying the total effect of horror, but it is a controlled
and lucid horror, achieved by the patient laying on of apposite details,
like bricks, usually in pairs: first the captains, then the soldiers; first

the maimed, then the slain; first the decapitated bodies, then the dis-
embodied limbs; first the weapons, then the steeds. Turmoil and hubbub
are rendered with a certain pictorial sharpness of outline by the antithetic rhetoric, as in a tapestry, while the free play of detail helps keep
the symmetries unobtrusive.

After the battle the antitheses and oppositions surge more insistently
into view, and begin to mesh more closely with the stage action. As
the king finishes hearing the reports from the campaign, the victorious
Spanish army crosses the stage, with Balthazar led between Lorenzo
and Horatio. The two Spanish warriors, flanking their prisoner, provide
a visual image of their rivalry for the honour of his capture. The king
inquires into the circumstances of the capture:

> KING. But tell me, for their holding makes me doubt,
> To which of these twain art thou prisoner?
> LORENZO. To me, my liege.
> HORATIO. To me, my sovereign.
> LORENZO. This hand first took his courser by the reins.
> HORATIO. But first my hand did put him from his horse.
> LORENZO. I seiz'd his weapon and enjoy'd it first.
> HORATIO. But first I forc'd him lay his weapons down.
> KING. Let go his arm, upon our privilege.
>
> (I. ii. 152)

The plot here involves a symmetrical antagonism, mimed simultaneously in the language and in the stage action. At the king's bidding,
the Spanish knights release their captive, who now explains his position
for himself:

> KING. Say, worthy prince, to whether didst thou yield?
> BALTHAZAR. To him in courtesy, to this perforce:
> He spake me fair, this other gave me strokes:
> He promis'd life, this other threaten'd death:
> He wan my love, this other conquer'd me:
> And truth to say I yield myself to both.
>
> (I. ii. 160)

Again the antitheses in the language are mirrored by the antithetic
gestures with which Balthazar designates his captors, as he particularises
by turns their treatment of him. His final line, surprisingly, collapses
the vivid contrast back into a noncommittal unity. Here we meet one

of the perils of rhetoric. It is true that Balthazar is merely answering the king's question, and that he has, in fact, surrendered to both Horatio and Lorenzo. It hardly follows, however, from the opposition between courteous and peremptory treatment elaborated in the first four lines, that he should end by casually abandoning the distinction. The sharply registered preference for the one who offered gentle usage cannot be so limply disowned without making retrospective nonsense of the rest of the speech. Kyd's penchant for the reconciliation of opposites seems to have led him to enfeeble the force of his own disjunction at a crucial moment. And this leads to the further suspicion that the odd ascription of harsh behaviour to Horatio and generous behaviour to Lorenzo springs itself from the passion for disjunctions.

The king next mediates the contention by awarding Balthazar's weapon and horse to Lorenzo, but his ransom to Horatio; the custody of him to Lorenzo, but his armour to Horatio. All claims are scrupulously adjudicated, both the rights and rewards arising from the combat itself, and the larger issues arising from the unequal social rank of the rivals. The latter, in fact, interfere with the former, and prevent true justice; the king awards the armour to Horatio as a compensation for depriving him of the prisoner himself. The competing claims of the two knights, then, can be regulated only in part, even by a king renowned for his equity. When conflicts arise in a situation more resistant to justice, such as the rivalry between Horatio and Balthazar for the favours of Bel-imperia, tragedy ensues, and justice flees to heaven.

For the moment, however, justice is done as it was in Hades: competing extremes are moderated by compromise. The patterning in the language, clearly, is more than a perfunctory verbal manœuvre; it reflects the patterning in the plot, and helps to delineate it. In the episodes leading up to the murder, the patterns become more pronounced; Kyd uses them to reinforce the relationships on the stage, to intensify the mood, and to underline the varying temperaments of the *dramatis personae*. When Bel-imperia finishes her first frank avowal of love to Horatio in II. ii, our attention shifts to Lorenzo and Balthazar, hidden, by pre-arrangement, above, to spy on the lovers:

BALTHAZAR.   O sleep mine eyes, see not my love profan'd,
                Be deaf my ears, hear not my discontent,
                Die heart, another joys what thou deserv'st.

LORENZO.   Watch still mine eyes, to see this love disjoin'd,
                Hear still mine ears, to hear them both lament,
                Live heart, to joy at fond Horatio's fall.

                                        (II. ii. 18)

Balthazar's speech and Lorenzo's belong to the kind of 'conceited verse'
that Fraunce praised in Sidney, where the same grammatical scheme
recurs a number of times in sequence, with its key words—subject,
verb, object—shifted like interchangeable blocks. Each speaker pursues a formula of systematic invocation, directing his eyes, ears and
heart in turn to react to love, to sorrow, and to joy. But the two
speeches are also antithetical, and Lorenzo's forms an answer to
Balthazar's. Balthazar invites his faculties to abandon their function,
to wrap him in insensibility and death. Lorenzo, following the same
grammatical scheme, instructs *his* senses to redouble their activity.
The first speech expresses defeatism and passivity, the second violence
and aggression; so that while the symmetry reflects the close partner-
ship between the two eavesdroppers, the antitheses reflect the contrast
in their dispositions, the self-abandon of the one and the vindictive
energy of the other.

These speeches, perhaps, should be spoken like incantations. During
the speaking of them, there is nothing for Horatio and Bel-imperia to
do but remain silent and motionless below. When they resume their
interrupted duet, Kyd capitalises brilliantly on the interval of enforced
silence. Bel-imperia is still waiting for an answer to her declaration
of love; Horatio is still lost in his own thoughts.

BEL-IMPERIA.   Why stands Horatio speechless all this while?
HORATIO.   The less I speak, the more I meditate.
BEL-IMPERIA.   But whereon dost thou chiefly meditate?
HORATIO.   On dangers past, and pleasures to ensue.
BALTHAZAR.   On pleasures past, and dangers to ensue.
BEL-IMPERIA.   What dangers and what pleasures dost thou mean?
HORATIO.   Dangers of war, and pleasures of our love.
LORENZO.   Dangers of death, but pleasures none at all.
BEL-IMPERIA.   Let dangers go, thy war shall be with me.

                                        (II. ii. 24)

Even more strikingly than before, the patterned language here, with
its intricacies of repetition and echo, translates itself into stage

rhetoric. Balthazar and Lorenzo, unseen, unheard, give the reply to Horatio and Bel-imperia, grimly converting each cheerful presage into a menacing one. The repetitions bind the two levels of the stage together into a unity, and charge the love dialogue with heavy irony. Caught up as we are in the vigorous rhythm of the patterning, we scarcely notice such blemishes as the fatuousness of Bel-imperia's question, 'What dangers and what pleasures dost thou mean?'

In the wooing scene in the arbour, the intimate reciprocity between word and stage gesture becomes even closer:

BEL-IMPERIA. If I be Venus, thou must needs be Mars,
              And where Mars reigneth there must needs be wars.
HORATIO.   Then thus begin our wars: put forth thy hand,
              That it may combat with my ruder hand.
BEL-IMPERIA. Set forth thy foot to try the push of mine.
HORATIO.   But first my looks shall combat against thine.
BEL-IMPERIA. Then ward thyself, I dart this kiss at thee.
HORATIO.   Thus I retort the dart thou threw'st at me.
BEL-IMPERIA. Nay then, to gain the glory of the field,
              My twining arms shall yoke and make thee yield.
HORATIO.   Nay then, my arms are large and strong withal:
              Thus elms by vines are compass'd till they fall.
BEL-IMPERIA. O let me go, for in my troubled eyes
              Now may'st thou read that life in passion dies.
HORATIO.   O stay awhile and I will die with thee,
              So shalt thou yield and yet have conquer'd me.
                                              (II. iv. 34)

Here the language dictates physical gesture nearly line by line; the governing analogy between love and war completes itself in a series of bodily movements. The hand, the foot, the lips, the glance of each lover advance with ceremonious gravity, to be parried by their counter-parts from the other, just as the sallies of the Portingale troops were repulsed by the counter-assaults of the Spaniards. As with infernal justice, as with the campaign between the neighbouring kingdoms, as with the dispute over the capture of Balthazar, initial oppositions are here more than ready to merge into a dialectal unity, when the killers rush in with drawn swords and rend the fabric of reconciliation for good. Open antagonisms can be mediated and compromised; stealth cannot. From this point on the dialectic retreats into the inner spirit of Hieronimo, as he wrestles to reconcile his impulse toward revenge with the sanctions against it.

In all these cases we find Kyd using imaginatively and incisively the same rhetorical materials used so inanely and ineffectively by Mundy and the author of *The Rare Triumphs*. Sometimes, however, the use of the figures involves Kyd in the sort of decorative writing in which the decorativeness obscures narrative clarity instead of sustaining it. Balthazar's celebrated Euphuistic lament in II. i, though it establishes him as a despairing Petrarchan wooer, does so at some strain to the known facts of the plot; most of its details have the air of having been improvised hastily, and none too accurately, for the occasion. A more damaging illogicality creeps into the symmetrical flourish at the end of the same scene, when Balthazar expresses his fury with Horatio:

> I think Horatio be my destin'd plague: ·
> First in his hand he brandished a sword,
> And with that sword he fiercely waged war,
> And in that war he gave me dangerous wounds,
> And by those wounds he forced me to yield,
> And by my yielding I became his slave.
> Now in his mouth he carries pleasing words,
> Which pleasing words do harbour sweet conceits,
> Which sweet conceits are lim'd with sly deceits,
> Which sly deceits smooth Bel-imperia's ears,
> And through her ears dive down into her heart,
> And in her heart set him where I should stand.
> Thus hath he ta'en my body by his force,
> And now by sleight would captivate my soul: . . .
>   (II. i. 118)

It is of at least passing interest to notice Kyd's especial fondness for this figure of climax, or 'Marching figure', as Puttenham terms it (p. 208). Its propulsive forward motion makes it in a sense intrinsically dramatic, lends it particular power to create sequences of cause and effect. Kyd ordinarily uses it as he does here, to forge a chain in which A brings about B brings about C, each effect becoming in turn a new cause. His partiality to the figure reflects the causality ingrained in his thinking, his penchant for intrigue and concern for motivation, and the densely sequential texture of his language in general.

A chain, however, is no stronger than its weakest link, and the present ladder contains a number of shaky rungs, offences against the facts of Kyd's own story. We know that Horatio gave no dangerous wounds to Balthazar. Had he done so, we should have heard about them earlier, and, strictly speaking, they would have made it impossible for Balthazar to appear before the king to explain the circumstances of his capture. If Horatio did not dangerously wound Balthazar, by the same token he did not, with those wounds, force Balthazar to yield. And least of all did he, by the alleged wounds, make Balthazar his 'slave'; he has not even acquired nominal custody, much less privilege of restraint over him.

Of the second half of the dyptych, lines 124-9 may be allowed as the resentful fantasies of an envious rival, though we may notice that they are founded on mere conjecture; Balthazar has no information about what prompted Bel-imperial to love Horatio. It is the concluding couplet, however, that effects a final divorce between sound and sense: 'Thus hath he ta'en my body by his force, / And now by sleight would captivate my soul'. Here the pressure of the antithetic patterning requires attributing 'sleight' to Horatio in his wooing, to match the 'force' of his soldiership, and it requires, even more bizarrely, charging him with the aim of enslaving Balthazar's 'soul', to correspond to his previous capture of his 'body'. At the moment of the ringing final rhyme on 'soul', the rhetorical pattern thus reaches its satisfying auricular conclusion, and the plain prose sense of the speech, as a reflection of the humble facts of the narrative, collapses into absurdity.

The failure here, if it is not to be ascribed to a deliberate attempt to show Balthazar as the victim of his own words, as I think it is not, illustrates the tendency of figural rhetoric to strew hidden reefs in the path of its own smooth sailing. The figures develop an impetus of their own, which can carry them athwart the dramatic current as well as along with it. The danger lies not, as an older school of critics might have said, in the fact that 'passion runs not after' exact schemes and tropical symmetries, but in the tendency of the schemes and symmetries to coerce thought. They bend somewhat reluctantly to quick shifts in feeling; they pursue a statelier, more galleon-like course; they tend to promote an effect of ritualized abstraction, so that it takes a sure hand to keep them obedient to all the particulars of a given dramatic context. Perhaps there is some justice in Moody Prior's charge that 'ostentatiously rhetorical art of any sort endows almost any sentiments with an academic, generalised quality' (p. 51).

Kyd is nevertheless often strikingly successful in projecting even extreme emotion within the bristling geometry of the figures. Hieronimo's much parodied outburst in III. ii brings to the stage, for a moment of clamorous passion, a scheme derived ultimately from Petrarch, which Sidney had already used, or would shortly use, in *Astrophil and Stella*:

> O teares, no teares, but raine from beautie's skies,
>   Making those Lillies and those Roses grow,
>   Which ay most faire, now more then most faire show,
> While gracefull pitty beauty beautifies.
> O honied sighs, which from that breast do rise,
>
> .   .   .   .
>
> O plaints conserv'd in such a sugred phraise,
>   That eloquence it selfe envies your praise,
> While sobd out words a perfect Musike give.
>   Such teares, sighs, plaints, no sorrow is, but joy:
>   Or if such heavenly signes must prove annoy,
> All mirth farewell, let me in sorrow live.
>   (*Poems*, ed. W. A. Ringler (1962), p. 231)

Sidney's use of the figure creates a sense of majestic calm. Each quatrain, through a spacious suspension, elaborates on one of the beloved's attributes of sorrow—her tears, her sighs, her plaints—and all three are made to converge at length under the sign of joy rather than sorrow. The theme of the poem is the transformation of apparent sorrow into pleasure through the beloved's beauty. Kyd, by packing the three successive apostrophes into three successive lines, and stressing the correspondences between them, achieves an effect of swollen passion breaking loose:

> O eyes, no eyes, but fountains fraught with tears;
> O life, no life, but lively form of death;
> O world, no world, but mass of public wrongs,
> Confus'd and fill'd with murder and misdeeds;
> O sacred heavens! If this unhallow'd deed . . .
>   (III. ii. 1)

In Sidney, the lady's manifestations of sorrow remain on the same level of importance and intensity; they do not evolve, except perhaps in the direction of increasing articulateness. Kyd proceeds climactically, through circles of widening significance: eyes, life, world, heavens—organ, organism, social milieu, cosmos. The theme is the progressive perversion of all order and health into disease and disorder through the murder of Horatio. Each of the first three members of the series represents a realm felt to be deranged by the murder. In the case of the final realm, the heavens, the question is left open—left, indeed, for the heavens themselves to answer.

Hieronimo's sense of cosmic dislocation leads him to a second series, in which he enumerates forces that spur him to revenge: the night, the ugly fiends, the cloudy day. Finally, in a recapitulation—what Puttenham would term a 'collection'—of the sort adopted by Sidney in line 12 of his sonnet, Hieronimo gathers together all the phenomena he has discoursed upon, and appeals to them for aid in the discovery of the identities of his son's killers:

> Eyes, life, world, heavens, hell, night, and day,
> See, search, shew, send, some man, some mean, that may—
>
> (III. ii. 22)

At which point, the stage direction informs us, '*A letter falleth*'. Hieronimo's recapitulation thus serves a dramatic as well as a rhetorical purpose. It constitutes a plea for action, and it leads up to a significant bit of stage business, the dropping of Bel-imperia's letter with its disclosure about the murderers. What is remarkable is that Kyd has worked out the schematism of the speech with a high degree of precision—no rhetorical treatise of the day would have had to apologise for offering it in illustration of the figures it uses—yet with enough flexibility in detail, especially prosodic detail, to make it convincing as an expression of Hieronimo's grief. What Elizabethan audiences found exciting and memorable in the language of *The Spanish Tragedy* was precisely such moments of high artifice as these. The numerous parodies of Hieronimo's lament, and of Balthazar's complaints, testify to the auricular impact of Kyd's theatrical tropes—testify, that is, to the pleasures of rhetoric, as well as, by their scorn, to its perils.

One problem faced by the bereaved Hieronimo throughout is how to find adequate expression for his feelings. When we meet him first, after the battle in Act I, he only with difficulty refrains from pleading his son's cause against Lorenzo. He refrains not out of any mistrust of his own eloquence, but because the king's well-known wisdom makes eloquence unnecessary; the king can be counted on to decide justly.

Despite its evident scrupulosity, however, the king's justice, bending
as it does to the pressure of the world's prejudices, inspires little confidence. Hieronimo, along with the rest, accepts it without protest,
but it is not long before he is plunged into a situation in which he can
find neither justice nor relief for his anguished feelings. The latter,
indeed, becomes as cardinal a necessity as the former, and a main
spur to revenge; revenge alone can provide a satisfactory outlet for
his grief and outrage. 'Where shall I run to breathe abroad my woes',
he cries, entering distractedly shortly after the murder,

> My woes, whose weight hath wearied the earth?
> Or mine exclaims, that have surcharg'd the air
> With ceaseless plaints for my deceased son?
> (III. vii. 1)

The immensity of Hieronimo's desolation demands cosmic scope for
its utterance. Even his adjutants, the compassionate winds, who have
vexed nature in his behalf, have wrought too feebly, for 'still tormented
is my tortur'd soul/With broken sighs and restless passions'. Words,
even when they denote extremest woe, remain words. Even when
reinforced by the eloquence of the blustering winds, verbal plaints
remain insufficient to express the fullness of grief. Still less can they
bring about justice or revenge. Words, indeed, as Hieronimo comes to
feel, are 'unfruitful', and yet, they are all he has.

> But wherefore waste I mine unfruitful words,
> When naught but blood will satisfy my woes?
> I will go plain me to my lord the king,
> And cry aloud for justice through the court,
> Wearing the flints with these my wither'd feet,
> And either purchase justice by entreats
> Or tire them all with my revenging threats.
> (III. vii. 67)

If language cannot be made to relieve his feelings, or accomplish
justice, at least it can be turned into a weapon of harassment, and
used to disturb the peace of mind of his foes.

The fact that his cries go unheard—partly through his own impru-
dence, partly through Lorenzo's cunning—deepens Hieronimo's
skepticism toward the efficacy of speech. The decision to revenge,
which crystallises in the *Vindicta mihi* soliloquy (III. xiii. 1), carries
with it the realisation that henceforth, in order to combat those who

have violated the natural current between speech and feeling, he must tamper with it himself. Having been driven, by abnormal circumstances, to adopt a course of action abhorrent to him, he must embrace the unnatural methods that will enable him to accomplish his purpose. He must enjoin his eye to 'observation', and his tongue 'To milder speeches than [his] spirit affords' (III. xiii. 40). From this moment on, he must turn language into something opaque and deceptive, instead of revelatory and transparent.

The apparition of Don Bazulto, the forlorn *senex* who stands mutely by at the sessions, proffering the humble supplication for his murdered son, acquaints Hieronimo with a kind of silent eloquence that he recognises as more potent than mere speech. Convinced of the futility of spoken words, Don Bazulto refuses to give voice to his distress. Instead, he presents the supplication. Ink must 'bewray', he explains, what blood began; passion must be reduced to formal writ, to documentary petition, to visible emblem. As the writ serves Bazulto, so the bloody napkin dipped in Horatio's wounds serves Hieronimo, as a mute testimony or dumb significant, helping to express the inexpressible. The old man himself, returning to the stage to confront Hieronimo alone, suddenly becomes an image in a hallucination, the ghost of Horatio, until Hieronimo awakens to the realisation that he is staring at a simulacrum of himself. The scene bears fresh witness to Kyd's power to make figured rhetoric convey intensity of feeling:

> Ay, now I know thee, now thou nam'st thy son,
> Thou art the lively image of my grief:
> Within thy face, my sorrows I may see.
> Thy eyes are gumm'd with tears, thy cheeks are wan,
> Thy forehead troubl'd, and thy mutt'ring lips
> Murmur sad words abruptly broken off,
> By force of windy sighs thy spirit breathes,
> And all this sorrow riseth for thy son:
> And selfsame sorrow feel I for my son.
>   (III. xiii. 161)

Gazing at the old man gradually becomes, for Hieronimo, a process of self-discovery, an act of mirror-gazing. As on previous occasions, the patterned rhetoric participates deeply in the configuration of action: the anaphora, the repetitions, the near-identity of the two last lines, all express the growing identity felt by Hieronimo between himself and

Bazulto. Bazulto is his semblable, as the audience already knows. The patterning in the language allows Hieronimo to make the discovery himself, as the two bereft old fathers stare hopelessly into each other's faces.

By this time, words scarcely avail Hieronimo at all, either as vehicles of woe, or vessels of truth. Like Lorenzo, he will henceforth keep his own counsel: 'pocas palabras, mild as the lamb' becomes the motto (III. xiv. 118); a distrust of all language replaces his former fluent security with it. When asked to contribute some 'pleasing motion' to entertain the visiting Portingales, he answers with a bit of autobiography:

> When I was young, I gave my mind
> And plied myself to fruitless poetry:
> Which though it profit the professor naught,
> Yet is it passing pleasing to the world.
>
> (IV. i. 71)

Hieronimo may arraign the fruitlessness of poetry out of bitter experience. His skill has in fact already diverted the court once before, in the show of knights and scutcheons in Act I, but it has not enabled him to give proper utterance to his grief, or to secure justice, earthly, celestial or infernal. The play commanded for the visiting monarch will allow him, at last, to validate his poetical talent by translating it into action— reprehensible action, to be sure, but action none the less. For once, fruitless poetry will bear fruit. And it will do so in terms suitable both to the distracted poet and to the ceremonious audience. Suitable to the distracted poet in being an incomprehensible medley of tongues, expressive of the chaos in Hieronimo's spirit; suitable to the court in being 'tragedia cothurnata, fitting kings' (IV. i. 160)—appropriate in stateliness and style to the pompous occasion it is intended to honour.

In view of the sustained emphasis in The Spanish Tragedy on verbal artifice, it seems reasonable to think that the original audience did indeed hear the play within a play spoken 'in sundry languages'. An audience that had already listened to various miscellaneous scraps of Latin, Italian, and Spanish in the course of the afternoon, including Hieronimo's 14-line dirge recited over the bleeding body of Horatio, would not have been likely to balk at the brief polyglot interlude of Soliman and Perseda. Even if the original script, in its sundry languages, ran to the same length as its English translation, the plot had already

been fully explained in advance; it would twice be interrupted
for further explanation while in progress, would be interrupted a
third time for a spectacular stabbing and was capable of being
mimed vividly throughout so as to heighten and clarify its essential
gestures.[3]

The effect, perhaps, would have been to suggest the extremes to
which language can evolve, the lengths to which verbal ingenuity
can be carried and how unintelligible words can become when they
lose their moorings in the realities they are meant to express. The
jabbering in four languages turns the whole phenomenon of speech
under a strange phosphorescent glare, revealing it as a kind of dis-
embodied incantation, a surrealistic dance of abstractions, divorced from
roots in lived existence. Hieronimo's experience has involved a progressive alienation of language, a breakdown of the links between
rhetoric and reality. To this alienation the playlet forms a fitting
climax. It acts out the insubstantiality of words, sets them at logger-
heads with motives and at cross-purposes with each other, shows them
as the fantasms they threaten to bec me, and cancels them out, finally,

[3] The presence of a puzzling note from the printer at IV. iv. 10, to the
effect that the playlet would be *set down in English . . . for the easier understanding
to every public reader*, together with some other oddities of this scene, have led
editors to suspect textual corruption in this portion of the play. Edwards
(pp. xxxiii–xl) advances an ingenious and intricate hypothesis concerning the
copy in an attempt to account for the difficulties: (1) In order to shorten
The Spanish Tragedy for performance, Kyd revised the original ending by
striking out the English playlet and substituting a pantomime with a few
snatches of gibberish ('*sundry languages*'). But the original ending had already
been printed in the first edition of the play, now lost. (2) The printer of the
extant 1592 edition, when setting up this part of the play, had recourse both
to the earlier printed text and to Kyd's manuscript revision. Confused he
failed to see that he was dealing with alternate versions of the same scene, and
so printed them as successive episodes, but did recognise the discrepancy
between Hieronimo's promise of sundry languages and the actual English
provided in the earlier text, and so inserted his note to explain the anomaly.

My own view, which concurs generally with that of S. F. Johnson, '*The
Spanish Tragedy*, or Babylon Revisited', in *Essays on Shakespeare and Elizabethan Drama*, ed. R. Hosley (1963), is that the printer's note may be taken at
face value, and that the finale of the play is essentially intelligible as it stands.
Certain problems remain, chiefly the discrepancy between Hieronimo's speech
of explanation to the court and his subsequent refusal to explain, coupled with
references to a mysterious 'vow' he has made, but it is doubtful whether the
problems require a hypothesis so drastic as that of Edwards.

F

by a stroke of the sword. The disclosure of Horatio's mutilated body
provides a more devastating climax, a silent spectacle of woe for which
words serve humbly as interpreters again:

> See here my show, look on this spectacle:
> Here lay my hope, and here my hope hath end:
> Here lay my heart, and here my heart was slain:
> Here lay my treasure, here my treasure lost:
> Here lay my bliss, and here my bliss bereft:
> But hope, heart, treasure, joy and bliss,
> All fled, fail'd, died, yea, all decay'd with this.
>   (IV. iv. 89)

The patterned litany, with its insistent anaphora on the adverb 'here',
pins us relentlessly to this moment in time and this point in space. It
enforces repeatedly on us the reality of the visible, palpable fact and so,
momentarily, restores the wholeness of the fractured image.

Having thus published to the world what heretofore he confided
only to the winds, the night, and the churlish heavens, Hieronimo
ends with the declared determination to 'as resolute conclude his
part / As any of the actors gone before'. When, at the king's command, the guards bar his flight, he concludes his long agony by biting
out his tongue. The final lunatic gesture betrays the final despair at
the uselessness of talk, the berserk resolve to have done with language
forever. And not spoken language only—the knife he is given to mend
his pen he plunges into his heart; the last instrument available to
facilitate expression he uses savagely to annul all further possibility of
expression.

The Spanish Tragedy, then, with its thickets of figural rhetoric, is
also to some degree a critique of rhetoric, an assessment of the limits
of impassioned speech. We might term it a theatrical digression on a
familiar Senecan text: *Curae leves loquuntur; ingentes stupent.* Language,
including the patterned language borrowed from the sonneteers,
proves able to meet the expressive requirements of epic narration in
Act I, and the portrayals of love and hate in Act II. With the murder
of Horatio, the world's equilibrium is upset; justice goes awry, and
language with it. An unnatural state of divorce sets in between thought
and word, word and deed; speech deteriorates as an instrument of
reality and an agent of truth. In the distracted climax, it horribly apes
the confusions of the world, sending them back magnified and further

deformed as from a distorting mirror. The Babel-Babylon playlet does not so much reflect the visible ceremony of the Spanish court as its inner ethical chaos.

Action, in nondramatic poetry, remains of necessity verbal action. The poet, rebuffed by his mistress or the world, withdraws, perhaps, into frustration, or comes to terms with his plight rhetorically—through argument or retort, through objurgation, defiance, or self-inflicted melancholy. In the drama, words must be affirmed or denied by other acts—coupled with blows, or mingled with kisses. Under normal conditions, words and acts complete and complement each other: a half-angry, half-submissive Balthazar displays both anger and submissiveness to his captors and his captor king, and yields himself to both; a proud Hieronimo beguiles the triumphant court with vignettes of an earlier epoch when England invaded the Iberian peninsula. When the healthy reciprocity between words and acts is fractured, they develop independent and dangerous lives of their own; instead of confirming and corroborating each other, they delude and destroy. When the divorce becomes chronic, it leads, ultimately, to the splintering, shattering finale of *The Spanish Tragedy*, in which all communication breaks down, the community collapses in horror, and the stage is left littered with silent corpses for whom there is nearly no-one alive to mourn.

*   *   *   ·

The heir to Kyd's innovations with theatrical rhetoric, as to Marlowe's, was of course Shakespeare. Shakespeare's early plays, especially those of the so-called 'lyric' period, revel in verbal artifice. They exploit far more intensively than Kyd does the expressive possibilities of the schemes and figures, making them into a distinct mode of apprehending experience while at the same time using them to comment on the inadequacies of that mode. They also adopt some of Kyd's experiments in staging. The balcony scene in *Two Gentlemen of Verona* rings new and complex changes on the eavesdropping episode of *The Spanish Tragedy*; the overspying climax of *Love's Labour's Lost* transposes the same pattern into a comic key; and the balcony scene in *Romeo and Juliet* carries the device to its brilliant conclusion. In all these instances Shakespeare borrows from Kyd the arrangement of the split stage—now split into as many as three levels—in which one character or set of characters, transcendently placed with respect to the rest, listens to the rhetoric of the rest, completes it, mockingly, bitingly, or sadly, and in so doing reveals the limitations of it, or of his own rhetoric, as a vehicle of feeling. By eavesdropping on artifice, we find ourselves placed, if not beyond artifice, at least in the more inclusive and spacious domain of the natural.

The falling in love of Romeo and Juliet at the Capulets' ball plays other variations on the arbour idyll of *The Spanish Tragedy*. Again two lovers, oblivious of the menacing presences around them, perform a ceremony of union—rhetorically, in the sonnet that requires their interlinked speeches for its completion, and physically, in the conjunction of palms and lips that seals the verbal union. In a related play, the wretched Richard II throws himself despairingly to earth like the Viceroy of Portugal in *The Spanish Tragedy*, refusing, like the Viceroy, to be consoled for a loss that has not yet occurred, persisting in grief, abandoning himself to a torrent of schemes and figures to describe it, and so, in his case, making the loss real. Kyd's treatment of the Viceroy merely hints at a connection between self-indulgence in lament and an excessive fondness for patterned language. In Shakespeare the connection becomes insistent. Richard's verbal preciosity is precisely the index of his shallow feelings, his insufficient sense of himself and of the world. Like Hieronimo, Richard learns the limits of rhetoric through suffering, reaching, in the abdication scene, an awareness of the degree to which his true misery lies 'all within'.

Ultimately Shakespeare absorbs the figures into his richer and more flexible mature style. Where they continue to call attention to themselves, as with Polonius or Claudius, they usually serve as negative examples of what art cannot do, or of how feelings can be trumped up or disguised by them. The burning away of the more obvious figures leaves a style increasingly individualised, increasingly able to express unique raptures and incomparable sufferings. Where rapture and suffering become so intense as to blot out consciousness, they blot out figuration also—the fragmentary mutterings of Lear as he bends over the body of Cordelia, the ravings of Othello before he falls swooning at Iago's feet. From these extremes Shakespeare returns us to a more balanced world, where enough remains of rhythm, recurrence, and ceremonious phrase to suggest an ordered existence, but where the individual accent predominates, so that the schemes and figures, in their primitive stiffness, now seem like fossils from an archaic epoch in stylistic evolution, when the speech of the individual was still scarcely differentiated from that of the tribe, and characters could express their most intimate passions only by borrowing the heavily patterned language common to the entire society.

Note

Biography. Christopher Marlowe was born in 1564, the same year as Shakespeare. He was educated at the King's School, Canterbury, and went as a scholar to Corpus Christi College, Cambridge. The university authorities refused him a degree on the grounds of non-residence, but relented after an intervention from the Privy Council. This is usually taken to imply that Marlowe's absences had been on government business, probably as a spy on Catholic exiles. In May 1593 he was arrested on suspicion of blasphemy, but before the charge was heard he was murdered in Deptford by a disreputable trio, who since some at least of them had also been government spies, may have been concerned to keep Marlowe's mouth shut. (See also Note on Kyd preceding Chapter III.)

Works. *The Tragedy of Dido, Queen of Carthage* (?1587; printed 1594); *Tamburlaine the Great,* parts I and II (?1587–8; printed 1592); *The Jew of Malta* (?1589–90; printed 1633); *The Massacre at Paris* (?1590–92; printed edition undated); *Doctor Faustus* (?1592–3, possibly 1589; printed 1604 and 1616); *Edward II* (?1591–3; printed 1594). Marlowe also translated from Ovid and Lucan and wrote *Hero and Leander* (unfinished; printed 1598).

Modern Editions. *The Works of Christopher Marlowe* were edited by C. F. Tucker Brooke (1910), *The Plays* by L. Kirschbaum (1962) and *The Complete Plays* by I. Ribner (1963).

References in this chapter are to the following single play editions: *The Life of Marlowe* and *Dido,* ed. Tucker Brooke (1930); *Tamburlaine,* ed. U. M. Ellis Fermor (1930); *The Jew of Malta* and *The Massacre at Paris,* ed. H. S. Bennett (1931); *Edward II,* ed. H. B. Charlton and R. D. Waller, revised F. N. Lees (1955); *Dr. Faustus,* ed. J. D. Jump (1962) and *Poems,* ed. L. C. Martin (1931).

Scholarship and Criticism. A. P. Rossiter's *English Drama from Early Times to the Elizabethans* (1950), and *A Guide to English Literature,* 2, ed. B. Ford (1955) have important references to Marlowe, and D. M. Bevington's *From 'Mankind' to Marlowe* (1962) considers the development of his dramaturgy from the Interludes. P. H. Kocher, *Christopher Marlowe* (1946), H. Levin, *The Overreacher* (1954), D. Cole, *Suffering and Evil in the Plays of Christopher Marlowe* (1962) and J. B. Steane, *Marlowe* (1964) are critical studies of Marlowe's career. J. P. Brockbank's *Marlowe: Dr. Faustus* (1962) is a detailed 'reading' of the play.

C. Leech has edited *Marlowe: A Collection of Critical Essays* (1964) and the *Tulane Drama Review* has published an issue devoted wholly to Marlowe (1964).

M. M. Mahood's study of Marlowe's Heroes is reprinted in *Elizabethan Drama: Essays,* ed. Kaufmann.

For texts of *Cambises* and *Mankind* see notes to Chapters I and II.

IV

Marlowe the Dramatist

NICHOLAS BROOKE

*

MARLOWE'S quatercentenary in 1964 was inevitably overshadowed by the Shakespeare celebrations; but it produced some notable events, from which I would select two: the production, by Clifford Williams with the Royal Shakespeare Company, of *The Jew of Malta*; and the publication, by the *Tulane Drama Review*, of a volume of newly written essays on Marlowe. It is true that the success of *The Jew* was attributed by many reviewers to what Philip Hope-Wallace (in *The Guardian*) called the 'sending-up' of Marlowe's play, apparently assuming that it was being played for laughs that would have disconcerted Marlowe. Yet nearly fifty years ago T. S. Eliot called the play a savage farce,[1] and his point has been respected (often uneasily) in most subsequent criticism. The ways divide, not simply on how good a play Marlowe wrote, but on what *sort* of play. The definition of what is dramatic has been drastically changed in this century, and in ways that promote this new theatrical success for Marlowe in a mode quite different from that in which he was supposed to excel.

A similar point is made by J. R. Brown in *Tulane Drama Review*; and it is remarkable that at least two thirds of the essays there are given to vindications either of Marlowe's structural methods, or of his theatrical skill. These are precisely the abilities which critical tradition denied him, and it is only fifteen years since a critic as distinguished as A. P. Rossiter (whose book was certainly not regarded as old-fashioned) wrote:

[Kyd] is . . . a true dramatist in his plotting; Marlowe, except in

[1] 'It is the farce of the old English humour, the terribly serious, even savage comic humour, the humour which spent its last breath in the decadent genius of Dickens.' *Selected Essays*, reprinted in *Marlowe: A Collection of Critical Essays*.

Edward II, is a dramatist only in his dramatic poetry—in great vistas of *mind*, rather than of the slip-knot of fate or events pulling tight on human lives. (p. 160)

Rossiter's words had a specific purpose in pointing to the significance of Kyd, and this may explain the narrow sense in which he used 'dramatic' here; if we are to see Marlowe as a dramatist we shall have to enlarge that term to include forms of theatrical experience that have little enough to do with 'the slip-knot of fate'. But Rossiter did at least allow that Marlowe's poetry was dramatic; it is still not uncommon to find Marlowe regarded as an epic or lyric poet involved in drama only because it was the dominant literary form of his time; whereas, in fact, it was not until he made it so. It may therefore be worth restating briefly the view that Marlowe's dramatic poetry is radically unlike his other work (the translations of Ovid, or *Hero and Leander*), and that its nature and function, in the use of verse itself, are in fact intensely dramatic.

DRAMATIC POETRY

The point can be conveniently made about Tamburlaine's famous line 'And ride in triumph through Persepolis'. The words in fact occur three times; first as a relatively prosaic prediction by Menaphon when the latent rhythm holds no more than sycophancy; it is only after Tamburlaine has repeated them, and then led back into a final repetition as the climax of a rhythmic build-up through three powerful lines, that the stress is shifted from 'ride' to 'triumph', and Persepolis is translated from a geographic fact into an imaginative El Dorado:

> MENAPHON.   Your majesty shall shortly have your wish,
> And ride in triumph through Persepolis.
> TAMBURLAINE.   And ride in triumph through Persepolis!
> Is it not brave to be a king, Techelles?
> Usumcasane and Theridamas,
> Is it not passing brave to be a king,
> And ride in triumph through Persepolis?
> (I, *Tam.*, II. v. 48)

This transformation of routine statement into sensuous vision is specifically a *dramatic* effect, the use of poetry *for* dramatic effect. It is also the transformation of routine blank verse into Marlowe's 'mighty line': in final form it is, as Marlowe's verse is said always to be, 'end-stopped'—on that depends its peculiar rhythmic splendour. Marlowe's effective use of this device may be clearer if we scotch an oft-repeated historical fallacy, that English blank verse was normally end-stopped until Shakespeare released it: it was not normally end-stopped in Surrey's *Aeneid*, or in *Gorboduc*, or in lesser works until Marlowe stopped it to contain the rhythmic splendour of such lines as this.

The dramatic intensity here is emphasised by the flatness of Techelles' response:

> O, my lord, 'tis sweet and full of pomp!

Usumcasane and Theridamas improve on this:

> USUMCASANE.   To be a king, is half to be a god.
> THERIDAMAS.   A god is not so glorious as a king . . .

But at an ironic hint of reproof from Tamburlaine, Theridamas retreats hastily:

> TAMBURLAINE.   Why say, Theridamas, wilt thou be a king?
> THERIDAMAS.   Nay, though I praise it, I can live without it.

Tamburlaine's teasing has possibilities for laughter. But teasing is the prerogative of the bully, which Tamburlaine certainly is; the play would be dull if it had not established the added dimension of imaginative splendour, a dramatic extension of the situation beyond the scope of 'plot', and the kind of effect which an over-obtrusive plot would inhibit.

The climax of this movement, after the brief scene vi, comes in Tamburlaine's famous speech over the dying Cosroe:

> Our souls, whose faculties can comprehend
> The wondrous architecture of the world,
> And measure every wandering planet's course,
> Still climbing after knowledge infinite,
> And always moving as the restless spheres,
> Wills us to wear ourselves and never rest,
> Until we reach the ripest fruit of all,
> That perfect bliss and sole felicity,
> The sweet fruition of an earthly crown.
>   (II. vii. 21)

It is an obvious failure of critical response to take the last lines as *mere* bathos: the whole force of the sustained build-up of the passage is to establish its end as a climax. But the climax that needs all that support is in the nature of a tour-de-force: the dramatic effect depends on the paradox of a *concrete* aspiration that is not just vague dreaming. Outside the play, this would be no more than impressive nonsense (lop off the last three lines, and it would be an innocuous day-dream); inside, it is the core of the drama—something at once splendid and horrible, the horror kept before us by the presence of the dying Cosroe.

For it is quite wrong to suppose that Marlowe underrates the horror. I have already called attention to the simultaneous bully and hero in Tamburlaine: the quality of the play is to see that the hero cannot exist in human experience without being a bully. In the same way, as the triumphs mount, so do the horrors: Tamburlaine's triumph over Bajazeth is celebrated in jeering laughter at the banquet in IV. iv.

The romantic fallacy in Marlowe criticism offered these passages of splendid verse as moments of 'inspiration', when Marlowe's imagination 'caught fire', and by putting them together out of context added up an idea of Marlowe's 'mind' which excluded the rest of the plays as 'inferior'. To this I would oppose the proposition that such passages are functional, and significant as part of (decidedly *not* the whole of) a much more complex dramatic development. This is as true of *Faustus* as it is of *Tamburlaine*: the celebrated address to Helen is not an isolated effusion of genius, but the climax of a dramatic sequence in which its distinctive quality of verse has a specifically dramatic function. Helen has appeared before, earlier in the scene, to a chorus of admiration from the scholars:

> No marvel though the angry Greeks pursu'd
> With ten years' war the rape of such a queen,
> Whose heavenly beauty passeth all compare.
> (xviii. 30)

On that the Old Man enters, with the specific warning that 'This magic . . . will charm thy soul to hell.' He proceeds in quiet but effective verse to develop a concept of Christian redemptive love:

> For, gentle son, I speak it not in wrath
> Or envy of thee, but in tender love
> And pity of thy future misery;

> And so have hope that this my kind rebuke,
> Checking thy body, may amend thy soul.
>
> (l. 50)

The tone is governed by the adjectives 'gentle', 'tender', 'kind'; but a modern audience has no difficulty in grasping how this paternal love provokes the reaction of despair in Faustus. His recalling of Helen is at first a gesture of defiance, to 'extinguish clear / Those thoughts that do dissuade me from my vow'. To make it more than that calls (as in *Tamburlaine*) for a tour-de-force:

> Was this the face that launch'd a thousand ships
> And burnt the topless towers of Ilium?
>
> (l. 99)

The radical change of rhythm makes this infinitely more than mere 'magic' or a glutted longing: the expectation of squalid sensuality is dramatically transformed into the realisation of sexual love as a positive experience, in direct contrast to the concept of Christian love:

> Sweet Helen, make me immortal with a kiss.
>
> (l. 101)

The two ideas of Love are co-existent and irreconcilable; and just as Tamburlaine's rhapsody on the sweet fruition of an earthly crown is spoken in the presence of a dying king, so here the old man re-enters as reminder of the other values which Faustus' equally concrete imagination is in conflict with. The point could not be made with a less effective verse; and that, more than inspiration, explains its presence here.

Marlowe as poet, then, is essentially a dramatic poet. Verse, in these celebrated passages, is used for specific dramatic effect, and not for a merely routine superiority to prose. It is used where it is relevant; so it is in *The Jew of Malta*: it is not relevant in slapstick scenes, and it is not used in them. Marlowe was not a poet who lacked dramatic talent, he was the reverse; a dramatist who had the resources of a great poet at his command, when required.

DRAMATIC STRUCTURE: (i) *The Jew of Malta* and *Tamburlaine*

The dramatic context of Marlowe's verse, then, is demonstrable: it is an intensely *theatrical* experience. The problem is the nature of his dramatic construction: whether there is an adequate structure on which to rest such climactic utterance. An answer may be suggested by the theatrical success of the production of *The Jew* to which I have already referred, for that was achieved with very little help from the poetry: the best verse was allowed about as much eloquence as a symphonic theme tapped out on drums alone (in London: there was some improvement in Stratford). The kind of bafflement evinced in criticism can be represented most clearly through two opposite accounts. One is Eliot's, already referred to, calling it a farce: with much of the play this is satisfactory, but not for all of it, for at times it has a seriousness unrelated to farce. The opposite is the general view against which Eliot was reacting, which can be summed up in Rossiter's words (though I must stress that Rossiter was *not* thinking of this play): 'the slip-knot of fate or events pulling tight on human lives'. In a very limited sense the play does show this; but not in any sense that fits with the traditional idea of Greek tragedy from which I suppose that definition to derive. Thus *The Jew* was supposed to be a failed tragedy: a play which ought, perhaps, to have attended consistently to its plot like *The Spanish Tragedy*, but failed to do so, and finally fell into 'mere melodrama' as Barabbas fell into the boiling pot.

This idea of the significance of plot involves a belief that structure is necessarily logical in form. It applies as well to Eliot's idea of farce, for he had Ben Jonson's *Volpone* in mind; and though *The Jew* was obviously a model for Jonson's play, they differ precisely in that Jonson supplied a coherence of plot and moral rectitude that Marlowe did not attempt. The fact is that classical structure and moral orthodoxy are about the last things which could have been derived from Marlowe; they are what Jonson imposed on his model, not what he found there. Either way, seen as tragedy or as farce, Marlowe's play fails to satisfy the expectation of logical structure.

A totally different approach is necessary, for there is something absurd about a critical account which can only accept about half a dozen speeches from a full-length play as being 'worthy' of what it is supposed to be. This is why I stressed 'theatrical experience', for obviously the relevant structure, whether or not it is logical, must be a deployment of related and co-ordinated theatrical experiences. One might do worse than begin with the ending. Seen visually, it achieves an emblematic tableau of one of the basic themes of traditional pictorial art—the fires of hell.[2] A very moral conclusion, one might suppose; but the trick by which Barabbas is consigned there is as funny as it is startling. And its agent is not God but Ferneze, so that the ironically open moral with which the play leaves us is in Ferneze's words:

> So, march away; and let due praise be given
> Neither to Fate nor Fortune, but to Heaven.
>
> (V. v. 123)

Audiences nowadays may laugh too easily at that, but there is no sense that their laughter offends the play's solemnity. Christian orthodoxy can no doubt accept this, and the Machiavel does not return to refute it; but his prologue returns to memory most eloquently here:

> I count religion but a childish toy,
> And hold there is no sin but ignorance.
>
> (l. 14)

Morality is simultaneously satisfied and repudiated in the simultaneous violence and laughter of the conclusion.

That is, of course, an intensely dramatic achievement; but it is not one which corresponds at all to formulations of a 'tragic' or a 'comic' experience. It is the perfect conclusion to a form of drama alien to either; and it is a dramatic form which I have described in terms of visual action much more than words in the text: not to undervalue words, but because they have no coherence divorced from the stage. Furthermore it is a dramatic climax which cannot be defined satisfactorily in terms of the hero. What Barabbas is, or what Marlowe thought of him, is only of marginal concern in this dramatic effect: Barabbas is the central actor in a play that has ranged through imaginative perception, human passion, violent cruelty, farcical slapstick, and so on; and the actor has ranged with it. This is a range which a drama committed to narrative logic and character study cannot possibly encompass.

Now if these reflections have any validity, the accepted lines of critical discussion of Marlowe's work must be seen to have very little relevance. The solution lies in exposing another historical fallacy

[2] For the cauldron, see G. K. Hunter: 'The Theology of Marlowe's *The Jew of Malta*', *Journal of the Warburg and Courtauld Institutes* (1964). Marlowe's frequent use of traditional iconography for his stage spectacle is noted by M. C. Bradbrook in 'The Inheritance of Christopher Marlowe', *Theology* (1964), and by J. Powell in the Marlowe issue of *Tulane Drama Review*.

no less complete than that about blank verse: the widely assumed existence of a kind of tragedy as a genre in which Marlowe was or ought to have been writing, fitfully illuminating it with genius, but elsewhere doing it so badly as to expose himself to derisive laughter. This supposed line of descent from a type of play trying hard to provoke pity and fear, but lapsing from sheer incompetence into absurdity, is a complete fiction. Forty years' study of Shakespeare's transformation of the chronicle play into his histories led to the discovery that there had been no chronicle plays for him to transform. In exactly the same way, Marlowe did not take hold of a popular ranting melodrama in King Cambises' vein, there was no such thing. There was no English tragedy before Kyd and Marlowe outside the Inns of Court, where it was amateur, private and incredibly dull.

I have not, of course, seen a full production of *Cambises*, but I have seen most of it in action with a stage practice class of students,[3] and seen it with continual surprise and unexpected pleasure. I had assumed that it was—as usually described—an almost unbelievably crude and incompetent attempt to assimilate Senecan blood tragedy with the popular lineaments of a morality. An attempt to be serious so preposterously beyond Preston's powers that it would sink any attempt at performance. A foolish assumption when one considers that sophisticated audiences could be expected to remember this play at least thirty years after its first performance. It turned out in fact to be very different, in some ways at least that should have been quite obvious: principally in that, though it is about Cambises, it is essentially Ambidexter's play—he is its presenter, a frequent commentator, and he enters freely into all parts of the action and at all social levels. He is far more than pleasant mirth mixed into the lamentable tragedy, as the title-page had it, for the play has a consistent framework of his sardonic and malicious humour—and it is, frequently, very funny. Within this ambidextrous frame, Cambises himself is frequently funny too, in the sense that the play invites and assumes laughter at him. But the sardonic evil that Ambidexter offers is met by glimpses of the really shocking and appalling: the irresistible corruptions of power in Sisambes and Cambises are funny, but frightening too; and surrounding them the strongest

[3] In the University of East Anglia; inevitably only a crude approximation to theatre conditions, but near enough to reveal forms of theatrical impact such as one rarely guesses at in mere reading. The dramatic structure of *Cambises* is discussed in Chapter V, below.

fear is engendered in the sense of what life is like in a tyrant-dominated society. Through our laughter we become aware of the total collapse of any reliable forms of behaviour. This predominantly, but not exclusively, farcical treatment is a much less aristocratic response to social instability than Surrey's subdued stoicism, which was not far removed from it in time; but farce with a frightening edge is a more convincing image than Surrey's elegant sonnets.

Cambises is no masterpiece, and Preston was certainly not a genius; but nor is the play a merely silly failure. It seems to me likely that when Shakespeare mocked King Cambises' vein he was not so much mocking the play, as accepting its derision of its ranting actor. The number of references, including Shakespeare's, might itself suggest some kind of respect. Preston did not invent the form, of course: one could extend this kind of observation backwards into stricter moralities like *Mankind*, where it would be naïve indeed to describe the play simply in terms of its overt moral, which is as often parodied as endorsed.

What I am getting at is that these plays are not serious drama gone silly in deference to a clownish audience: they represent a form of play which can move between the polarities of straightforward seriousness and outright farce, not by alternating different sets of actors in separate plots, but by varying use of the same performers in a manner no more bewildering to the audience than the alternations between patriotism, satire, slapstick and pathos in a modern review. It is a curiously ambiguous sort of drama, in which some scenes are simply funny, some simply painful, but many more exist in a sort of limbo where you may laugh, or may not, but you will be pained as well, either way. It is, in fact, in these respects very like the ambiguous plays of Ionesco or Pinter: not as fantastic as Ionesco, nor as limited in scope as Pinter. Such plays do not lose their force when you laugh—indeed the more you laugh, the more the play bites. To grasp the form of plays like *The Jew of Malta* we have to forget the idea of 'unintended laughter'.

Now once one sees that this, and not some degenerate broken-backed tragedy, is the tradition in which Marlowe wrote *The Jew*, one's view of it changes considerably. It is not at all an imaginative tragedy in which Marlowe lost interest, nor is it strictly a farce; it is a *Cambises*-type play given an additional twist in the added dimension of some brilliantly imaginative writing for Barabbas himself. The structure of such a play cannot be considered in simply narrative terms (though there is of course a narrative sequence) because the rapid changes of

theatrical mode which are its chief resource have no narrative significance; still less can it be considered in terms of character, for the actor
who takes Barabbas' part will have to display a range of theatrical
power in which character-definition (though existing) will be quite
different things at different times. It is a range which Alleyn quite
certainly possessed. It is therefore, I think, true (as A. P. Rossiter said
(p. 143)): 'The step [from *Cambises*] to *The Jew of Malta* is not so great
as from that to Iago.' But my account of *Cambises* has differed somewhat
from Rossiter's, and my respect for it is greater. It seems to me that
Marlowe realised the potentialities of this form of play, and that his task
was to fulfil them as richly as possible. The starting-point is therefore
theatrical situations, rather than linguistic ones. The use of a major
poetic utterance is one such situation: but it is in no sense a 'norm' to
which the play does or should conform.

In one respect the play is formally different from *Cambises*: there is
no precise equivalent for Ambidexter. In part his ubiquitousness, of
mind and role, is assumed by Barabbas, as I have already suggested.
But Barabbas' role is also partly derived from Cambises himself: his
violence can be laughed at, as much as his comic vitality can be laughed
with. And the play has a separate presenter in Machiavel. A prologue
figure who does not appear anywhere in the play became common
later, but is unusual in 1590. Yet the force of Machiavel's stated attitudes
is felt throughout the play, and his cap fits every single actor in it,
Christian, Jew, prostitute or pagan slave. We never in fact forget his
words, and remember them most vividly, as I remarked, in the play's
last lines. Thus his non-appearance actually gives him a ubiquitousness
beyond even Ambidexter's capacity, and is a successful structural
experiment. It probably had the additional advantage of encourag-
ing satiric implications (e.g. of Christianity) which it would have
been dangerous to have stated more explicitly. Self-protective ambiguities can be found elsewhere in the play: whatever can be taken as
anti-Christian satire can also be seen as conventionally acceptable anti-
papist diversions, and some scenes can never be much more.

This means, of course, that parts of the play are cheap enough. In a
sense, my suggestions about the theatrical form Marlowe is fulfilling
may seem to be all too permissive: where a play in its nature ranges
from tragic intensity to mere slapstick, this is not to be avoided. For
violence is an ingredient of slapstick, and slapstick is a major theatrical
response to violence; it has its necessary place here, far more intimately

involved in the whole than it can be in later plays when relegated to a sub-plot. But the relationship between parts and tones is, sometimes at least, more precisely established. The successful poisoning of an entire nunnery in Act III may well seem a merely vulgar joke when regarded in isolation; but its full effect depends on its fulfilling the fantasy of evil in Barabbas' well-known speech to Ithamore in II. iii:

> As for myself, I walk abroad a nights
> And kill sick people groaning under walls:
> Sometimes I go about and poison wells . . .
>
> (l. 175)

The ambiguity of tone here is unmistakable: it is absurdly funny, but it develops a paranoic vision as well. Obviously such an effect cannot be altogether contained within a naturalistic framework of revealed character, but a context is provided for this extravaganza as a testing of Ithamore's readiness for crime. It is not, that is to say, offered simply as 'self-revelation', but it has that quality in grotesque form. And, once again, the difference is felt between the rhythmic momentum of Barabbas' verse, and the merely commonplace echo of it in Ithamore's response. When, with the dying nuns in III. vi, this fantasy is translated into action, the proportion of our responses necessarily changes: it is one thing to laugh at the idea of mass-murder, another to see it done. We laugh still; but differently. For a moment the reality of death is looked at in Abigail's confession, torn between loyalty to her father, her dead lover, and her new religion. The moment of pathos is scarcely established before its ironic inadequacies are returned to farce:

ABIGAIL. Death seizeth on my heart: ah, gentle friar,
Convert my father that he may be sav'd,
And witness that I die a Christian!　　(Dies.)
FRIAR.　Ay, and a virgin too; that grieves me most.　(l. 38)

So far, then, from being a dramatist who couldn't construct a play, Marlowe emerges as one for whom the type of structure used is fundamentally important. As soon as one looks at his output in this way one can see that each play is strikingly different from any other—that in fact he was actively enough interested in dramatic structure to experiment with as many different forms as he wrote plays. *The Massacre at Paris* is too fragmentary to be judged; and with this sense of Marlowe's work we must be very cautious of making statements about *Tamburlaine*. The squeamish printer of 1592 complacently boasted of omitting

G

'certain fond and frivolous gestures' which he thought would 'prove a great disgrace to so honourable and stately a history'. What we have, therefore, is the epical structure which the printer abstracted from Marlowe's text; it serves well to establish the human deity which constitutes Tamburlaine's heroic stature, a figure commonly referred to as the typical renaissance Man. But this does Marlowe less than justice, for once again there are no precedents (in English at least) for this figure. The structure *supports* the hero; it gives all too little scope for criticising him. Yet the play does approach farce at times, even in part I. In IV. iv, for instance, the baiting of Bajazeth is a sort of cabaret turn at Tamburlaine's feast, written in a prose which contrasts sharply with the high-flown verse before and after:

USUMCASANE.   Nay, 'twere better he killed his wife, and then she shall be sure not to be starv'd, and he be provided for a month's victual beforehand.

TAMBURLAINE.   Here is my dagger; despatch her while she is fat, for if she live but a while longer, she will fall into a consumption with fretting, and then she will not be worth the eating . . . Go to; fall to your meat. What, not a bit? Belike he hath not been watered to-day; give him some drink.   (l. 46)

As it stands, this seems a slightly uncomfortable extravagance; it might be very different if it were suspended between the play's polarities of barbaric splendour which we have, and farcical slapstick which is presumably what we have lost. The anti-body of Calyphas in part II, whose disturbing combination of cowardice, lechery, lethargy and sensitivity provokes Tamburlaine's most shocking murder, may similarly have been more integrally related to the play's original form. This is mere guess-work, for which we can only curse the printer. The plays can never have been anywhere near *The Jew* in form for they are by no means short and the printer cannot have cut a great deal; but it may well have been enough to distort their structure fatally.

DRAMATIC STRUCTURE: (ii) *Dr. Faustus*

If *Tamburlaine* is obviously different from *The Jew of Malta*, that in its turn is in many ways unlike *Dr. Faustus*, which is a more radical experiment. For *The Jew*, a play about society and politics, the sphere of the Machiavel, Marlowe revived the form of *Cambises*; for *Faustus*, about mankind in the universe, he went to the religious morality itself, and fulfilled more richly than ever all the ambivalences the form offered him. *Faustus* is supremely a play that has been distorted by wilful pre-conceptions about what it *ought* to be. Basically, the complaint made about it amounts to this: that it embarks on the tragic narrative of Faustus' career, invites us to see him as a tragic hero, and then deviates bewilderingly into slapstick with a horse-courser, a Pope, and an Emperor. In a sense the opening chorus seems to invite this expectation; true, it dismisses heroic war and love as themes, but it goes on:

> Only this, gentles—we must now perform
> The form of Faustus' fortunes, good or bad.
> (l. 7)

It might be pressing that a bit hard to remark that it is the *form* which is good or bad, not simply the fortunes; but in any case, the expectation of narrative we attach to these words is *our* expectation, based on experience of three centuries of the development of the novel. A slight acquaintance with Elizabethan fiction, whether at the level of courtly romance or popular jest-book, will immediately remind us that their notion of 'story' was much more devious. But the reference here need not be so vague—the Chorus continues:

> And now to patient judgements we appeal,
> And speak for Faustus in his infancy.

Which sets the form of Faustus' fortunes firmly in a morality of the Seven Ages of Man—or rather, since this is obviously the point of the earlier disclaimer of heroic status—of mankind. The comparison is, I think, enlightening so long as I am not misunderstood to claim direct connection with the old play. The only morality to which explicit reference may be suspected is *The Conflict of Conscience*, but that was a poor specimen of the genre, and Marlowe's knowledge was obviously wider. I have no reason to suggest Marlowe knew *Mankind* itself, but he certainly knew the type. Nothing in *Mankind* offends Christian doctrine outwardly, and the idiotic farce of poor Mankind's flirtation with the devil ultimately justifies the unbendingly severe forgiveness he receives. Yet the play is alive, if not actually with protestantism (it

sounds like Lollardry at times), at least with protestation: Mercy as a
feudal overlord is a strange and striking image; and Mercy and Mischief
as born brothers, to whom the helpless image of ourselves is committed
in sad if silly slavery, is a very suggestive conception. Marlowe's Lucifer
and Christ are not brothers; but they are closely related images of
submission for Faustus. His oscillation between them is variously
heroic, anguished, pathetic, feeble and farcical; echoing through it is
the refrain 'Faustus be resolute', which is painfully impossible amid
these varying senses of mankind. When the play turns tragic in its final
twist, Faustus' collapse is into simultaneous submission to both his
bosses:

> See, see where Christ's blood streams in the firmament!
> One drop would save my soul, half a drop. Ah, my Christ!—
> Rend not my heart for naming of my Christ;
> Yet will I call on him. O, spare me, Lucifer!—
>
> (xix. 146)

Faustus is torn to pieces between Love and Fear: either requires submission and so depends on a failure of resolution. That failure appears
variously as comic, tragic or farcical: it is always dramatic.

Once this is grasped we need no longer force ourselves to blink at
everything that departs from tragic dignity; nor to pretend that the
opening scene is in fact more elevated than the rest of the play—too
many discussions have proceeded as though we were asked to take
seriously a tragic hero whose error was merely to overestimate the
length of twenty-four years. That is absurd; and so, of course, is the
raising of devils. The Elizabethans were not as credulous as they are
sometimes reported, and Wagner's scene with the clown not only
mocks Faustus himself, it works from outside the play's whole assumption and mocks conjuration, belief in devils, everything. Further, the
idea that the play somehow 'goes off' after scene vii and scarcely
recovers until scene xviii, seems to neglect the purely farcical incidents
in which Faustus is involved in scene v, when (for instance) he gets a
hot whore from hell for a wife. This, and much else besides, is in fact
slapstick, and the actor who takes Faustus will have to play that as well
as the briefer moments of tragic perception.

The play, in short, is not a tragedy in structure; though it is ultimately
more comprehensively and variously moving than most plays that are.
Its *form* is that of the popular morality, twisted by imaginative genius,

in various and contrasting directions. The old sense of man as small
and feeble co-exists with the demi-god; Faustus' intellectual imagination with his sensual vision; and as well as Faustus' conflict of conscience there are also brilliant passages for Mephostophilis and (more
surprisingly still) the beauty of heaven. And this too can breed comic
perception: one of the funniest lines in English drama is Faustus' saying
to the devil beside him 'I think hell's a fable'. What is wrong with the
later scenes is surely not that many of them are slapstick, which is
appropriate, but that there is not enough variety amongst them (there
is in fact more than is usually allowed). The consequence is, of course,
one of the most fascinatingly ambiguous plays ever written, and it
is scarcely surprising that attempts to fix its attitude by analysing its
moral argument are no more successful than earlier efforts to find its
significance in the character of Faustus: it doesn't have an argument, and
Faustus doesn't have a character. The play is an outstandingly full
realisation of the potentialities of the particular form; it resists any
single formulation, not because it lacks directive intelligence, but
because here that intelligence is precisely concerned to explore the
ambiguities of the human predicament. It is no doubt also true that
the ambiguity functions as self-protection: evidence of hostility to
Christianity in the play is abundant, though not of a kind that would
stand up in a court of law. But the ambiguity reaches beyond that,
because there is also some strikingly perceptive writing from a Christian
standpoint.

DRAMATIC STRUCTURE: (iii) *Edward II*

It will be clear that I think efforts to trace a line of development in
Marlowe through observing the stature of his heroes from Tamburlaine
to Mortimer are dangerously ignoring the structure of the plays; and
that it is more important to observe that the structures themselves are
different in kind, than to assume that one is necessarily an advance upon
another. The contention that Marlowe's plays are all experiments in
form is even more obvious when one comes to *Edward II*, which has
been called an advance because it is superficially more accessible to
later notions of what a play ought to be. It is, more or less, consistent in
tone—unlike *The Jew* or *Faustus*, which both exploit radical shifts of
tone—but it has also proved curiously baffling, at least partly because
that tone is so largely (not quite entirely) muted; and because, as several

critics have remarked, it does not seem to have a coherent theme.[4] It does, however, tell a story: the sad story of Edward's relations with his barons, his minions and his queen, finally simplifying to the rise and fall of Mortimer in Act V, dovetailed with the moving scenes of Edward's torture and death. It is a curiously exclusive play, lacking any serious interest in politics or the structure of a state; there is a sense of kingship, as power, but not as divine right; no sanction is provided for Edward's authority beyond the personal ability to exercise it, which he lacks. The motives, his own or Gaveston's, the barons' or Mortimer's, are never clear in other terms than the sensual, in which they are all and always unrequited. It is in puzzlingly sensual terms that Edward is punished, kept endlessly and horribly moving on through the sewers of Gloucestershire. The effect of the play is cumulative, an expansion of Mephistophilis' 'Why this is hell, nor am I out of it.'

In other words, if it is true that this is better constructed than Marlowe's other plays, it seems also to be true that it has much less to construct. It omits, very largely, the positive elements of his work, as it seems deliberately to resist the afflatus of end-stopped verse. But that is not the only conspicuous omission: its structure seems to owe much to Shakespeare's earliest histories, but whereas in the other structures he adopted, Marlowe richly fulfilled their potentialities, here one might almost say he does the opposite. Through the *Henry VI* plays Shakespeare develops a number of derivatives from the morality tradition towards an increasingly elaborate superstructure of Divine Order overriding historical events, and a multi-level sense of the State afflicted by civil war. There is none of this in *Edward II*—no commons cry, or wise counsellor, no ghosts, soothsayers, spirits or any trace whatever of the supernatural: no divine order, and no state. Whereas in *Faustus* Marlowe revived the overt form of the morality, here he eliminates all trace of it. He finds, in fact, as radically different a form as one can imagine. Once one grasps that structure, so far from being Marlowe's weakness, was in fact one of his central interests, then this radical contrast between *Faustus* and *Edward II* becomes the most significant point to grasp. However one dates them (and the maximum gap is four years), they were not far apart in time, written in total contrast to each other.

The form of *Edward II* has, then, the air of deliberate choice: this is a play about *men*, as they are strong or weak—as deliberately *not* a

---

[4] See M. C. Bradbrook: *Themes and Conventions in Elizabethan Tragedy* (1935), and J. C. Maxwell in *A Guide to English Literature*, ed. B. Ford.

morality as *Faustus* is one. The muted verse is obviously part of this deliberation: man, here, is as unlovely as he is inglorious; the cruelty outgoes the glimpses of delight. The play does end with a restoration of order by the new king, but there is no reference to God; most un-usually for an Elizabethan play, and almost blasphemously, the judge-ment rests solely with man. Edward is not consigned to hell, he is in it: the tortures of the last Act form an image of hell, darkness, damp, rats and all; and their climax is his final baiting and murder by Lightborne. Lightborne—as editors say—is not in Holinshed; but he *is* in fifteenth-century miracle plays. He is the tragi-comic devil that falls with Lucifer, and the connection is very suggestive: a familiar devil brought into the human context. The murder he inflicts as a man is more horrible than anything he conceived as a devil; yet his wit still makes us laugh, more grotesquely than ever. It is, of course, the murder described by Holin-shed (despite Charlton and Waller's statement to the contrary):[5] Matrevis and Gurney are sent to heat a spit; and it is that, not being smothered by a table, which provokes the horrid cry they fear will wake the town; the table is precisely to suppress the cry. Lightborne pushes the red-hot spit up Edward's anus in full view of the audience. It is a viler scene than any in Elizabethan drama, until perhaps Glouces-ter's blinding in *King Lear*; more horrible than anything in *Titus Andronicus*, for there the crimes are distanced by formality of speech and staging whereas here the play's careful naturalism makes the horror more immediately felt. Yet I do not think this is simply a medium for unnecessary sadism. In *Lear*, Gloucester's torture is moralised: 'The gods are just, and of our pleasant vices make instruments to plague us.' The moral is appalling, but it has its place in the play. In *Edward II* no moral whatever is drawn; if it were, it would have to be that Edward's punishment fits the crime with appalling exactitude. It is conspicuous that the barons persistently hold against him, not his weakness as a ruler, but his devotion to his minions, his homosexuality: and the devil's relish is to kill him where he loved.

This moral, I said, is not drawn; and it cannot be, it is intolerable. But yet, in a sense, it is there. If you take a play morally, this is the most moral one ever written; if you see poetic justice as an affirmation of divine order, then this becomes profoundly vile. But the action which

[5] See their notes to V. iv. 39 and V. v. 30. My view is strongly supported by C. Leech in 'Marlowe's *Edward II*: Power and Suffering', *Critical Quarterly* (1959).

the moralist should attribute to God is very like the role which Marlowe elsewhere assigns to Him, of the avenging Jehovah. The play has, then, the material of Christian moral drama, and totally excludes the moral. It follows that this scene is in a sense a trap—if plays should be moralities, moralise this one if you dare. If you cannot, then you are forced towards the fatalistic implications of the play's only explicit moral, which follows in Mortimer's dying speech:

> Base Fortune, now I see, that in thy wheel
> There is a point, to which when men aspire,
> They tumble headlong down: that point I touch'd,
> And, seeing there was no place to mount up higher,
> Why should I grieve at my declining fall?
>
> (V. vi. 59)

After Lightborne we have Lucifer's headlong tumble; but Mortimer too is a man and not an angel/devil; and so for him there is only chance and a stoical response to it, as there was for Barabbas.

CONCLUSION

Seen thus, *Edward II* fits with *Dr. Faustus*: *that* used the fullest potentiality of the morality structure so that the conventional moral idea became untenable; *this* is its precise opposite, a play from which morality is totally excluded: and both tend to the same effect. But this is a relationship which, I suggest, can only be grasped when one realises the significance of dramatic structure in Marlowe's work: his plays are not the carelessly half-written throw-outs of poetic genius, but successive experiments in different dramatic forms.

It may well be urged that this account of Marlowe ascribes to him a complexity, even a subtlety, that is more characteristic of twentieth-century critics than of sixteenth-century dramatists. The case is in fact more subtle to set down than to experience: despite all warnings, we are still prone to think of a play in terms of its planning rather than its execution; but the significance of my suggestion that Marlowe was exploiting the potentialities of existing dramatic forms is that this, though it calls for creative intelligence, does not require total planning from scratch; rather, it supposes imaginative opportunism and might well produce a result more complex than the intention. There are modern plays which seem to develop in a similar way, but they are more sophisticated precisely because they have no traditional form to exploit. Brecht, of course, did sometimes take up old plays for this very reason; I have already referred to Ionesco; a more striking instance is the *Marat/Sade*, which provoked an interesting bewilderment in reviewers. It was found to be moving, funny, acutely painful, and intellectually disturbing in fairly equal degrees; but the complaint was made that nobody knew what it was about, that its structure of ideas was incoherent. It seems to me that the consistency of the play is to something quite different from logical argument: that it depends on constructing a situation—of lunatics dramatising recent historical events—that has immensely varied dramatic potentialities; and it is the full development of those potentialities, not a resolution in terms of ideas, which constitutes the structural quality of the play. Weiss's play is indeed more sophisticated than Marlowe's; and if it seems a more exotic growth, that is partly because Weiss has to construct what he exploits, whereas Marlowe found his forms in the popular dramatic tradition: for *The Jew*, in plays like *Cambises*; for *Faustus* in the earlier moralities; and for *Edward II* partly in the new histories and partly in the oldest form of all, the miracles. But if *Edward II* was structurally his most original play, we should not be surprised to find that it was also dramatically his thinnest.

Note

Texts. All quotations in this chapter from interludes and romantic narrative plays are from facsimile editions. In the Malone Society Reprints: *Clyomon and Clamydes* (1913), *The Interlude of Vice* [*Horestes*] (1962), *Patient and Meek Grissell* (1909), and *The Rare Triumphs of Love and Fortune* (1930). In the Tudor Facsimile Texts: *Cambises* (1910), and *Mucedorus* (1910). In the Yale Elizabethan Club Reprints: *Common Conditions* (1915).

There is no uniform modern edition of the plays cited, but Dodsley's *Old English Plays*, ed. W. C. Hazlitt (1874) contains *Cambises* (vol. iv), *Mucedorus* (vol. vii), and *The Rare Triumphs of Love and Fortune* (vol. vi). A recent edition of *Mucedorus* is in *Three Elizabethan Plays*, ed. J. Winny (1959). *Clyomon and Clamydes* appears in *Peele's Works*, ed. A. H. Bullen (1882); *Common Conditions* in *Five Anonymous Plays*, ed. J. S. Farmer (1908); and *Horestes* in *Illustrations of Old English Literature*, ed. J. P. Collier (1886).
Sidney's *Apology* is quoted from G. G. Smith (ed.), *Elizabethan Critical Essays*, 2 vols. (1904).

Criticism. There are no detailed studies of each specific play. The most useful work on the subject deals with theatrical conventions of the period in general; see especially D. M. Bevington's *From 'Mankind' to Marlowe* (1962), M. C. Bradbrook's *The Growth and Structure of Elizabethan Comedy* (1955) and *The Rise of the Common Player: A Study of Actor and Society in Shakespeare's England* (1962), and T. W. Craik's *The Tudor Interlude: Stage, Costume and Acting* (1958). For a discussion of the influence of the Vice's motiveless compulsion to destroy, see the study of Iago in B. Spivack, *Shakespeare and the Allegory of Evil* (1958).

V

Romantic Narrative Plays: 1570–1590

PATRICIA RUSSELL

*

THE dramatised tales of chivalric adventure, the loosely structured, wide-ranging gallimaufries that made up a large part of the popular drama of the 1570's and 1580's contained flaws in dramatic construction immediately apparent to a sophisticated critic. Sir Philip Sidney's words on the lack of artistic coherence in the plays and Stephen Gosson's on their lack of moral substance have been quoted many times in demonstrating again the weaknesses of this exuberant, and often grotesque, drama:

> Where you shall have Asia of the one side, and Afric of the other, and so many other under-kingdoms, that the player, when he cometh in, must ever begin with telling where he is, or else the tale will not be conceived. Now ye shall have three ladies to walk to gather flowers, and then we must believe the stage to be a garden. By and by, we hear news of shipwreck in the same place, then we are to blame if we accept it not for a rock. Upon the back of that comes out a hideous monster with fire and smoke, and then the miserable beholders are bound to take it for a cave; while in the meantime, two armies fly in, represented with four swords and bucklers, and then what hard heart will not receive it for a pitched field? . . . ordinary it is, that two young princes fall in love; after many traverses she is got with child, delivered of a fair boy; he is lost, groweth a man, falls in love and is ready to get another child; and all this in two hours' space; which, how absurd it is in sense, even sense may imagine . . . But, besides these gross absurdities, how all their plays be neither right tragedies nor right comedies, mingling kings and clowns, not because the matter so carrieth it, but thrust in clowns by head and shoulders to play a part in majestical matters, with neither decency nor discretion; so as neither the admiration and commiseration, nor the right sportfulness, is by their mongrel tragi-comedy obtained. . . . I know the ancients have one or two examples of tragi-comedies,

as Plautus hath *Amphytrio*. But, if we mark them well, we shall find
they never, or very daintily, match hornpipes and funerals.

(Sidney, *Defence of Poesie*; Smith, i. 198-9)

Sometime you shall see nothing but the adventures of an amorous
Knight, passing from country to country for the love of his lady,
encountring many a terrible monster of brown paper, & at his
return, is so wonderfully changed, that he cannot be known but
by some poesie in his tablet, or by a broken ring or a handkircher
or a piece of cockle shell. What learn you by that? When yᵉ soul
of your plays is either mere trifles, or Italian bawdry, or wooing
of gentlewomen, what are we taught?

(Gosson, *Plays Confuted*; quoted *Eliz. Stage*, iv. 215-16)

'A terrible monster of brown paper', 'a hideous monster with fire and
smoke'—the only surviving examples of exactly this kind of play, *Sir
Clyomon and Sir Clamydes* (c. 1570) and *Common Conditions* (c. 1576),
are in some ways as monstrous as the beasts that appeared on the stage.
These plays can be criticised from many standpoints—for their taxing of
the suspension of disbelief beyond measure, for their expansion beyond
the decorous ordering of time and action, for their sudden, unmotivated
transitions from serious to funny and back again, for their use of sup-
posedly unsubstantial subject-matter, for their adherence to the essentially non-dramatic form of the episodic tale, and for their language:

BOTTOM.   But stay, O spite!
                     But mark, poor knight,
             What dreadful dole is here!
                     Eyes, do you see?
                     How can it be?
             O dainty duck! O dear!
                     Thy mantle good,
                     What! stain'd with blood?
             Approach, ye Furies fell.
                     O Fates! come, come;
                     Cut thread and thrum;
             Quail, crush, conclude and quell.
                     (*A Midsummer Night's Dream*, V. i. 268)

The lines from Peter Quince's play of 'very tragical mirth' sound like
direct parody of speeches in *Clyomon and Clamydes* and *Common
Conditions*:

CLYOMON.   Ah wofull *Rumor* raunging thus, what tidings do I
                  heare,
            Hath that false King of Norway stolne my love and
                  Lady deare?
            Ah, hart, ah hand, ah head and mind, and every
                  sence beside,
            To serve your maisters turne in need, do every one
                  provide.

                             (*Clyomon and Clamydes*, l. 1211)

LAMPHEDON. Though depe dispaire doth drive in doubt dew
                  honor to disgrace.
            Though dredful domps doth dau[n]t ye minde being
                  in uncoth place
            Though hart is harded to hasard forth in ladies cause
                  to try.

                             (*Common Conditions*, l. 1276)

Thomas Preston's *Cambises*, an interlude written before the romantic
narrative plays of the 1570's and 1580's (*c.* 1561), plainly declares itself
on the title-page to be a 'lamentable Tragedie, mixed full of plesant
mirth'; and the lament of Otian, a youth whose father Sisamnes is to be
executed by the tyrant Cambises, is practically indistinguishable from
Bottom's ranting vein:

> O father deer, these words to hear, that you must dye by force,
> Bedews my cheeks with stilled teares, ye King hath no remorce,
> The greevous greefes and strained sighes,
> My hart doth breake in twaine:
> And I deplore most woful childe, that I should see you slaine.
> O false and fickle frowning dame, that turneth as the winde:
> Is this the joy in fathers age, thou me assignest to finde?
> O dolefull day, unhappy houre, that loving childe should see:
> His father deer before his face, thus put to death should be.
> Yet father give me blessing thine, and let me once imbrace:
> Thy comely corpse in foulded arms, and kiss thy ancient face.[1]

                             (*Cambises*, C2^v)

Not only is the dramatic rhetoric far from the 'height of Seneca his
style', but there is, as well, a roughness in the manner in which the play
is constructed which can serve as an example of a frequent weakness in
the dramaturgy of interludes and romantic narrative plays. *Cambises*

[1] See, also, Chapter II, p. 53, above.

contains a comic action running parallel to the serious main plot—a comic action headed by the Vice, who has the potential of making a parody of the serious action and of deliberately changing the direction of the main plot, and in doing so to remove the audience from sympathetic involvement with the serious tale and make it aware that what it is watching is stage illusion.[2] Yet often in *Cambises* the potential remains unfulfilled. The entrances of the Vice, Ambidexter, seem often completely arbitrary, merely imposed on the serious action, not actively changing its direction but serving only to hold it up to ridicule. After Cambises has executed Sisamnes and has been cautioned by his counsellor Praxaspes to leave his wicked ways, the King continues in evil by slaying Praxaspes' child and this atrocity is followed by the long lament of the child's mother which succeeds in creating some true pathos; yet, before the serious tone is firmly established, Ambidexter enters and gives the audience a much lighter view of the King's tyranny, turning attention from the distraught mother and extolling the King's ability to play at 'both hands'. Though the Vice's traditional method of operating is always by swift, whimsical, arbitrary disruptions of the serious action, in *Cambises* Ambidexter's mocking comments seem often to distance the audience from the main plot with uncomfortable suddenness. The episodes which deal with Cambises' tyranny seem to come in fits and starts, with no firm progression from one to the next. After Ambidexter's interruption of the mother's lament, a new stage of the serious action begins—the downfall of Cambises' brother Smirdis, introduced here for the first time. Ambidexter has an active rôle in this episode, for it is he who begins the slanders against Smirdis; but just as the treacherous plots are developing to a climax, just before Cruelty and Murder enter to slay Smirdis, Ambidexter suddenly makes the audience see the affair in a comic light:

> Are ye gone? [*to the King*] straight way I will follow you.
> How like ye now my maisters? doth not this geere cotten?
> The proverbe old is verified, soone ripe and soone rotten.
> He will not be quiet til his brother he kild.   (D3-3ᵛ)

Surely this is a blithely undecorous mingling of hornpipes and funerals; yet the device itself contains great dramatic potential. It remains a principle of English dramaturgy throughout the Jacobean period, and in Shakespearean drama the effect of distancing brought by

[2] See Chapter II, pp. 50–1, above for earlier Vices.

the sudden introduction of a comic view of things permits the audience to stand apart from the action for a moment and to see the play as artifice—or, as in *A Midsummer Night's Dream*, as an artifice that sometimes reveals more than nature does. The presence of the simple mechanicals in the magic woods and at the court of Athens not only provides a parody of the language of earlier drama; but, also, Bottom and his crew, through their rock-bottom realistic interpretation of dramatic illusion, cause the audience to puzzle out the shifting relation of 'reality' and 'dream'. Bottom at first makes no distinction between their play and the world outside ('Masters, you ought to consider with yourself to bring in—God shield us!—a lion among ladies is a most dreadful thing . . .' (III. i. 27)). At the end, the mechanicals accept the illusion of their play more easily than do the courtiers (the foolish mortals who have not been able to see that the previous night's 'dream' really happened), who disrupt the progress of 'Pyramus and Thisbe' and make sure they prove that Moonshine is in fact a man.

*   *   *

Generalisations about the romantic narrative plays of 1570 to 1590 are based on a few remaining plays, no two of which are quite alike, which makes a strict classification 'popular romantic narrative drama' impossible. While *Clyomon and Clamydes* and *Common Conditions* are the only surviving plays of the type Sidney and Gosson ridiculed,[3] E. K. Chambers, when describing extant popular romantic drama, includes with these three earlier plays: Thomas Preston's *Cambises* (c. 1561), John Phillip's *Patient and Meek Grissell* (c. 1559), and John Pickering's *Horestes* (1567). Yet it seems that the descriptive phrase 'hybrid interlude' would fit these earlier three plays more exactly; for, while there are great similarities, *Clyomon and Clamydes* and *Common Conditions*

---

[3] Lists of lost plays indicate that the number of plays similar to these must have been quite large. *Herpetulus the Blue Knight* (c. 1570), *The Irish Knight* (c. 1576), *The Solitary Knight* (c. 1576), *The Knight of the Burning Rock* (c. 1579), *The Soldan and the Duke of* . . . (c. 1580), were probably based on tales of chivalric adventure. But the category of 'romantic narrative' might be extended to include plays the titles of which suggest that the sources for the plays were Hellenistic prose 'romances'—pastoral romance (*Daphnis and Chloe*) and 'romance of adventure' (*An Aethiopean Romance*): e.g., *Chariclea* (c. 1572), *Philemon* (c. 1574), *A Greek Maid* (c. 1579), *Phyllida and Corin* (c. 1584), *Felix and Philiomena* (c. 1585), *The Mad Priest of the Sun* (c. 1587). (See Harbage, *Annals of English Drama: 975-1700* (revised 1964).)

follow the mood and nature of the pure romantic tale more closely than do the 'interludes', with their pervasive tone of moral instruction. *The Rare Triumphs of Love and Fortune* (1582), *Mucedorus* (c. 1590), *Fair Em, the Miller's Daughter of Manchester* (c. 1590), *George a Greene, the Pinner of Wakefield* (c. 1590), and Robert Wilson's *The Cobbler's Prophecy* (c. 1590) have also a kinship with *Clyomon and Clamydes* and *Common Conditions*; but the somewhat more sophisticated dramaturgy of these later plays marks them as late developments of the popular 'gallimaufrey' rather than as primary examples of a hornpipe and funeral play. However, from *Cambises* of 1561 to *The Cobbler's Prophecy* of 1590 the central dramaturgical problem of a romantic play remains—that of bringing artistic coherence to a form which has as its essence a large action that ranges from the houses of the gods, to earthly courts, to common streets and fields, that has room for joke, dance and prayer, and that attempts, in spite of what Gosson declared, to be more than a 'mere trifle', and strives, though not always successfully, to teach by delighting. The development of popular drama from *Cambises* to *Mucedorus* can perhaps be considered as an attempt to give romantic substance a proper dramatic form.

Plot summaries of *Clyomon and Clamydes* and *Common Conditions* give some idea of the vast scope of action in these plays. The action of both takes place in the never-never land of the fabulous tale, ten leagues beyond man's life. *Clyomon and Clamydes* tells of the adventures of the two knights Clyomon and Clamydes, who at times are combatants who try to prove one's honour finer than the other's, but who in the end are reconciled and obtain their respective loves. Clamydes, at the opening of the play, has been sent by his lady Juliana, princess of Denmark, on a quest to slay the Flying Serpent. Juliana is (unknown to Clamydes) the sister of Prince Clyomon, who has been missing from the Danish court many years. Clyomon, meanwhile, has met with 'Subtill Shift the Vice', who promises to serve him, but is always ready to change loyalties.

Before Clamydes sets out on his quest, Clyomon, for no particular reason except to further the erratic action, 'steals' Clamydes' knightly honour by pushing Clamydes aside at the moment when Clamydes' father is about to knight him. The mace falls on Clyomon, and thus begins the rivalry between the two men. Clamydes pursues Clyomon to the court of Alexander the Great, and a day of trial at arms is set, so that their chivalric feud can be resolved. While waiting for the tournament, Clamydes pursues the Serpent to the Forest of Marvels, where he meets the cowardly enchanter Brian sans Foy. Clamydes slays the Serpent, but Brian (aided by Subtill Shift) steals its head, puts Clamydes in prison, and goes off to claim the hand of Juliana. Meanwhile, Clyomon travels in search of adventure, but is shipwrecked on the Isle of Strange Marshes, where he meets and falls in love with the King's daughter Neronis. Each knight—Clamydes, by being imprisoned, and Clyomon, by being shipwrecked—has missed his day of battle and thinks his honour lost. The truth unknown to them is that neither knight's honour is lost, since they are both absent from Alexander's court.

Neronis, in the meantime, is kidnapped by the King of Norway; but she escapes and flees to the forest disguised as a man, where she is befriended by Corin, a pastoral figure who is more rustic clown than classical swain. Clyomon slays the King of Norway, but Neronis mistakes the King's grave for Clyomon's, because Clyomon has hung his shield on it. Believing her lover dead, Neronis is about to slay herself; but she is stopped by the sudden intervention of Providence, who gives her a written testimony that Clyomon is alive.

The separate adventures of the two knights join when Clyomon, representing Neronis' mother in her rightful claim to the throne of the Isle of Strange Marshes, fights Clamydes, who represents the pretender to the throne. The knights do not know each others' identity, but they are nevertheless fulfilling the earlier tournament arrangements each thought he had broken. Their honours are redeemed; and finally, when their identities are known, friendship grows from enmity.

A general look at the structure of *Common Conditions* shows a series of adventures of the romantic heroes and heroines brought about, interrupted, and redirected by the motiveless pure mischief-making manipulations of Common Conditions the Vice. The only reason Conditions grants to the audience as explanation for his whimsical control is that he strives, as does his kinswoman Dame Fortune, to keep men in the way of 'mediocritie', neither too happy nor too sad:

> . . . for my owne advantage beleeve me you may.
> As nere as I can ile use a mediocritie by the way.
> And *Mediocritie* is my name though conditions they mee call,
> Nere kin to dame fortune to raise and to let fall.[4]   (l. 164)

[4] Conditions here follows the methods of his fellow Vices, taking delight in making sure that his name (real or assumed) is clearly established. This

Conditions' policy and slander have caused the exile of Duke Galiarbus and his children Sedmond and Clarisia from the Arabian court. As the romantic characters start on their adventures, the tone of serious lament dominates, but is soon cut off by Conditions' explanation of his tactics (ll. 156–210) and by the entrance of three tinkers, the English rustics Shifte, Drifte, and Unthrifte, who rob and separate Clarisia and Sedmond. The tinkers' song of 'Hay tifty tofty' begins the hornpipe. This kind of alternation of tones and quick succession of episodes continues through the play. Clarisia (whose wanderings have brought her to Phrygia) falls in love with Lamphedon. They exchange vows of devotion and constancy in true courtly fashion, but no sooner have they plighted troth than Conditions gives a reductive, satiric view of the situation:

CLARISIA.   If all the *Trojan* knights were here, or *Grecian* in like
                   case,
             Whose valiant courage did surpas eche wight in
                   every place:
             Clarisia doth protest, as she is Lady true,
             To rest thy love while life indure hap so what shall
                   ensue. . . .

                                                          (l. 658)

             Here enter CONDITIONS *sodeinly.*

CONDITIONS. God give you joy I hartely pray, and send you both
                   good lucke
             And if I might you should be sure to have hornes
                   like a Bucke.

                                                          (l. 695)

Conditions' connivings cause the separation of the two lovers, but when the despairing Lamphedon is about to kill himself, the comic action (here, the sudden entrance of 'Mariners with a songe') prevents his self-destruction:

LAMPHEDON.   Draw forth thy lingering blade with speede, & give
                   thy self a wound,
             Sith that her joy was joy to thee, let her death be
                   thine also,

---

tradition of the Vice's formal self-identification appears in Autolycus' first speeches to the audience (*The Winter's Tale*, IV. iii. 23–31).

> And with this goring blade of thine devide this hart
> from wo.
>
> *Here entreth the Mariners with a songe.*
>
> Lustely, lustely, lustely, let us sayle forth,
> The winde trim doth serve us, it blowes at the north.
>
> (l. 1122)

Successive rises and falls of fortune could continue *ad infinitum*. The action drags its slow length along without coming to a definite climax or conclusion. The play ends in mid air, with the seeming death of Lamphedon and the imminent death of Clarisia; and the stories of the other characters are never finished. The Epilogue, faced by the prospect of another two thousand lines of dialogue needed to untie the tangled action, concludes in despair:

> So time saith to us seace now here, your audience much ye wrong
> If farther now to weary them the time ye do prolonge.

In *Clyomon and Clamydes*, though the play is more 'finished' in that the narrative tale is brought to an end, the action, as in *Common Conditions*, is carried forward not by a careful building of tension and progressive interlocking of situations, but rather by sudden, unmotivated changes in the fortunes of the characters, which permit the story to take a new turn. The device of surprise is difficult to handle and in these plays produces awkward moments, but it is part of the essence of dramatic romance; and to remove it from the plays is to destroy the ability of romance to break without warning from the world of the tangible to the world of the illusory that suddenly becomes 'real', or from the world of despair and bad fortune to the world in which the happy lover is granted everything. In the successful dramatic romance the device is exploited, not eliminated.

★   ★   ★

Taking a broad look at the popular narrative plays from *Cambises* to *Common Conditions*, one notices what appears to be an attempt to make coherent dramatic use of the device of sudden change. *Cambises* is brought abruptly to a close by the only event that seems sure to stop what would otherwise be an endless succession of events: Cambises' death. No warning that the King's life is in danger is given to the audience, until, just before the event, Ambidexter enters and forecasts the action:

> . . . I will lay twenty thousand pound:
> That the King himselfe doth dye by some wound.
> He hath shed so much blood, that his will be shed:
> If it come to passe in faith then he is sped.

> *Enter the King without a gowne, a swoord thrust up into his*
> *side bleeding.*

KING.   Out alas what shal I do? my life is finished:
Wounded I am by sodain chaunce, my blood is minished.

(F 3ᵛ)

In *Clyomon and Clamydes* and *Common Conditions* an attempt is made to work some of the sudden new developments of the story into a unified action. The episode of Clamydes' encounter with Brian sans Foy is prepared for, before Brian enters, by Subtill Shift's description of the cowardly villain (l. 524); and, though Brian then disappears from the play for over a thousand lines, he reappears at the end and aids in bringing the play to its conclusion, by posing as Clamydes to claim Juliana's hand (l. 1903). D. M. Bevington notices a similar attempt to combine surprise and logical plot progression in *Common Conditions*, when describing the sudden appearance of the three tinkers Shifte, Drifte, and Unthrifte:

> The author presents this episode for its traditional comic appeal, but transforms his vice lieutenants into tinkers and robbers. The episode has potential as sub-plot: these pillaging escapades more substantially resemble those of Shakespeare's Gadshill highwaymen than do those of Haltersick and Hempstring, or Huf, Ruf, and Snuf [the low comedy 'vice lieutenants' of *Horestes* and *Cambises*, who enter for a few moments of horseplay]. Furthermore, the comedy has a closer relationship to the main plot than that of *Horestes* or *Cambises*. These 'vice lieutenants' actually enter into the action of the story. It is their attack that separates Sedmond from Clarisia, producing two strands of the plot. At the same time the scene serves as comic diversion in a romantic story, occupying the dramatically potent second scene.

(p. 192)

The dramatic handling of the devices of romance is far from being completely successful in these plays of the 1570's. The shifts of locality, the rises and falls of fortune, seem completely arbitrary. Frequently in *Clyomon and Clamydes*, as in the earlier interludes, the major episodes are concluded before preparation for the next is made; all suspense and tension are lost, even though surprise abounds. Clyomon's lady, Neronis, disguised as a page in her flight from the tyrant king of Norway, sees Clyomon's golden shield on Norway's grave and, like Imogen in *Cymbeline*, wrongly imagines that her lover is dead (l. 1533). She despairs at once, sings her death song, and raises Clyomon's sword to kill herself, when she is stopped by the sudden descent of Providence: 'Stay, stay thy stroke, thou woful Dame, what wilt thou thus dispaire?' Providence gives her a piece of writing, which immediately informs Neronis that Clyomon is alive and that she has mistaken Norway's grave for his. Both Neronis and Providence exit, and the next episode begins with the appearance of Clyomon himself. Similarities between the episode of Neronis' errors and several incidents in *Cymbeline* are at once apparent, but in Shakespeare's play the device of sudden revelation is handled quite differently. Imogen's mistake in thinking that Cloten's body is Posthumus' is not at once rectified. Though the appearance of Lucius leads toward the resolution of tangled matters, the manner in which the golden chance will grow from misfortune cannot be foreseen. Posthumus, chained in the Roman camp, believing Imogen dead, is granted a vision of Jupiter, who leaves him the written prophecy as proof that the vision did not proceed from false imagination. But all doubts are not immediately resolved, as they are after the descent of Providence to Neronis. Posthumus' situation has changed only in that he now has questions where before he believed only in the certainty of his wife's death; and he is left in puzzled wonderment, knowing merely, when he reads the veiled prophecy, that some 'golden chance' has been given him:

> Poor wretches, that depend
> On greatness' favour, dream as I have done:
> Wake and find nothing. But, alas, I swerve;
> Many dream not to find, neither deserve,
> And yet are steep'd in favours; so am I
> That have this golden chance, and know not why. . . .
> 'Tis still a dream, or else such stuff as madmen
> Tongue, and brain not; either both or nothing,
> Or senseless speaking, or a speaking such
> As sense cannot untie.
>   (V. iv. 127, 144)

*   *   *

In the romantic narrative plays the problem of combining surprise and coherent action is in some measure solved by the activities of the Vice, who, though he is the chief causer of the sudden turns, the chief disrupter of the straightforward progress of the episodic tale, becomes at the same time a means for tightening the sprawling action. The Vice is able to see all the action at once and to manipulate its course. His position as overseer is superior to that of the audience, for he can be master of ceremonies as well as viewer. He ranges through all levels of action, from the heavenly to the earthly, mixing with courtly lovers and rustic buffoons and getting the better of both.

Politicke Persuasion, the Vice of *Patient and Meek Grissell* (1559), is an early representative of this energetic controller. He tumbles into the action at the opening of the play, falling from the dwellings of the classical gods; and the journey itself is a hodge-podge of places and times. But, in telling of his travels, Politicke easily unites Olympus, Heaven, and London in one vigorous, 'absurd', description:

> *Orpheus* the God of harmonie, was sent for to supper,
> And *Mercurius* for a present, a frend of mine old acquaintaunce,
> Brought to welcome me, a dishe of Almond Butter,
> Saint Peter fryed Pancakes a jolly good pace
> And sent them as daynties to *Jupiters* grace   (l. 15)

> Throughe the thicke cloudes I had a merveilous fall,
> That I had lyke to broke my necke on the tope of westminster hall
> But charinge cross was my frende and caught my lege in his hand
> The wethercocke of Paules to ayd me to his flight . . .   (l. 48)

What the Vice aims to accomplish is the complete disruption of the course of true love or the ordered government of a state; yet it is this lord of misrule himself who pauses in the midst of his antics to explain to the audience exactly what he is doing, to remind them of what has gone before, and to give them an idea of what the new direction of events will be.

Common Conditions in his play, written some eighteen years later, wants only to play the shifting knave and to bring about as many confusions as he can: 'Roome for a turne coate, that will turne as the wynde, / Whom when a man thinkes surest he knowes not where to finde' (l. 622). But his descriptions of his past and projected pranks supply points of coherence in the midst of the wild and whirling action:

Ah ah ah this geare cottens I may say to you.
I have wrought a fetch to set the[m] by yᵉ eares hap what shal ensue
By my honesty it doth me good that I so crafty should bee
For the Duches is fallen out with *Clarisia* long of mee. . . .
Thus I have set them together by the eares hap what hap shall,
And marke the end of this geare which way it shall fall.
For *Clarisia* having to unkle *Mountaynio* Kinge of *Thrace*,
Will no longer here abide but straight waies thither will trace.

                                        (ll. 895, 902)

In *Clyomon and Clamydes* (1570), Subtill Shift's soliloquies likewise
permit the audience to share with him the position of 'Like a demigod
here sit I in the sky, / And wretched fools' secrets heedfully o'er-eye'
and to see the entire scope of the linear action brought together at one
point in time. Shift has caused Clyomon to miss his day of battle with
Clamydes by betraying him into the enchantments of Brian sans Foy;
and now, as Clyomon awakes from the spell, Shift plans further mischief. He addresses the audience, putting the past and future action in
the perspective of an 'old tale':

Be your leave I came up so early this morning that I cannot see my
      way,
I am sure its scarce yet in the break of day.
But you muse I am sure wherefore these weapons I bring,
Well, listen unto my tale, and you shall know every thing.
Because I play the shifting knave, to save my selfe from harme,
And by my procurement, my maister was brought in this charme.
The ten daies are exspir'd, and this morning he shall awake,
And now like a craftie knave, to the prison my way I will take
With these same weapons, as though I would fight to set him free,
Which will give occasion that he shall mistrust, there was no
      deceit in mee.[5]   (l. 852)

Later in the play, when Clyomon has slain the wicked king of Norway,
hung his shield over the grave, then left to seek Neronis, Shift suddenly
interrupts the romance episodes and brings about what seems to be a

_____

[5] Again, at the end of the play Shift makes the audience see the action as a
fiction or artistic illusion, a comedy that ends true to formula, as Berowne's
'old play' does not; for in *Clyomon and Clamydes* Jack hath Jill:

        What is all things finished, and every man eased?
        Is the pageant packed up, and all parties pleased?
        Hath each Lord his Lady, and each Lady her love?
                                        (l. 2130)

complete change of direction (ll. 1477 ff.). He enters 'very brave', decked out in a rich gown, and says that he is no longer going to spend his time seeking the Knight of the Golden Shield, but that he has come to announce the development of rivalry for the throne of the Isle of Strange Marshes, a contest between Neronis' mother and the Queen's brother-in-law Musantius. By turning the story suddenly in this new direction instead of letting it continue in its slow straightforward course, Subtill Shift quickens its path toward resolution. The contest which seems to be an arbitrary development turns out to be the occasion for the long-awaited meeting of Clyomon and Clamydes.

The Vice's ability to surprise and at the same time to bring disparate parts of the action together and to hasten the resolution of the narra-tive tale is likewise Autolycus' skill in Shakespeare's much later *Winter's Tale*. His first entrance (IV. iii) is a surprise to the audience. He follows Polixenes' and Camillo's courtly prose with the first song in the play; with his entrance the wintry scene becomes the sweet o' the year. He, in common with Subtill Shift and Common Conditions, attempts to gull the rustics and control the lives of princes. After Florizel has resolved to flee with Perdita, Autolycus reveals to the audience his plans for foiling the rustics' journey to Polixenes and for assisting the Prince's course, pausing in the midst of the narrative action, as do his predecessors in mischief, to explain his purposes and to forecast the future:

> If I had a mind to be honest, I see Fortune would not suffer me: she drops booties in my mouth. I am courted now with a double occasion—gold, and a means to do the Prince my master good; which who knows how that may turn back to my advancement? I will bring these two moles, these blind ones, aboard him. . . .
>
> (IV. iv. 818)

But Autolycus, unlike the earlier Vices, is not a perfect manipulator. As *The Winter's Tale* draws toward its conclusion, the audience re-ceives the impression of the forces of the right workings of natural time controlling the progression of the tale. Autolycus' own actions, in spite of his desire always to play the knave, become honest. The vast and wide-ranging nature of the 'old tale' is given point and direction by the sure progress of the tale itself. A sense of dramatic unity is achieved as the narrative action assumes control, as the separate lives of all the characters—from shifting knave to virtuous wife—are gathered together. The Shakespearean solution to the problem of the creation of unified drama from romantic substance is, in part, to let the 'tale' itself dominate—to convey the final impression that it is the 'old tale' which represents the natural course of life in time and which has (as the audience in its 'here sit I in the sky' position comes to see) a formal order and coherence.[6]

*   *   *

Although Shakespeare's last plays do not depend upon a Vice figure to give a clear direction to the expansive romantic tale, the manner in which the narrative action in the last plays grows to contain more substance than a 'mere trifle' seems in some ways a development of what the Vice achieved in the earlier romantic narrative plays. The Vice distanced the audience from direct involvement with the tale by destroying the illusion that the tale was the 'true and perfect image of life indeed' and by parodying the romantic values of honour, faith, and love. Although in Shakespeare's last plays the romantic story never becomes entirely a thing of ridicule, there are times when it is made deliberately artificial, when the audience is invited to view the story from the vantage of a larger world in which one can see the action simultaneously as serious and funny. (Such times occur when Prospero, somewhat in the manner of an all-seeing Vice, surveys the trials of Ferdinand and Miranda, and when the Gentlemen in *The Winter's Tale* describe in conceited, courtly rhetoric the reunion of Leontes and Perdita.) The romantic narrative plays made early use of the potential of dramatic romance to contain a parody of itself, seeing the satyr in the pastoral landscape.[7]

In the 'hybrid interludes' of the 1560's, the Vice and his 'lieutenants' accomplished, in their scenes of rollicking slapstick, a sudden reversal of values the heroic characters have established, or have pretended to

[6] In *The Tempest*, Prospero is a successful manipulator, but even he has worked, all through the play, to the strict deadline of six o'clock. The same tightening and gathering of action that occurs at the end of *The Winter's Tale* is found here: at the end, Prospero renounces his magic powers to become subject to natural time.

[7] The idea that parody and satire are to be included in romance and pastoral probably originated with a semantic confusion between 'satyr' and 'satire'. (See E. M. Waith's *The Pattern of Tragicomedy in Beaumont and Fletcher* (1952) for a full discussion of satire in late renaissance pastoral drama.) One notices in the romantic narrative plays an early appearance of what became characteristic of pastoral drama in the early seventeenth century—both in Italy and in England.

establish. In *Cambises* the King speaks with seeming bravery of his proposed campaigns against Egypt: 'To *Egypt* land now forth with speed, my voyage I will take . . .' (A4). That the King's bravery is shallow and his honour merely show is not surely established until the Vice Ambidexter enters in rag-tag armour and immediately presents the audience with quite a different view of Cambises' campaign:

> *Enter the Vice with an old Capcase on his head, an olde paile about his hips for harnes, a scummer and a potlid by his side and a rake on his shoulder.*   (A4ᵛ)

The three ruffians Huf, Ruf, and Snuf join Ambidexter, and the warfare they carry on for the King degenerates into a quarrel about who will sleep with Meretrix, the old whore. In this battle even Ambidexter's forces are defeated, for Meretrix wins the day, reversing their standards of manly valour. She whips them all and concludes:

> Tut, tut, in the Campe such Souldiers there be:
> One good woman would beat away two or three.
>
> (B3ᵛ)

Horestes begins, not with the serious action of Horestes' revenge for Agamemnon's death, but with a low comedy revenge story, set in motion as the Vice tries to gull the bumpkins Rusticus and Hodge. His aim is merely to pick a quarrel, for any reason, at any cost; and when Hodge scoffs at the false name 'Patience', which the Vice gives out as his, the Vice vows revenge (l. 119). He tells Rusticus that his hog is dead, killed by a dog—Hodge's dog in fact—and thus sets the two men quarrelling. Rusticus vows revenge for his hog, but the rift is soon healed and revenge is forgotten as Hodge and Rusticus shake hands and go off to drink ale. This is the state of affairs when Horestes enters, speaking in high-sounding rhyming fourteeners of the noble act of revenge against his murderous mother.

The parody of heroic revenge provided by *Horestes*' Vice seems, as does Ambidexter's parody of military valour in *Cambises*, to have come into the play almost by chance, not through carefully planned dramatic intention. The low comic scenes break suddenly into the action and have no firm connection to the main plot. Huf, Ruf, and Snuf, Rusticus and Hodge never appear again; the touch of parody has gone by in a flash and is not sustained. Although whenever *Horestes*' Vice appears on stage he introduces a point of view in opposition to the heroic, he does not actively change the direction of the story, as later Vices began to do. This is found, for the first time in an extant play, in *Patient and Meek Grissell*. Politicke Persuasion is a commentator on the serious action while providing in his own deeds a different set of values, like the *Horestes* Vice, but at the same time he influences the main plot: it is this that becomes an essential quality of later Vice figures, from Subtill Shift and Common Conditions to Falstaff and Autolycus, and perhaps Iago.

Politicke Persuasion's statement of his cynical view of marriage does not stop with asides to the audience, but causes Gautier's resolve to try Grissell's patience and virtue. Although his comments to the audience distance the romantic tale, making it appear an impossible illusion to the eyes of a mischief-making realist, when Politicke attempts to bring Gautier to his way of thinking, he enters the main action—and at once the separation between heroes and commentator, or the boundary between 'tale' and 'real life', becomes indistinct. Like Iago's, Politicke's confidences to the audience have a real effect on the world he mocks:

> I will not cease prively her confusion to worke.
> For under Honnie the proverbe saith poyson maye lurke:
> So though I simulate externally Love to pretend,
> My love shall turne to mischife . . .   (l. 897)

And so reductive comments of Subtill Shift and Common Conditions provide a running parody of the main plot that is more sustained and clearly formed than in the earlier *Horestes* and *Cambises*. Since their mischiefs are potent enough to frustrate the quests and desires of the heroes, the Vices' view of things is more than comic relief. The opening episodes of *Clyomon and Clamydes* best reveal the nature and methods of the shifting manipulator. Clamydes has dedicated himself to Juliana: 'Yet for to win a Lady such, I do account it least / Of travels toyle to take in hand . . .' (l. 101); but Shift's first description of his kind of wooing shows a world far from the lovers': 'in a dirtie Ditch with a woman . . .'. The reduction of courtly love is continued when Shift falsely identifies himself as 'knowledge', which knowledge extends as far as having as good skill in a woman as any man, whatsoever he be:

> For this I am certaine of,
> let me but lie with her all night,
> And Ile tell you in the morning,
> whither she is maide, wife, or spright

After Clyomon defines his heroic purpose, in grand language that extolls soldierly courage, Shift, left alone on stage, defines his shifting nature, which becomes a parody of the knightly courage and constancy Clyomon has praised. Shortly afterwards, when the scene changes to Clamydes' father's kingdom, the parody is counteracted by the King of Suavia's advice to his son: 'Know thou therefore *Clamydes* deare, to have a knightly name / Is first above all other things . . .' (l. 231). The organisation of this play can be seen as a shifting between two standards of judgement: 'keep . . . faith and troth in every thing' (l. 235) and 'to shift for my selfe I am fully decreed' (l. 356), as parody and serious action interact. Though the play does not overcome the 'piecemeal' effect determined by its episodic construction, the organising principle of the rapid succession of statement and parody is an intricate one and far from an indiscriminate matching of hornpipes and funerals.

Though Subtill Shift and Common Conditions mock romantic constancy and disturb the smooth course of love with sudden jars, they nevertheless do not succeed in deflating for ever the realm in which romantic love is a serious thing. The expansiveness of the genre can become an advantage, in permitting the development of a form large enough to contain its own parody. In both interlude and narrative play the serious action reasserts itself after the comic reduction. In *Horestes* the hero's choice of revenge over filial love for Clytemnestra is called into question through the parody revenges, which make the act seem ridiculous—Rusticus' revenge on Hodge and the braggart soldier Haultersyke's revenge on his companion Hempstring (for a box on the ear). Haultersyke manages to combine both a brave statement of revenge and a cowardly postponement of effecting his resolve (l. 468). Hempstring pursues the coward; and, after this, Horestes' immediate entrance in full ceremony and his prayer for the honourable 'band' (made up of the roisterers the audience has just seen) could easily become ludicrous:

> HAULTERSYKE.   In dede I must saye, I have cought the worst,
> But I wyll be revengyd, or eles I shall bourste.
> Yf tyme did not call me, from hence to departe,
> I should anger the hempstring, even at the hart:
> Therefore farwell, tyll an other daye,
> But hearste thou take this, to spend by the waye.
>
>   *Give him a box on ye eare & go out.*

HEMPSTRING.   Goges oundes is he gon, naye after I wyll,
               And of the slave by his oundes, I wyll have my fyll.

               let ye drum playe and HORESTES *enter w[ith] his*
               men & then lette him knele downe & speake.

HORESTES.   Oh godes be prosperous I praye, & eke preserve my
                   band,
               Show now [that] ye be gods in ded, stretch out
                   your mighty hand
               And give us hartes & willes also, where by we may
                   prevayll
               And suffer not you godes I praye, our courragis to
                   fayll.   (l. 467)

But as Horestes continues to speak, the serious nature of what he
says becomes stronger than the previous tone of parody. The goddess
Nature descends to him (l. 486) and, pleading with him not to contrive
against his mother aught, establishes the heroic dilemma of the play, the
conflict of the strict law of revenge and the natural law of filial piety.
Later in the play, when Horestes is besieging the castle of his mother
Clytemnestra, the Vice breaks into the action and sings his own praises
as a brave revenger (l. 776) and takes on himself the 'person of Revenge'; but the serious tone of the main action is reasserted in Clytemnestra's pleas for mercy (ll. 870–879). Here the presence of the Vice,
instead of parodying the main action, leads the play away from tragedy
and toward its happy conclusion by not allowing the pathos of Clytemnestra's situation to dominate:

CLYTEMNESTRA. Yf ever aney pytie was, of mother plante in the,
               Let it apeare Horestes myne, and showe it vnto
                   me.
HORESTES.   What pyttie thou on father myne, dydest cur-
                   sedly bestowe,
               The same to the at this present, I purpose for to
                   showe.
               Therefore Revenge have her a way, and as I
                   judgment gave:
               So se that she in order lyke, her punishment dew
                   have.
VYCE.   Let me alone, com on a way, that thou weart out
                   of sight,
               A pestelaunce on the crabyd queane, I thinke thou
                   do delyght,

> Him to molest, com of in hast, and troubell me
>   no more,
> Come on com on, ites all in vaine, and get you on
>   a fore.   (l. 990)

In *Common Conditions* and *Clyomon and Clamydes*, the Vice, by his
mockery of the misfortunes of the lovers, permits the audience to view
the action from a distance, and by his jests and shifts prevents the development of the action toward tragedy, but whenever he leaves the
stage the figures of romance assume control and the audience becomes
once more directly involved with the tale. In *Clyomon and Clamydes*,
after Clamydes has slain the Flying Serpent and set the prisoners of
Brian sans Foy at liberty, Subtill Shift asserts his own quite different
mode of conduct. He plunders Brian's store of gold and, in his parting
shot to the audience, establishes shifting craft over knightly valour
(ll. 983 ff.). Neronis, Clyomon's beloved, then enters, seeking her
knight. Judged from high dramatic standards her words are stilted
and sentimental and the dramaturgy is naïve; but, even with its obvious
flaws, this moment in the play accomplishes finely and firmly the effect
desired—the return to serious action. The ornate formality of Neronis'
lines re-establishes the world of romance; and her lines become a kind
of charm, bringing the audience back to the courtly, 'artificial' land:

SHIFT.   Well, its not best to tary too long behinde, lest my
                 maister over-go,
             And then some knave knowing of my money, a peece
                 of cosonage sho.

                                                        Exit.

         Enter NERONIS.

NERONIS.   How can that tree but withered be
             That wanteth sap to moist the roote?
             How can that Vine but waste and pine,
             Whose plants are trodden under foote?
             How can that spray but soone decay,
             That is with wild weeds overgrowne?
             How can that wight in ought delight
             Which showes, and hath no good will showne?
             Or else how can that heart alasse,
             But die by whom each joy doth passe?

                                                   (l. 988)

Similar moments occur several times throughout the play, as well as in *Common Conditions*. At one point, just after Conditions has planned with the pirates to rob Lamphedon and Clarisia, Sabia (the heroine of the unconcluded subplot, in love with Nomides of Arabia (Sedmond in disguise?)) enters and expresses her love for Nomides, which will remain constant despite the seemingly impossible hope of fulfilment. Instead of controlling the present moment by shifts and reversals, she waits with hope for the favourable turn of fortune (ll. 1096 ff.). The code of the Vice is reversed by the lovers' hopeful patience, and theirs is the standard that controls the final direction of the play.

The quality of early romantic narrative plays to include both statement and parody, and for each to have its moments of supremacy, remained an essential feature of dramatic romance. In *Mucedorus*, first performed around 1590 and probably the most popular play of its time,[8] the technique is used to good effect. The hero Mucedorus, the prince of Valencia disguised as a shepherd, is about to be banished from Aragon as a result of the jealous manipulations of Segasto, an evil counsellor. His traditional lament at being forced to leave Aragon (the country of his new-found love the Princess Amadine) is made ridiculous by the comic asides of Mouse, the clowning Vice:

MUCEDORUS.	Ah luckelesse fortune worse than *Phaetons* tale,
	My former blisse is now become my bale.
CLOWN.	What wilt thou poison thy selfe?
MUCEDORUS.	My former heaven is now become my hell.
CLOWN.	The worst ale house that I ever came in, in al my life.

(C3^v)

The Clown sings the decree of banishment as a rag-tag jingle, after which Mucedorus' lament sounds like exaggerated sentimentality:

CLOWN.	Shepheard stand foorth and heare thy sentence,
	Shepheard begone within three dayes in payne of,
	My displeasure, shepheard begon, shepheard begon,
	begon, begon, begon, shepheard, shepheard, shep-
	heard. *Exit.*
MUCEDORUS.	And must I goe, and must I needs depart?
	Ye goodly groves . . . (C4)

Yet, as the action continues with Amadine's entrance a few lines later,

<hr>

[8] The play was printed in 1598, then reprinted in 1606. The revised, amplified version was printed in 1610, reprinted in 1611, 1613, 1615, etc.

the tone of the serious exchange of vows is sustained enough to over-ride Mouse's comments. When Mouse enters again it is with Segasto, and here the effect of his presence is, in making the villain look silly and harmless, to temper the tragic implications of the tale and to suggest the possibility of a happy outcome.

Further developments of these basic techniques appear in *The Winter's Tale*. Autolycus' gay songs of loose living and loose loving, his blithe, conscienceless trickery, expand the play beyond the roman-tic main plot. Though romantic love, in his view, becomes a slight or non-existent thing, when the lovers appear, in IV. iv, their vision con-trols. The largeness that results from the presence of clowns and lovers does not indiscriminately match hornpipes with funerals, but includes them both 'very daintily' to create the distinctive quality of the play, in which the swift and sudden transition from one mood to another, or from one level of perception to another, is easily accomplished. The suggestion of comedy in Leontes' agony, the often deliberately ex-travagant language as in Paulina's accusation of Leontes (III. ii. 172 ff.) or Antigonus' description of the 'dead' Hermione (III. iii. 19 ff.), the appearance of the Clowns, and the sudden entrance of Autolycus, all prepare the audience for a subtle shifting of moods or expansion from 'the far to the distant or the distant to the near'. As the play draws to its conclusion, this expansive quality becomes part of its meaning; for the play shows, in the reunion of those long separated and in the waking of Hermione's statue, the full breadth of a world in which both art and nature operate with power, and demonstrates that the distinction be-tween the two (like that between the serious and the funny or between 'stage' and 'audience') is not always clear. Toward the end of *The Winter's Tale* all aspects of the action (not merely the Vice figure alone) come to cause in the audience the shift from one way of seeing 'reality' to another. The transition is brought about by what occurs within the romantic tale as well as by what comic characters say about the tale. The lovers themselves are capable of creating the transition, as Perdita does when she suddenly sees herself as performing a 'rôle' in her dis-tribution of flowers:

> . . . bold oxlips, and
> The crown-imperial; lilies of all kinds,
> The flow'r-de-luce being one. O, these I lack
> To make you garlands of, and my sweet friend
> To strew him o'er and o'er!

FLORIZEL.   What, like a corse?
PERDITA.   No; like a bank for love to lie and play on;
             Not like a corse; or if—not to be buried,
             But quick, and in mine arms. Come, take your flow'rs.
             Methinks I play as I have seen them do
             In Whitsun pastorals. Sure, this robe of mine
             Does change my disposition.

                                        (IV. iv. 125)

The belt of rule that gives formal coherence to dramatic romance does not do so by excluding either 'Asia of the one side and Afric of the other'. The extant popular dramatic romance of the 1580's, that written following the period of the chivalric gallimaufries, omits few of the elements of the earlier plays, but rather attempts to give the constant features of romance a form of 'decency and discretion'. In *Mucedorus, The Rare Triumphs of Love and Fortune* (1582), and *George a Greene* (c. 1590), the fanciful, the marvellous, and the sudden shifts in mood are given dramatic immediacy by placing the characters not in the never-never land of the Isle of Strange Marshes but in realms and situations which resemble life on the audience's side of the stage. Villains are not Brian sans Foys, but political intriguers; the love story has more in common with the tale of intricate comic love tangles (as in the Italian novella) than with a purely fanciful fairy tale. Mundy's *Earl of Huntington* plays (1598) combine their central tale of Robin Hood with a satiric view of human folly and courtly corruption, and *As You Like It* (also c. 1598) has both Touchstone and Jaques to challenge its pastoral world. The general impression is that what happens takes place not ten leagues beyond man's life, but, perhaps, 'now and in England'. But whatever is 'realistic' about dramatic romance from 1580 onwards, does not have the effect of making the audience reject the fanciful as false, rather it gives to the fairy tale a local habitation and a name.

Solutions to the essential difficulties in writing dramatic romance were sought in popular drama from *Clyomon and Clamydes* through *Mucedorus*, and the plays seem to be an attempt to create—as *The Winter's Tale* creates—an old tale that is nearer to Sidney's ideal of teaching delightfully than to his scorned 'gross absurdity'.

I

Note

Plautus and Terence. The best general studies are by W. Beare, *The Roman Stage* (1950; rev. ed., 1955), and G. E. Duckworth, *The Nature of Roman Comedy* (1952). The Loeb Classical Library provides good modern texts together with parallel translations: *Plautus*, 5 vols., ed. P. Nixon (1916–38), and *Terence*, 2 vols., ed. J. Sargeaunt (1918). A useful collection of translations is Duckworth's *Complete Roman Drama*, 2 vols. (1942).

Influence on Renaissance Drama. Important general studies dealing with classical and Renaissance comedy are Madeleine Doran's *Endeavors of Art* (1954) and Northrop Frye's *Anatomy of Criticism* (1957). Renaissance critical theory is treated by Doran and by M. T. Herrick in *Comic Theory in the Sixteenth Century* (1950). The influence of Roman comedy and of the Christian Terence on Elizabethan comedy is treated by M. W. Wallace in the introduction to his edition of *The Birth of Hercules* (1903). A significant specialized study is Alfred Harbage's 'Intrigue in Elizabethan Tragedy', in *Essays on Shakespeare and Elizabethan Drama in Honor of Hardin Craig*, ed. R. Hosley (1962). A study which stresses both Roman comedy and the *commedia erudita* is H. B. Charlton's *Shakespearian Comedy* (1938). Productions at the Universities are listed by F. S. Boas in *University Drama in the Tudor Age* (1914); at Cambridge, by G. C. Moore Smith in *College Plays in the University of Cambridge* (1923).

The commedia erudita. Good treatments of various aspects of the *commedia erudita* may be found in Vincenzo de Amicis' *L'imitazione latina nella commedia del XVI secolo* (1897), Ireneo Sanesi's *La commedia*, 2 vols. (1911–38), R. W. Bond's introduction to *Early Plays from the Italian* (1911), D. C. Boughner's *The Braggart in Renaissance Comedy* (1954), Herrick's *Italian Comedy of the Renaissance* (1960), and Louise G. Clubb's *Giambattista della Porta, Dramatist* (1965).

The Illustrations. Plate 1 reproduces two woodcuts from the Venice Plautus of 1518. These are of interest since they suggest that the comedies of Plautus and Terence need not always, in Humanist productions, have been performed with entrances bearing the names of the chief characters, as depicted in the well-known illustrations of the Lyons Terence of 1493. The cuts are reproduced through the courtesy of the Folger Shakespeare Library. Plate 2 reproduces a photograph of the lower end of the hall of Gray's Inn, in which the *Supposes* was performed in 1566 and *The Comedy of Errors* in 1594. (The hall itself was built in 1556–60, the screen during the late 16th century.) The hall screen, with its two entrance-ways and gallery over the passage, was presumably used as a tiring-house in the production of *The Comedy of Errors*. The photograph (courtesy of the Royal Commission on Historical Monuments) is reproduced with the kind permission of the Honourable Society of Gray's Inn.

VI

The Formal Influence of Plautus and Terence

RICHARD HOSLEY

*

POLONIUS, wishing to name a representative of comedy comparable to Seneca as a representative of tragedy, mentions Plautus rather than Terence: 'Seneca cannot be too heavy, nor Plautus too light.' At first glance, in view of the great preoccupation of Renaissance critics and moralists with Terence, the choice seems surprising. But it is not surprising in view of the greater number and variety of Plautus's plays, nor in view of the apparently greater formal influence of Plautus on Elizabethan comedy. (Admittedly Terence had a greater thematic influence.) That influence reveals itself chiefly in two areas: implicitly, in recorded productions of the plays of Plautus and Terence; and explicitly, in accepted uses of their plays by Elizabethan dramatists.

Production of Roman comedy at Cambridge in the sixteenth century provides a convenient index to the relative popularity of Plautus and Terence. The high tide of such production, to judge from the researches of G. C. Moore Smith, was the period from 1548 to 1583. During those thirty-five years there were seventeen productions of at least twelve of Plautus's plays: the *Amphitruo, Asinaria, Aulularia, Bacchides* (twice), *Curculio, Menaechmi* (twice), *Mostellaria, Persa* (twice), *Poenulus, Pseudolus, Stichus* (twice), *Trinummus*, and an unspecified 'commedie'. The colleges in question were Trinity (ten productions), Queens' (three), Jesus (two), King's (one), and St. John's (one). During the same period there were five productions of three of Terence's plays: the *Adelphoe* (three times), *Eunuchus*, and *Phormio*. The colleges in question were Trinity (two productions), Jesus (two), and Queens' (one). Thus Plautus, in the seed-time of Elizabethan comedy, was performed at Cambridge more than three times as frequently as Terence.

A number of Elizabethan plays reveal a limited influence by Plautus or Terence in their use of a general situation or a specific scene or device taken from the Roman dramatist. (Plays whose indebtedness to Roman comedy involves only the use of a braggart soldier are not here considered because of the difficulty of distinguishing the influence of Plautus from that of Terence—or, for that matter, the influence of Roman comedy from that of Renaissance Italian comedy.) At least thirteen plays appear to be indebted in this manner to Plautus: *Jack Juggler* to the *Amphitruo*; *Roister-Doister* to the *Miles Gloriosus*; the *Supposes* (through Ariosto's *Suppositi*) to the *Captivi* and the *Trinummus*; *The Bugbears* (through Grazzini's *Spiritata*) to the *Mostellaria*; *The Taming of the Shrew* to the *Trinummus*, the *Mostellaria*, and (through the *Supposes*) the *Captivi*; *The Merry Wives of Windsor* and *Epicene* to the *Casina*; *The Alchemist* to the *Mostellaria*; *The Tempest* to the *Rudens*; *No Wit like a Woman's* and *A New Way to Pay Old Debts* to the *Captivi*; *A Very Woman* to the *Curculio*; and *The Cunning Lovers* to the *Miles Gloriosus*. At least five plays appear to be indebted in this manner to Terence: *Roister-Doister* to the *Eunuchus*, *The Bugbears* to the *Andria*, the *Supposes* to the *Eunuchus*, *Misogonus* to the *Heauton Timorumenos*, and *The Taming of the Shrew* (through the *Supposes*) to the *Eunuchus*. (*Mother Bombie* is so generally indebted to Roman comedy that it is difficult to narrow the influence to one or the other dramatist.) Since the particular use made of Plautus and Terence varies considerably from one to another of the cited plays, the present comparison is necessarily imprecise. Nevertheless, it seems safe to say that Plautus had at least twice as much influence of this kind as Terence.

A number of Elizabethan plays reveal a strong influence by Plautus or Terence in their use of a whole plot taken from the Roman dramatist. Six plays are indebted in this manner to Plautus. In *The Comedy of Errors* Shakespeare adapts the *Menaechmi* and fuses it with part of the *Amphritruo*. In *The Case is Altered* Jonson uses the *Captivi* as the basis of his primary action and the *Aulularia* as the basis of his secondary action. In *The Birth of Hercules* the anonymous author makes a free adaptation of the *Amphitruo*. And in three instances Heywood adapts a play by Plautus. Act 2 of *The Silver Age* is a shortened version of the *Amphitruo*, the main action of *The Captives* is taken from the *Rudens*, and the secondary action of *The English Traveller* is adapted from the *Mostellaria*. One play is indebted in this manner to Terence. In *All Fools* Chapman adapts the *Heauton Timorumenos* and fuses it with part of the *Adelphoe*. It seems clear that Plautus had considerably more influence of this kind than Terence.

It is possible (and desirable) to differentiate the formal influence of Plautus from that of Terence in respect of plot. In all but two or three of his twenty extant plays Plautus used a single plot; in five of his six plays Terence used a double plot. (The exceptions are the *Aulularia*, the *Bacchides*, and the *Poenulus*; and the *Hecyra*.) Now Elizabethan examples of the double-action plot are often said to be in imitation of Terence. In a general sense this is true enough. Yet in a more restricted sense it is only half true. Plays like the *Adelphoe*, the *Andria*, and the *Eunuchus* are certainly double-plot plays in comparison with such single-plot plays as the *Amphitruo*, the *Menaechmi*, and the *Miles Gloriosus*. But the two plots (if they may be so spoken of) of a Terentian double-plot play are generally more tightly unified than the two actions of an Eliza-bethan double-action play. The two plots of a Terentian double-plot play are like the two sides of a coin; the two actions of an Elizabethan double-action play are like two separate coins lying together. This is not to say that the separate actions of a good Elizabethan double-action play are not linked together; usually they are. But normally the two separate actions are more distinct in respect of atmosphere, character-isation, theme and conduct of the action than the two plots of a Ter-entian double-plot play; and we sometimes acknowledge their loose integration by calling them *parallel* actions. Probably the development of the tightly-knit double-plot play of Terence into the more loosely-knit double-action play of Elizabethan comedy (and tragedy) is to be attributed in part to the work of Lyly and Greene but chiefly to Shakespeare's achievement in such plays as *The Taming of the Shrew*, *The Merchant of Venice*, *Much Ado About Nothing*, and *Twelfth Night*.

However that may be, it is necessary to consider, in addition to Roman comedy, the influence of the *commedia erudita*—through such double-plot plays as Ariosto's *Studenti*, the *Calandria* of Bibbiena, the *Ingannati* of the Sienese Intronati, Secchi's *Interesse*, and Pasqualigo's *Fedele*. For despite the pious concern of the Italian critics with unity of plot, the general practice of Italian writers of comedy, except in relatively few examples such as Machiavelli's *Mandragola*, Ariosto's *Suppositi*, and Dolce's *Marito*, is to produce a tightly unified double-plot play in the Terentian manner. Thus it looks as though the formal influence on Elizabethan comedy of the Terentian double plot was exercised in part through the medium of the *commedia erudita*. It need hardly be added that the parallel actions of tragedies like *King Lear*, *A*

Woman Killed with Kindness, The Atheist's Tragedy, and *The Changeling* are derived from the tradition of Terence, the *commedia erudita,* and Elizabethan comedy.

*   *   *

Much of the formal influence of Plautus and Terence is general in the sense that the influencing element is common to both dramatists. Hence it is convenient to speak of the abstraction, Roman comedy. In some respects Dryden's definition, in the *Essay of Dramatic Poesy* (1668), is the best. Of the plot of Roman comedy Dryden has this to say:

> In their comedies the Romans generally borrowed their plots from the Greek poets; and theirs was commonly a little girl stolen or wandered from her parents, brought back unknown to the city, there got with child by some lewd young fellow who, by the help of his servant, cheats his father; and when her time comes to cry,— *Juno Lucina, fer opem,*—one or other sees a little box or cabinet which was carried away with her, and so discovers her to her friends, if some god do not prevent it by coming down in a machine and taking the thanks of it to himself.

This is both witty and accurate (excepting the lapse about denouement by *deus ex machina*). Dryden rightly emphasises (as many other critics do not) the heroine's occasionally giving birth to her lover's child during the action of the play. This occurs in the *Aulularia,* the *Adelphoe,* the *Andria* and (with a difference) the *Amphitruo*; there are strong echoes in *Pericles, The Winter's Tale* and *Henry VIII.* Dryden also rightly emphasises what may be called the device of the 'foundling revealed'— the frequent *anagnorisis* in which it is learned that the heroine was lost as a baby, is actually a citizen, and hence may be married. Of this device it should be noted that, as employed in Roman comedy, the foundling is usually a girl. (Compare the use of a male foundling in the *Oedipus Tyrannus* of Sophocles.) A boy foundling crops up in Roman comedy only in that most exceptional example the *Captivi* of Plautus.

Further, it is interesting that Dryden presents his typical plot, not— as do Plautus and Terence—by hastening *in medias res,* but by narrating it *ab ovo*—in much the same fashion as did the illustrator of the Strassburg Terence of 1496, printed by Johann Grüninger. Here understanding of the formal influence of Plautus and Terence is much indebted to

Madeleine Doran's brilliant insight, in *Endeavors of Art* (1954), into the nature of the typical Roman-comedy plot:

> Unlike the illustrations in the Lyons edition of 1493, printed by Jean Trechsel, which show stage settings, the cuts in the Grüninger edition are illustrations of the story of each play. They are compositions in the manner of many illuminations and medieval paintings with narrative subject matter; that is, various incidents in the story appear within one frame, the same character reappearing in different parts of the picture wherever required by the episodes illustrated. The *Figur* for *Andria* [reproduced as Miss Doran's frontispiece] is particularly interesting. Houses with the appropriate characters grouped around them appear in the foreground and in the middle distance. Crito, in the center, with a finger pointing towards Glycerium, Pamphilus' mistress, is indicated as the character who brings the clue to her identity and hence the solution to all difficulties. In the background at the top of the picture is a scene illustrative of Glycerium's romantic past, when, as Pasibula, the daughter of Chremes, she was lost in a shipwreck. The scene is a seascape showing an abandoned ship, the head of Phania, her uncle, near drowning, the child Pasibula afloat on a raft, and 'Andria insula', fortified with towers and battlemented walls, in the midst of the waters.
>
>   In the play, of course, the action is confined in classical fashion to the critical moment in Pamphilus' affairs when his father is on the point of marrying him off to Philumena, his friend Charinus is suspecting him of breach of faith in taking her away from him, and his mistress Glycerium is giving birth to his child. The revelation of Glycerium's past comes in the last act as a means of untangling what looks to be a hopelessly complicated knot. The effect of the illustration, on the other hand, is to give the romantic background even more prominence than the critical action of the play. It is a narrative, not a dramatic, illustration, without focus on a single moment of action. The story, if not fully set forth, is at least implied from start to finish. The illustrations for the other plays are of the same narrative type, although no other carries the story so far back.

Miss Doran concludes with the point that 'the plays of Terence were readily assimilated to the tradition of medieval romantic narrative'. (The fortunes of Marina in *Pericles* provide an enlightening comparison with those of Pasibula in the *Andria*.) The apperception is true also, of course, of the plays of Plautus. It may be added that writers of the *commedia erudita* generally retained the crisis plot of classical comedy, as in the *Suppositi*, whereas writers of Elizabethan comedy tended to tell the story from the beginning, as in the secondary action of *The Taming of the Shrew*.

Another important insight into the formal influence of Plautus and Terence is Alfred Harbage's suggestion that the characteristically Elizabethan tragedy of intrigue involves an adaptation of the basic technique of Roman-comedy plot to the requirements of tragedy. In this context 'intrigue' is not merely a plan to kill someone, as in the *Agamemnon* and *Macbeth*, but the artful manipulation of a person or object toward some deadly end, as in *The Spanish Tragedy* and *Othello*. Thus Harbage sees Elizabethan intrigue tragedy as cross-bred from comedy—a kind of comitragedy. The suggestion is the more striking in that intrigue tragedy appears to have originated, full-blown, only in the late 1580's, in *The Spanish Tragedy*. The Italians, needless to say, and the French after them, keep the plots of their tragedies uncontaminated by intrigue, the dominant technique of Roman-comedy plot.

Further important insights (of a general nature) into the formal influence of Plautus and Terence have been made by Northrop Frye, in *Anatomy of Criticism* (1957). These include the basically Oedipal quality of the frequent opposition between father and son, the analysis of comic characters into the general types of *alazon*, *eiron*, *bomolochos*, and *agroikos*, the deeper significance of blocking character and scapegoat, the transition, during the course of the play, from an established society in opposition to the lovers to a new society of which they are the approved centre, and the feast (symbolising the new society) with which so many comedies end and to which the audience are sometimes playfully invited.

★   ★   ★

Dryden continues his definition with some remarks on the typical characters of Roman comedy:

> By the plot you may guess much of the characters of the persons. An old father who would willingly, before he dies, see his son well married; his debauched son, kind in his nature to his mistress but miserably in want of money; a servant or slave who has so much wit to strike in with him and help to dupe his father; a braggadochio captain, a parasite, and a lady of pleasure.

This too is accurate, though the comment resembles that of many another critic. But Dryden makes a further point:

As for the poor honest maid on whom the story is built, and who ought to be one of the principal actors in the play, she is commonly a mute in it; she has the breeding of the old Elizabeth way, which was for maids to be seen and not to be heard; and it is enough you know she is willing to be married when the fifth act requires it.

This observation (which relatively few critics make) is of some help in understanding the formal differences between Roman and Elizabethan comedy. To it should be added, however, the companion observation that in many Roman comedies the young heroine does not even come on stage as a mute. In the six plays of Terence, for example, only two young heroines come on stage: Antiphila in the *Heauton Timorumenos* and Pamphila in the *Eunuchus*. Pamphila is a *muta persona*. The situation is generally similar in many Italian comedies of the early sixteenth century (for example, Ariosto's *Suppositi*, *Lena*, *Negromante*, *Studenti*, Piccolomini's *Amor Costante*); but by mid-century the Italians had developed active young heroines who not only play a prominent part in the plot but also figure prominently in the stage-action (for example, the *Ingannati*, Secchi's *Interesse*, Della Porta's *Tabernaria* and *Chiappinaria*). Needless to say, the English do this too, not only in late examples such as *Campaspe*, *Friar Bacon and Friar Bungay*, *The Merchant of Venice*, *As You Like It*, and *The Fawn*, but also in early examples such as *Fulgens and Lucrece* and *Roister-Doister*.

The formal influence of Plautus and Terence is much evident in the stock characters of Elizabethan comedy. But again we must consider the influence of the *commedia erudita*. Many of the character-types of Roman comedy are frequently used by Renaissance writers of comedy. A few appear infrequently. Some are altered. And there are additions, occasioned both by the demands of new plots drawn from the *novelle* and by changed social conditions of the Renaissance. For convenience of discussion the characters may be divided into three groups: primary male characters, primary female characters, and secondary characters.

Primary male characters are the *adulescens*, the *senex*, and the *servus*. In Renaissance Italian comedy the *adulescens* becomes the *giovane* or *innamorato*, in Elizabethan comedy the Young Man or Lover. Usually the Renaissance character-type plays a more active rôle in the plot than his classical prototype, in compensation apparently for the less active rôle usually played by his servant. The Italians somewhat deepen the Lover's sentimental qualities, and the English carry this development even further. The Young Man of Renaissance comedy is also more often a Rival Suitor than in Roman comedy.

The *senex* of Roman comedy has several aspects: Father, Husband, Aged Philanderer, Helpful Friend. In Italian comedy the *senex* becomes the *vecchio*, in Elizabethan comedy the Old Man. Usually he is a father. However, where the *senex* of Roman comedy is the father only of a son, the Old Man of Renaissance comedy can be the father of a daughter as well. (Vincentio in *The Taming of the Shrew* is an example of the one kind of father, Baptista of the other.) Sometimes the Old Man is a husband, and here an important development occurs in that he can be a Jealous Husband (the effect of the satire varying accordingly as he is or is not a cuckold) or an Aged Husband (usually a cuckold). These types, not found in Roman comedy, were obviously designed to accommodate another Renaissance innovation, the Adulterous (or possibly Adulterous) Wife. Sometimes the Old Man of Renaissance comedy is an Aged Suitor, this function corresponding approximately to the *senex*'s occasional function of Aged Philanderer.

The *servus* (whether clever or stupid) becomes the *servo* of Italian comedy, the Manservant of Elizabethan. The character-type is essentially the same in Renaissance comedy as in Roman comedy, except of course for his manumission—which brings with it the possibility of leaving his master's service (Lancelot Gobbo). A decided difference, however, is that the *servo* or Servant is used much less frequently as the manipulator of a plot to aid the Young Man his master; in Renaissance comedy the Young Man, and in some cases even the heroine, often takes over the scheming usually performed by the *servus* of Roman comedy (Callimaco in the *Mandragola*, Rosalind in *As You Like It*, Dulcimel in *The Fawn*, Dauphine in *Epicene*).

Primary female characters are the *virgo*, the *meretrix* and the *matrona*. In Italian comedy the *virgo* or *puella* becomes a *giovane* or *innamorata* or *donzella* or *fanciulla*, in Elizabethan comedy the Maid. In two respects the Renaissance character-type differs greatly from the classical. (1) In Roman comedy the heroine is usually a slave-girl, hence not a citizen, hence not marriageable. The generality holds, though sorely tested by the citizen heroine of Plautus's *Persa*. (Menander's *Dyskolos* provides another exception.) On the other hand, in Renaissance comedy the heroine is marriageable; and thus a condition essential for romantic comedy is provided—the heroine can be wooed, with marriage rather than seduction as a goal. (2) In Roman comedy the *virgo* rarely comes on stage (more often in Plautus than in Terence), and when she does come on she is sometimes a mute. The Italians followed Roman convention in this matter during the first decades of the sixteenth century, and for much the same reasons, as Giraldi Cinthio makes clear in his *Discourse on the Composition of Comedies and Tragedies* (1554):

> For the most part the comic stage is bawdy, and on it appear panders, courtesans, parasites, and other similar kinds of people of a bawdy and unchaste way of life; and therefore it seems not suitable to the decorum of a young virgin for her to come and speak on such a stage and among these characters.

However, the Italian writers of comedy were already, by mid-century' developing conventions that would permit the heroine to come on stage and even to play a prominent rôle in the conduct of the action. Thus the heroine might appear at a window, on the threshold of a door of the house, or with an attendant on the way to a convent; or she might appear in transvestite disguise, a device which greatly adds to the prominence of the heroine because of its possibilities for intrigue. English writers of comedy are generally freer than Italian in permitting the heroine to come on stage and even to dominate the action (compare the early sixteenth-century examples *Fulgens and Lucrece* and *Calisto and Melebea*); but they too delight in the comic irony and the potentialities for intrigue made possible by the device of the transvestite heroine.

The *meretrix* becomes a *meretrice* or *cortigiana* (sometimes simply a *putana*) in Italian comedy, a Courtesan in Elizabethan comedy. In general, despite interesting exceptions (Marston's *Dutch Courtesan*), the character-type does not appear nearly so much in Renaissance comedy as in Roman comedy, for the reason apparently that the chief female rôles have been taken over by Wives and Maids. The Roman-comedy *meretrix*, like the *virgo*, is unmarriageable, whereas the Renaissance Courtesan can be married—a difference occasionally of some importance to plot.

The *matrona* of Roman comedy appears from time to time in Italian comedy, where she is known by the same term *matrona*, but very infrequently as a Matron in Elizabethan comedy (an example is the Countess in *All's Well That Ends Well*). The general absence of Matrons from Elizabethan comedy is striking. But then a new character (foreshadowed in Alcmena) is created, in Italian comedy the *donna* or *moglie*, in Elizabethan comedy the Wife. Or, if you like, the Roman-comedy *matrona* bifurcates into the relatively rare Renaissance Matron and that younger variation, the Wife. In any case the Wife derives in part from the *novella* tradition, with the traditions of *fabliau* and farce not far in the background. In view of such derivation it is not surprising that the Wife of Renaissance comedy is often an Adulterous Wife, a character-type not found in Roman comedy since adultery is not there depicted or even much considered as a possibility. (Alcmena, of course, though seduced by Jupiter, is not guilty of adultery.) The Adulterous Wife makes possible the corresponding character-type of the Aged Husband or Cuckold (Lucrezia and Nicia in the *Mandragola*); and the Chaste Wife, the type of the (unjustifiably) Jealous Husband (Mistress Ford and Ford in *The Merry Wives of Windsor* or Celia and Corvino in *Volpone*). Another new female character-type is the *vedova* or Widow, who appears occasionally in both Italian and Elizabethan comedy (Dame Custance in *Roister-Doister*). Since she is usually marriageable, the Widow's characteristics and plot-function tend to be similar to those of the *innamorata* or Maid.

The secondary characters of Roman comedy include, more or less in descending order of their importance, the *parasitus*, the *miles gloriosus*, the *ancilla*, the *leno*, the *lena*, the *cocus*, the *trapezita* or *danista*, the *nutrex*, the *mercator*, the *medicus*, the *advocatus*, and the *piscator*.

Some of these appear infrequently in Renaissance comedy. The Roman-comedy *parasitus* becomes the *parassito* of Italian comedy, the Parasite of Elizabethan. But the Roman social type was alien to the Renaissance, and accordingly the Parasite's quality of free-loading tended to be assimilated to other character-types. (Sir Toby Belch is an example of the Parasite skilfully adapted to social conditions of sixteenth-century England.) The *leno* (the term being better translated, according to Duckworth, as slave-dealer than as pander or pimp) becomes a *ruffiano* or *maquerello* in Italian comedy, a Pander in Elizabethan. And the *lena* becomes a *ruffiana* or *mezzana* in Italian comedy, a Bawd in Elizabethan. These types appear infrequently in Renaissance comedy, however, since the heroines are normally in the control rather of a Husband or a Father than of a *leno* or *lena*. (Shakespeare provides approximate parallels to the classical types in the Pander and Bawd of *Pericles*.) The *trapezita* or *danista* appears very seldom in Renaissance comedy as a money-lender. (But Shylock seems to be essentially a development of this type.) The *piscator* also appears infrequently as a Fisherman (examples in *Pericles*).

Of secondary Roman-comedy characters who appear frequently in Renaissance comedy, the *miles gloriosus* is by all odds the most important. He becomes the *capitano millantatore* of Italian comedy, the Soldier or Braggart of Elizabethan. The type was elaborately developed both in Italy and in England but remains essentially the same in Renaissance comedy as in Roman: that is, the *capitano* or Soldier is (1) a braggart, (2) a coward, and usually (3) a fatuous would-be lover. An Italian-comedy development is the *bravo*, or thug (for example, Frangipietra in Pasqualigo's *Fedele*). This type appears rarely in Elizabethan comedy (Captain Crackstone in Mundy's *Fedele and Fortunio*) but may have an affinity with the Murderer of Elizabethan tragedy. The *ancilla* of Roman comedy becomes the *fantesca* of Italian comedy, the Maid-servant or Woman of Elizabethan. An interesting Elizabethan develop-ment is the Waiting Gentlewoman, who, being of rank, can become involved in a romantic action of her own (Maria in *Twelfth Night*). (Compare the *confidante* of seventeenth-century French tradition.) The Roman-comedy *cocus* becomes the *cuoco* of Italian comedy, the Cook or Servingman of Elizabethan. The type is essentially a variant of the *servus* or Servant. The *mercator* appears occasionally as the *mercatante* and Merchant, the *medicus* more frequently as the *medico* and Doctor, the *advocatus* even more frequently as the *avvocato* or *dottore* and Lawyer. The *nutrex* appears occasionally as a *nutrice* and (wet) Nurse. This character-type undergoes an interesting development during the Renaissance into the *balia* and (companion) Nurse. The type does not appear in Roman comedy, except perhaps tentatively in the *anus* or attendant, for the reason that young ladies of sufficient rank to support an attendant do not figure in the plots. The character is probably de-rived from the Renaissance social type, but a precedent exists in the female attendant of classical tragedy. In the plots of Renaissance comedy the *balia* or Nurse tends to take over the go-between functions of the *lena* in Roman comedy.

The Father of a Daughter, the Jealous or Aged Husband, the Aged Suitor, the Marriageable Heroine, the Adulterous Wife, the Widow, the *bravo*, the Waiting Gentlewoman, and the *balia* or Nurse are new character-types which developed out of Roman-comedy types during the Renaissance. Others are completely new. Of these the most important is the *pedante* of Italian comedy (foreshadowed, to be sure, in the old slave Lydus, tutor to Pistoclerus in the *Bacchides* of Plautus). Essentially a tutor, the *pedante* is brought into Elizabethan comedy as a Pedant but also there developed into the sub-type of the Schoolmaster. Perhaps next in importance is the *prete* or *frate* of Italian comedy, the Priest or Friar of Elizabethan. The type is occasionally a vehicle for strong anticlerical satire (Machiavelli's Fra Timoteo). An interesting type is the fake occultist, the *negromante* or *astrologo* or *alchimista*. The type appears in Elizabethan comedy as the fake Magician or Astrologer or Alchemist, and there is also an Elizabethan development in the true occultist or Magician. (Prospero, like Friar Bacon, belongs to the latter class.) A female fake occultist is the Italian *strega* or witch, a social type whose existence as a plague of Italian society is witnessed by Dante's comments in the *Inferno* (20. 121-3). The *strega* occasionally crops up in Elizabethan comedy as a Witch. (An example is Medusa in Mundy's *Fedele and Fortunio*, derived from the corresponding *strega* of Pasqualigo's *Fedele*.) A related Italian-comedy type is the *pinzochera*, a social type that was technically an aspirant to membership in a religious order but actually a kind of procuress, as her epithets *ruffiana* and *mezzana* indicate. The *pinzochera* is a rare type that appears not to have an Elizabethan equivalent. Finally, two nonclassical Elizabethan types, the Fool and the Clown, appear to have no counterparts in the *commedia erudita*.

*   *   *

Gascoigne's *Supposes*, performed at Gray's Inn in 1566 and again at Trinity College, Oxford, in 1582, may be used to illustrate some of the formal influences discussed in preceding pages. The *Supposes* is an especially useful illustration since it is a fairly close translation of Ariosto's *Suppositi* (1509) and since it was later reworked by Shakespeare, with significant variations, as the secondary action of *The Taming of the Shrew* (1593).

Certain of the characters of the *Supposes* are in the tradition of Roman comedy: Pasiphilo, the parasite; Erostrato, the *adulescens* involved in an amorous intrigue; Dulipo, the *servus* conducting an intrigue on behalf of his young master; and Philogano, the *senex* in the rôle of father to a young man. Other of the characters are in the tradition of Renaissance Italian comedy: Polynesta, the *inamorata* being courted in marriage; Balia, the *balia* or companion-nurse to a young lady; the feigned

Erostrato and Cleander, respectively the (fake) Rival Suitor and the Aged Suitor; and Damon, the *vecchio* in the rôle of father to a marriageable girl. Polynesta's promiscuity is characteristic of Roman comedy, and her hinted-at pregnancy echoes the pregnancy found in the *Andria* and other plays. Polynesta's small part in the stage-action is also in the tradition of Roman comedy—she comes on stage only twice, and in her second appearance she has no lines to speak. The play is typically Roman in its emphasis on fathers, of whom there turn out to be three (Damon, Philogano, Cleander), and typically Renaissance in its omission of a matron. There is a hint of what Northrop Frye calls the 'comic Oedipus situation' in the vying of father and son, Cleander and Dulipo, for the hand of Polynesta. The revelation of Dulipo's gentle birth in the denouement is typical of Roman comedy—though usually, because of the social station of the heroine and its importance to the plot, the foundling in Roman comedy is not a boy but a girl. (Plautus's use of a male foundling in the *Captivi*—generally considered to be Ariosto's source in this matter—is exceptional in Roman comedy.) And the *Supposes* aptly illustrates Frye's suggestion that a new society usually 'crystallises' around the lovers at the end of a comedy: the chief 'blocking' characters (Damon and Cleander) happily agree to the marriage which they have hitherto opposed between Polynesta and Erostrato.

In Shakespeare's version of Ariosto's story one of the classical character-types (the parasite) is eliminated. Two others are relatively unchanged: Tranio, the servant who manages an intrigue on his young master's behalf; and Vincentio, the father of a young man. Lucentio is changed in response to the different demands of a new, and characteristically Renaissance, plot: instead of seducing the girl, he runs away with and marries her. One of the Renaissance Italian character-types (the *balia*) is eliminated, apparently because, in view of the heroine's chastity, a go-between is no longer necessary. One other character-type is relatively unchanged: Baptista, the father of a marriageable girl. Others are changed. Bianca is altered, like Lucentio, for reasons of plot: instead of being seduced, she elopes with and marries her lover. And the values of Gremio and Tranio are altered, for, though the characters remain basically the Aged Suitor and the (fake) Rival Suitor, Shakespeare suppresses the recognition of Dulipo as the long-lost son of Cleander. Thus he eliminates Ariosto's echo of Plautus's *Captivi* in providing a last-minute rise in station for the faithful Dulipo, as well as the stroke of poetic justice whereby Cleander, who only wished to marry for the sake of begetting an heir, though disappointed of a wife nevertheless finds an heir. As a result, Gremio and Tranio seem to 'dangle' a bit at the end of the play—but Shakespeare's last Act was crowded with other matter. Shakespeare also provides two additional characters: a (true) Rival Suitor (Hortensio) and a Second Lady (the Widow) who make possible a double marriage at the end of the action. Ariosto retains the customary promiscuity of classical comedy while making his heroine, in the Renaissance style, marriageable; whereas Shakespeare makes his heroine not only marriageable but also chaste—in fact he presents the elopement leading to a 'stolen' marriage and the wedding feast which follows it. He also brings his heroine on-stage more than half a dozen times—considerably more than does Ariosto.

The *Supposes* is a single-action play in the Plautine manner, and it has a typically classical crisis plot: the action begins shortly after Damon discovers that his daughter has been carrying on an affair with her servant the supposed Dulipo, shortly after the supposed Erostrato has engaged the Scenese to pose as Erostrato's father, and just as the true father Philogano is about to arrive in town. The play, which has absolute unity of time and place, is an admirable example of the *in medias res* technique. In the light of Madeline Doran's suggestion, however, we can see the potential which the story has for treatment in the *ab ovo* manner. There are two major time schemes in the background of the *Supposes*. One extends back two years, to the day when Erostrato, newly arrived in Ferrara, first saw and fell in love with Polynesta. If the story were told as from this origin, the dramatist would begin with the lover's first glimpse of the girl, proceed with the stratagem of his taking service in her house and gaining access to her bed, and end with the events that are the whole subject of the action as we have it. This (saving Polynesta's promiscuity) is precisely what Shakespeare does in *The Taming of the Shrew*. He shows us Lucentio's first sight of Bianca, his falling in love with her, his taking service in Baptista's household, his gaining access to Bianca through his pose as a *pedante*, and so on. But there is another time scheme in the background of the *Supposes*. It extends back twenty years to the capture of Otranto by the Turks. If the story were told as from this origin, the dramatist would begin with Cleander's escape from Otranto, the capture of the infant Dulipo by the Turks, Dulipo's wanderings, his eventual sale as a household

I. Two Woodcuts from the Venice Plautus of 1518
(*top*) *from fol. LXXXVI verso.*
(*bottom*) *from fol. LIII.*

II. The Hall of Gray's Inn
(Courtesy of Royal Commission on Historical Monuments)

slave to Philogano, his growing up as Erostrato's servant, his coming to Ferrara with Erostrato and so on. Thus it seems clear that the plot of the *Supposes* has the same potential for handling in the romantic mode as does that of the *Andria*—or, for that matter, as does the plot of *The Comedy of Errors* and many another example. Furthermore, though Shakespeare chose to retell the story from the origin of Luc ntio's love of Bianca, in another, much later, play, he tells the story of a foundling from the very beginning: in *Pericles* he shows us the loss of the infant Marina in a shipwreck at sea, the situation of her growing up, her capture by pirates, her sale as a slave to the owners of a brothel, and her discovery in the brothel by the young man (Lysimachus) who will marry her when, at the end of the action, she is revealed to be of noble birth. Shakespeare's treatment of the Apollonius romance is not simply a dramatisation; it is a dramatisation which, while avoiding the retrospective plot of classical comedy, emphasises a common situation of the heroine in the comedies of Plautus and Terence.

K

Note

Biography. John Lyly was born in the early 1550's and was brought up in Canterbury where his father was an official of the diocese. The dramatist took his B.A. in 1573, and M.A. in 1575, at Oxford. He failed to get a fellowship, went to London and published *Euphues, The Anatomy of Wit*, a successful novel, in 1578; its sequel, *Euphues and his England*, followed in 1580. His first play, *Campaspe*, was performed in 1584 by the boy-actors of St. Paul's and the Queen's Chapel at Court and at the small, enclosed theatre at Blackfriars; and so were most of his seven other comedies, all written before 1595. Several of Lyly's letters to the Queen and Sir Robert Cecil seeking court preferment have survived, dated 1597–1601. He died 1606.

Texts. The plays were first published separately between 1584 and 1601; six were collected by E. Blount as *Six Court Comedies* (1632). The indispensable modern edition is by R. W. Bond (1902) in three volumes, including non-dramatic works; G. K. Hunter is preparing a new edition of the plays.

Criticism. The most recent and important study is *John Lyly: The Humanist as Courtier*, by G. K. Hunter (1962). Two earlier studies, both called *John Lyly*, are by J. D. Wilson (1905) and A. Feuillerat (1910). An excellent account of non-dramatic works is in C. S. Lewis, *English Literature in the Sixteenth Century* (1954). See also B. F. Huppe, 'Allegory of Love in Lyly's Court Comedies', *E.L.H.* (1947), P. A. Long, 'The Purport of Lyly's *Endimion*', *P.M.L.A.* (1909), and G. W. Knight, 'Lyly', *R.E.S.* (1939).

Background. Two works on the theory of play are important for this chapter: J. Huizinga, *Homo Ludens* (1949), and *Man, Play and Games*, by R. Caillois (1962). Studies of recreation in Tudor England are in *Shakespeare's England*, ed. O. Onions (1916); bibliographies are appended. For the play of language, wit, rhetoric and fancy see: Spingarn's *Critical Essays of the Seventeenth Century* (1908) and W. C. Crane, *Wit and Rhetoric in the Renaissance* (1937).

This chapter quotes Tudor and Stuart writers from T. Arbeau, *Orchesography*, tr. Mary S. Evans (1948); R. Burton, *The Anatomy of Melancholy*, Everyman's Library; Castiglione, *The Book of the Courtier*, Everyman's Library; Sir John Davies, *Orchestra*, in *Silver Poets of the Sixteenth Century*, Everyman's Library; Sir Thomas Elyot, *The Book Named the Governor*, Everyman's Library; T. Fuller, *The Holy State* (1642); S. Guazzo, *The Civil Conversation*, Tudor Translations (1925); Sir John Harington, *A Treatise on Play*, in *Nugae Antiquae*, ii (1779); Sir Thomas Wilson, *The Art of Rhetoric*, (2nd Ed. 1560), ed. G. H. Mair (1909); N. Breton, *The Court and the Country*, in *Prose Works*, ed. Ursula K. Wright (1929). An account of Melville's embassy is in *A Short History of Hampton Court*, by E. Law (1924). Brecht's critical writings have been selected by J. Willetts in *Brecht on Theatre* (1964).

VII

John Lyly and the Language of Play

JOCELYN POWELL

*

It's not the marbles matter, but the game
DUTCH PROVERB

A MODERN reader, approaching the works of Lyly for the first time, could be pardoned for wondering if they were not irredeemably precious. He could be pardoned; but he would be wrong. It is easy to find a sentence like the following jejune:

> Well, well, seeing the wound that bleedeth inwards is most dangerous, that the fire kept close burneth most furious, that the oven damned up baketh soonest, that sores having no vent fester inwardly, it is high time to unfold my secret love to my secret friend. (*Euphues*, i. 21)

High time, indeed. The pile of unremarkable proverbs, the punning parallelism of 'secret love' and 'secret friend', and the liberal spattering of alliteration, seem to occupy considerably more of the author's attention than the matter to be expressed. Also, considerably more space. One might agree with David Daiches that 'with these excessive efforts he [Lyly] wearies the reader and demonstrates clearly that Elizabethan prose had not grown up'; or with the two eminent French professors, Legouis and Cazamian, that Euphuism is 'a disease of language'.[1]

But isn't this to miss the point? The criticism is based on a presupposition: that prose is better the more direct the relationship is between the words and the ideas. This is a presupposition that needs to be questioned—that must be questioned if an understanding of Lyly is to be achieved (and surely the endeavour to understand and enjoy

---

[1] D. Daiches, *A Critical History of English Literature* (1960), p. 199; and Legouis and Cazamian, *A History of English Literature* (1957), p. 261.

the unfamiliar is one of the chief purposes of criticism). Why should one suppose that the only, or even the main, interest of words lies in the meaning behind them? C. S. Lewis took a contrary view when he wrote of *Euphues*: 'The book can now only be read, as it was chiefly read by his contemporaries, for the style. It is worse where it is least euphuistic' (p. 314).

The style may be absurd, self indulgent, and sensational, heaped with similitude, word-play, proverb lore, and unnatural natural history, but it is almost always sustained by a magnificent sense of extravagance and fun.

> He that always singeth one note without descant breedeth no delight, he that always playeth one part bringeth loathsomeness to the ear. It is variety that moveth the mind of all men.
>
> > (*Euphues*, i. 272)

Euphuism is essentially a game, and games are not merely childish.

It is only relatively recently that play has come to be regarded as important in its own right—a phenomenon with particular properties vital to the history of civilisation. History shows a need for organised forms of play in all societies, and Huizinga, in his book *Homo Ludens*, demonstrated the importance of play forms in the shaping of Law, and the rules of war, as well as philosophy, art, and literature.

That function of play of particular interest to aesthetic criticism is its apparent uselessness. Play 'interpolates itself as a temporary activity, satisfying in itself and ending there' (Huizinga, p. 9). It 'begins and ends in itself and the outcome does not contribute to the necessary life processes of the group' (p. 49). 'It is an activity connected with no material interest, and no profit can be gained by it' (p. 13). Play, in fact, is an apparently essential human activity which seems to lack any immediately obvious practical purpose; and Lyly, likewise, is a prime example of those authors who have to be approached from without the pale of utilitarianism which bounds so much literary criticism. His work may from time to time give evidence of moral sensibility, provide some relevant 'criticism of life', but even when it does so that is not what is important in it. What is important is its recreative function.

Play is as essential a part of experience as seriousness, recreation as work, and it is a mistake to think of the one as lighter, easier, or less important than the other. The Elizabethans themselves were well aware of the necessity for play, and prepared to spend some time about it. Castiglione's *Courtier* and Sir Thomas Elyot's *Governor*, to mention only two of the so-called 'courtesy' books, have long sections on a gentleman's recreation. But they too were worried about the uselessness of such pastimes:

> Those are the best recreations [writes Thomas Fuller], which, besides refreshing, enable, at least dispose, men to some other good ends. Bowling teaches men's eyes and hands mathematics and the rules of proportion . . . tilting and fencing is war without anger, and manly sports the grammar of military performance. (p. 173)

Elyot recommends painting for its usefulness to the military commander in the drawing of maps and devising of new machines of war (a function to which Leonardo Da Vinci was mercilessly applied), and dancing for its education in the virtue of prudence! To justify the latter activity Arbeau is even more practical in his *Orchésographie*:

> Dancing is practised to reveal whether lovers are in good health and sound of limb, after which they are permitted to kiss their mistresses in order that they may touch and savour one another, thus to ascertain if they are shapely or emit an unpleasant smell, like bad meat. Therefore, from this standpoint, quite apart from the many other advantages to be derived from dancing, it becomes essential in a well ordered society. (p. 12)

There is a basic materialism in human nature which revolts at any activity which is not directed to some end beyond itself. Every activity must demonstrate progress in a chain of cause and effect. As a matter of fact, play does so, and the Elizabethans knew this as we do now; but the chain is hidden, and so neither was then, nor is now, very easily admitted.

Sir John Harington, Queen Elizabeth's godson, and sometimes her favourite, beguiled his time by, among other things, writing a treatise on play:[2]

> Play, according to the ancient schoolmen (who were the narrowest examiners and subtlest distinguishers of words) is defined to be, *Ludus, id est, locutus vel operatio in quo nihil quaeritur nisi dilectatio animalis.* A spending of the time either in speech or action, whose only end is a delight of the mind or spirit. And therefore call it also

[2] He also wrote a treatise on the water-closet.

a remedy against the overburdening and dulling of the spirits.
(ii. 157)

Thomas Fuller, also, in spite of the condition quoted above, gives us
a similar, most beautiful definition:

> Recreations is a second Creation, when weariness has almost
> annihilated one's spirits. It is the breathing of the soul, which other-
> wise would be stifled with continual business. (p. 172)

One of the essential conditions of play, Huizinga tells us, is that it is
'different from ordinary life'. The recreative spirit turns the mind
away from life so that it may return to it refreshed. It re-creates the
mind in a world created for recreation which is without the inescapable
consequences that otherwise attend a human act, so that the mind is
refitted for human action. Such, in utilitarian terms is the purpose of
play. The manner by which the mind is refitted—and it is not a simple
matter of escape—the manner of which Lyly is a master, can be
ascertained by a further discussion of Elizabethan play forms.

*   *   *

As has been already suggested, play in Elizabethan England was a
serious matter, particularly for the courtier. The recreations of a gentleman all demanded a degree of skill and all took place very much under
the public eye. First there were the outdoor spots (falconry, the chase
and the tilt), all requiring specialised knowledge above the managing
of weapons and a good seat on a horse. Tilting, with all the panoply of
medieval chivalry was much in favour at Elizabeth's court, finding
particularly dramatic expression in the great annual tournaments
organised in honour of the anniversaries of the Queen's accession.

The court also indulged in many indoor pastimes. Dancing was of
course the chief, and in particular favour with the Queen. This was a
highly complex activity and the difficulty of many of the steps is
excellently demonstrated by the famous picture of Queen Elizabeth
dancing the La Volta with the Earl of Leicester. Music was also a
popular pastime. The Queen herself was an expert performer on the
virginals, and the ability to play some solo instrument or at least to
sing at sight was almost de rigeur. If the actual participation of the
Elizabethan gentleman in musical activity was neither so widespread
nor so adept as is sometimes supposed, it is certain he was willing to

apply his mind vigorously to the matter where he could not apply his fingers to the fact.

There were other games played at court some of which were perhaps less demanding. Chess was frequently played, though Castiglione thinks it a game that takes so much time to master that it is almost a virtue not to play it well. Elizabeth, in spite of her closeness, enjoyed a gamble at Primero. Cards were even played in the presence chamber. Sir John Harington justifies this practice in face of complaints from the older courtiers, in that it was important to have the presence chamber full and a man could not be expected to spend all day in talk. He suggests lightly that the room might be made more comfortable for the purpose; saying it would:

> As well become the state of the chamber to have easy quilted, lined forms to sit on (which fashion is now taken up in every merchant's hall) as great plank forms that two yeoman can scant remove out of their places, and wainscot stools so hard, that, since great breeches were laid aside, men can scant endure to sit on. (ii. 173)

It is possible to perceive behind all the above activities, except perhaps the cards, two important conceptions: exercise and display. What is not used, rusts. The games are designed to exercise every facet of the personality of 'Courtier, soldier, scholar, eye, tongue, sword,' and display each man's fitness for his place. To quote Arbeau again:

> Dancing is a kind of mute rhetoric by which the orator, without uttering a word, can make himself understood by his movements and persuade the spectators he is gallant and worthy to be acclaimed, admired, and loved. Are you not of the opinion that this is the dancer's own language, expressed by his feet and in a convincing manner? Does he not plead tacitly with his mistress, who marks the seemliness and grace of his dancing, 'Love me. Desire me'? (p. 16)

The court was a place of cut-throat competition. The Courtier played to catch his sovereign's eye. Sir Christopher Hatton was said to owe his position to his excellence as a dancer. Queens themselves were not above such rivalry. The Scottish Ambassador, Melville, coming to Elizabeth from Mary, Queen of Scots, was entertained for a week at Hampton Court and vouchsafed glimpses of our accomplished queen in all the activities at which she was most expert, including dancing and playing upon the virginals. After each demonstration the unfortunate man was confronted with the cantankerous question, 'which of us does such and such the better, your Queen or me?' The reasons for this are not entirely frivolous; play activities exercised the faculties of the soul and the body, they therefore made manifest the quality of the man.

If display was the aspect of play most crucial to the courtier, exercise was the basic principle. In moderation, according to Burton, it was essential to health, as one might see from the workings of the universe:

> The heavens themselves run continually around, the sun riseth and sets, the moon increaseth and decreaseth, stars and planets keep their constant motions, the air is still tossed by the winds, the waters ebb and flow, to their conservation no doubt, to teach us we should ever be in action.   (Vol. II, 69)

But when we read further in his chapter we find the conception of action distinctly curious. After discussing several of the more obvious sports he remarks:

> But the most pleasant of all outward pastimes is that of Aretaeus, *deambulatio per amoena loca.* . . . To disport in some pleasant plain, park, run up a steep hill sometimes, or sit in a shady seat, must needs be a pleasant recreation. (p. 75)

He particularly recommends angling, despite the disparagements of Plutarch:

> But he that shall consider the variety of baits for all seasons, and pretty devices which our anglers have invented, peculiar lines, false flies, several sleights, etc, will say that it deserves like commendation, requires as much study and perspicacity as the rest, and is to be preferred before many of them. Because hawking and hunting are very laborious, much riding and many dangers accompany them; but it is still and quiet: and if so be the angler catch no fish, yet he hath a wholesome walk to the brookside, pleasant shade by the sweet silver streams; he hath good air, and sweet smells of fine fresh meadow flowers, he hears the melodious harmony of the birds, he sees the swans, herons, ducks, water-hens, coots, etc, and many other fowl with their brood, which he thinketh better than the noise of hounds or blast of horns, and all the sport that they can make. (p. 74)

Here is indeed the complete exercise. All the faculties are involved, sight, sound, smell, touch, even taste, if the fish be caught, and all at their most delicate and subtle. Even the mind is employed, because it 'requires as much study and perspicacity as the rest' to master its techniques.

In fact Burton's conception of the recreation of the mind might strike a modern reader very hard. He advises, among other pastimes, the study of algebra:

> Than which, as Clavius holds, 'in all human disciplines nothing can be more excellent and pleasant, so abstruse and recondite, so bewitching, so miraculous, so ravishing, so easy withal and full of delight.'

The Elizabethans, indeed, were no strangers to the play of the mind. Harington has a category described as 'devotional play' which covers public and private worship as a refreshment to the soul. If there was algebra, there was also music:

> A custom inclining to virtue, which maketh the mind more apt to the conceiving of felicity, even as bodily exercise maketh the body more lusty. (*Courtier*, p. 75)

The complete gentleman should be versed in the liberal arts, so that, even if he does not practise them himself, he will be a proper judge of the performances of others. The gentleman's education had, as its base, the classical systems of logic and rhetoric; the penning of occasional verses was a common accomplishment, even if not every courtier was a Sir Philip Sydney. Their intellects were trained, as Sir John Davies would have it, for the dance of the mind:

> And those great masters of the liberal arts
> In all their several schools do dancing teach;
> For humble grammar first doth set the parts
> Of congruent and well according speech,
> Which rhetoric, whose state the clouds doth reach,
> And heavenly poetry do forward lead,
> And divers measures diversely do tread.
>
> For Rhetoric, clothing speech in rich array,
> In looser numbers teacheth her to range
> With twenty tropes and turnings every way,
> And various figures and licentious change;
> But poetry, with rule and order strange,
> So curiously doth move each single pace,
> As all is marred if she one foot misplace.

These arts of speech the guides and marshals are,
But logic leadeth reason in a dance,
Reason the cynosure and bright lodestar
In this world's sea to avoid the rocks of chance;
For with close following and continuance
One reason doth another so ensue
As, in conclusion, still the dance is true. (p. 335)

Not only does this passage describe the games of the mind—it also demonstrates them. The whole is a play upon words, and a play upon thoughts. One of the greatest discoveries of the renaissance was that words and ideas were general properties for the enjoyment of the many rather than of the few. There was a new sense that everyone had a mind, and that therefore its faculties, rational and fanciful, needed to be exercised and displayed. To this end one of the chief pastimes of the courtier offered itself immediately: the great game of conversation.

Conversation or discourse was, as was suggested above, the central occupation in the daily attendance in the Presence. Apart from this, the interest in formal conversation and debate as an after dinner pastime is attested by the literary dialogues of the period. Castiglione spends time on the courtier's need to be a good conversationalist for the recreation of his lord and companions:

> Therefore, for that I desire in the Courtier, it sufficeth to say (beside the matters rehearsed) that he be such a one that shall never want good communication, and fit for them he talketh withal, and have a good understanding, with a certain sweetness to refresh the hearers' minds, and with merry conceits and jests to provoke them to solace and laughter, so that without being at any time loathsome or satiate he may ever more delight them.[3] (p. 133)

The Italian, Stephano Guazzo, wrote a lengthy book on 'Civil Conversation', which was translated into English by George Pettie in 1581. He demonstrates that conversation was by no means a simple matter of saying what you mean:

> And therefore, as we have said already, it is needful to aid our-selves with a little art. For to set down things always in those bare and simple terms which our mother hath taught us, and to follow their plain property, doth but weary the hearer, who on the con-

---

[3] Castiglione's, as most other renaissance discussions of conversation, is largely based on the second book of Cicero's *Orator*.

trary is recreated and delighted with variety, and those figurative speeches which are not common to every one. (i. 137)

He then gives examples of how a witty man might ring the changes on the description of a dissembler by calling him, among other things, one that 'weepeth over his step-mother's grave'.

It was obviously important to decorate the general discourse with figurative speech. Thomas Wilson flatteringly remarks, in dedicating his *Art of Rhetoric* to Lord Dudley, that he will be driven:

> To set this simple treatise to your Lordship to school, that it may learn Rhetoric of your daily talk, finding you such an orator in your speech, as great clerks do declare what an orator should be.

Guazzo highly recommends what we know to have been a common practice, the carrying around of commonplace books, in which to note any phrases that come up in conversation that might be of use in the adorning of future discourse. He does however sound a warning note:

> I am of the opinion in this, that we suffer our ears to be too much tickled, whereby we give wrong judgment of the matter, being more attentive to the sound of the words than to the weight of the sentences, giving the title of orator to such a one as is but a brabbler, and altogether without learning. (i. 126)

Enough has been said, I hope, to show that play is by no means a facile or childish activity, and that its principles can usefully be employed over a wide area of human interest. Play, to the renaissance man, was an ordered exercising of the faculties of mind and body. Such is, in fact, the principle of all play. In playing, the physical and mental possibilities of man are explored to their furthest boundaries, and for the sake of pure discovery. A game is an expression of delight in a particular faculty or ability of the body, an exploration of the sensations and emotions aroused by its use. This principle is easily perceived even in the simplest play activities, hopping, singing, punning, and so on. Games are a way of grasping life. Different exercises go to display the whole potentiality of the man:

> The Earl of Leicester, knowing that Queen Elizabeth was much delighted to see a gentleman dance well, brought the master of a dancing-school to dance before her. Pish (said the Queen) it is his

profession, I will not see him. She liked it not where it was a master-quality, but when it attended on other perfections. (Fuller, p. 145)

Frobenius[4] describes the impulse to play in primitive societies as a kind of rapture: 'The experience of life and nature, still unexpressed, takes the form of a "seizure".' Play as exercise is a function of this impulse; it makes manifest the players' sense of thinking, feeling, being, that would otherwise be unexpressed.

The plays of Lyly give these impulses we have been discussing dramatic expression. They organise into an elaborate aesthetic game the exploratory, recreational activities of the court for which they were written. They reflect and absorb the multitudinous excitement of life in the royal presence, and give this excitement concrete expression:

> Oh, the gallant life of the Court, where so many are the choices of contentment, as if on earth it were the paradise of the world: the majesty of the sovereign, the wisdom of the Counsel, the honour of the lords, the beauty of the ladies, the care of the officers, the courtesy of the gentlemen, the divine service of morning and evening, the witty, learned, noble and pleasant discourses all day, the variety or wits with the depths of judgments, the dainty fare—sweetly dressed and neatly served,—the delicate wines and rare fruits, with excellent music and admirable voices, masks and plays, dancing and riding; diversity of games, delightful to the gamesters purposes; and riddles, questions and answers; poems, histories, and strange inventions of wit, to startle the brains of a good understanding; rich apparel, precious jewels, fine proportions and high spirits, princely coaches, stately horses, royal buildings and rare architecture, sweet creatures and civil behaviour: and in course of love such carriage of content as sets the spirit in a lap of pleasure. (p. 186)

In its magnificently random fashion this extravaganza by Nicholas Breton summarises those aspects of court recreation discussed above. There are the recreations of the spirit—worship, majesty, wisdom; of the mind—wit, discourse, art; of the body—riding, dancing; of the senses—sights, sounds and tastes. Lyly seizes upon all these. His plays address themselves to the courtier to replenish his faculties by use, exercising his reason by play of logic, his fancy by play of image, his memory by display of learning, and his senses, over all, with word, spectacle and music. This practice has an important aesthetic consequence. The experience that results in seizure in this kind of play is

[4] In *Kulturgeschichte*, quoted Huizinga, p. 16.

not the experience to which the words of the play directly refer; it is rather the experience of thinking, fancying, remembering. The plays are not about the ideas expressed; they are about the faculties employed.

*   *   *

Lyly's plays are games for the sense, and games for the mind. They are aimed at a difficult audience that was at least as interested in itself and its sovereign as in the play (Ben Jonson was later to complain of its behaviour). He attempted therefore to amuse easily and gracefully, drawing the attention to the play imperceptibly by catching at the senses, and holding it there by an elegant employment of matters close to a courtier's heart. He allowed the drama to play on every level, and further arranged that each separate part should lightly reflect the whole so that the attention could be detached almost at will without encountering any difficulty when it returned.

The settings for the plays are without exception fanciful and curious. *Campaspe* brings together a painter's studio, full of half-finished and finished pictures, the palace of Alexander the Great, the tub of Diogenes; *Sapho and Phao*, a river, the sybyl's cave, the forge of vulcan, as well as Sapho's palace; *Gallathea* gives us the nymphs of Diana on the Humber estuary; *Love's Metamorphoses* includes a tree which speaks with the voice of a nymph. The movement from scene to scene in the plays clearly demands some form of continuous staging, and so it seems certain that all, or almost all, of the scenic elements required would be present throughout, deployed about the playing space.

Against his spectacular background Lyly carefully orchestrates his action in order to create a continually changing visual pattern upon the stage. The first Act of *Sapho and Phao* is a good example. The play opens with a monologue for Phao, then a dialogue between Venus and Cupid and their encounter with Phao, then the appearance of a scholar and a courtier with their servants, followed by dialogue and a song for the servants, and then an extended conversation among the ladies of Sapho's court, six in all. This sequence illustrates two points: first the play of sight, solo, ensemble, dialogue; and second a consequent play of rhythm. This latter is emphasised by Lyly. He handles the different dramatic groups in a different dramatic manner, so that the play of movement is accompanied by a complementary play of mood. It is as well to note here that this mood is not dependent upon situation so much as upon character.

There are four main moods in the first Act of *Sapho and Phao*: the lyrical, represented in Phao's monologue, and the dialogue with Venus; the didactic, in the scene with the scholar and courtier; the farcical, in the parody of the pages; and the mannered, in the conversation of the ladies. Beneath all these lies a streak of mockery. The interest of the Act lies in our being aware of variety of pattern and difference of mood. One is fascinated by the interplay of mood and movement, and one's sense of the difference of several distinct modes of being is explored and sharpened.

> For as the spring time doth marvellously delight the eyes with sundry sorts of flowers which it bringeth forth, so these some, by the diversity and variety of their discourse, give wonderful refreshment to our minds.   (Guazzo, i. 188)

The delight of Lyly's plays is the delight of the courtier's conversation. One is playing with one's experience.

This effect is basic to the structure of the plays. In his organisation of plot and sub-plot Lyly juxtaposes, in almost every play (in *The Woman in the Moon* and *Love's Metamorphoses* mood is rather differently employed) contrasted dramatic moods and manners. Different groups of figures—Gods, courtiers, pages (the distinction is not always so obviously one of class)—have their particular rhythm of talk and life. Individual differences within the group are not strongly marked. Nor are differences attendant upon situation. The particular manner is important and persistent, and is sometimes heightened by excursion into song and dance—the love-songs of Sapho and Appelles, the dance of the fairies at the Lunar Bank, the grotesque routine of the Cyclops forging Venus' arrows, and the boisterous songs of the pages.

Curiously enough the effect of this variety of movement is one of stasis. This is Lyly's great dramatic discovery, for which, perhaps, Shakespeare is most indebted to him; it is the secret of the conversation piece. Narrative drama moves from each new situation on to the next, each development is in its turn a starting point, and the interest is held by curiosity as to what new possibility will obtain from each new situation. Such form is almost useless for the contemplation of ideas. It can develop, but it cannot discuss. The conversation piece is essentially discursive, and the problem inherent in this is the concentration of the attention upon a static concept and the possibilities inherent in it, when the form employed moves relentlessly forward. The conversation piece depends upon an extended stillness in which interest is centred wholly in the present, and not in movement from the present to the future. This stillness Lyly provides. The rhythmic contrasts assuage the desire for movement, while the short contrasted episodes, through which the rhythm is deployed, arrest in combination not in sequence. In this way the horizontal, melodic energy of drama is transformed into a harmonic energy. Melody extends, where harmony explores. Stillness achieved, the scene is set for the play of mind.

Most of Lyly's plays revolve around some sort of debate. Debate was in its own right an important entertainment form in the courts of the sixteenth century. Many occasional entertainments are couched in the form of argument between two sides on the relative merits of two opposed ideas or ways of life. The form is found in many moralities and interludes and owes its provenance to seasonal festivity, the flyting match, and the battles of summer and winter. Lyly uses the debate form as a base for plot, sub-plot, and conversation.

The plots of *Endimion* are united in their discussion of merits of fleshly and spiritual love; *Midas* opens with three courtiers counselling Midas as to which gift he should require from Bacchus, one counselling for Love ('I would wish to possess my mistress'), one for War ('I would wish to be monarch of the world'), and one for wealth ('I would wish that everything I touched might turn to gold'); in *Sapho and Phao* we find the age-old dispute between love and chastity argued in the contention between Venus and Sapho. Hunter defines the debate theme of *Campaspe* as: 'wherein lies true kingliness? Is it in the power to command others or in the power to command ourselves?' (p. 161) a theme which dominates the main plot and occurs again and again throughout the play. In a central scene Alexander argues the matter with his friend Hephaestion, who states the theme at length in a monologue:

> I cannot tell, Alexander, whether the report be more shameful to be heard or the cause sorrowful to be believed. What! Is the son of Philip, King of Macedon, become the subject of Campaspe, the captive of Thebes? Is that mind whose greatness the world could not contain drawn within the compass of an idle, alluring eye? . . . O Alexander, that soft and yielding mind should not be in him whose hard, unconquered heart hath made so many yield. . . . It is thought wonderful, among the seamen that the mugil, of all fishes the swiftest, is found in the belly of the bret, of all the slowest, and

shall it not seem monstrous to wise men that the heart of the greatest conqueror of the world should be found in the hands of the weakest creature of nature—of a woman, of a captive?

(*Campaspe*, II. ii. 29)

In *Sapho and Phao* such dialectic has a whole strand of the play to itself in the scenes between Trachinius and Pandion, the courtier and scholar, and in their dialogue with the court ladies. There is a similar level in the discussions in *Campaspe* between Clitus and Parmenio. Often the farcical characters are allowed to parody this type of formal argument. In *Midas* the discussion of the merits of singing, dancing, and telling tales, is placed as a complement to the earlier dispute on Wealth, Love and War. Debate is used to hold scenes together, to form a structure for conversation, and to set one episode off against another.

Debate and the techniques of debate are fundamental to the dialogue throughout the plays. Lyly has often been admired as the first writer to present conversation on the stage, and the closeness of his rhetorical style of discussion to the conversational manner of his day should by now be clear.[5] The renaissance rhetoricians, following Cicero, divided talk into two types—the discourse, and the repartee. The discourse was the personal amplification of the matter of the conversation; repartee was the neat turning of the arguments of another, the retort courteous. The rhythm of the plays is intimately dependent on the organisation of these two forms of discussion. One moves constantly from the light repartee of the pages, or the courtiers in the palaces of Cynthia and Sapho, to the more formal arguments of Geron and Eumenides in *Endimion*, or the Lords in *Midas*, and on to the discourses of Hephaestion or the Sibil, whose tone is taken up, more particularly, in the internal disputes of Sapho or Endimion.

'Judgment', wrote Hobbes, 'begets the strength and structure, and fancy begets the ornaments of the poem' (Spingarn, ii. 59). We have seen how the rational exercise of debate is the foundation of Lyly's plays; they are adorned throughout by the imaginative exercise of fancy. The exercise of fancy permeates the imagery of both plot and language.

It is in the lyrical episodes of the plot that fancy is naturally most apparent. Lyly adorns his themes with fables, and his fables with elab-

---

[5] Blount, in his 1632 edition of the comedies, actually remarked:
'That Beauty in Court which could not parley euphuism, was as little regarded as she which now there speaks not French.' (Preface)

orate and artificial symbolism. This symbolism, like the themes themselves, is drawn from the current fancy of the court—notably Italian
Neo-Platonism. As a result one feels continually, when reading, that
one has happened upon the incarnation of one of the allegories of
Botticelli. In *Gallathea* Neptune appears in his proper rôle as the
demon-king of Passion, demanding the sacrifice of a virgin to Agar the
sea-monster. Gallathea and Phillida, hidden from such a fate by their
doting fathers, none the less fall in love. Cupid invades Diana's nymphs,
and for his pains Diana captures him and clips his wings. The plot is
resolved when both Venus and Diana appeal to the raging Neptune.
After a debate it is decided that Neptune will forgo the sacrifice if
Diana will restore Cupid, so the virgins are saved for, in Spenser's
words, 'married chastity'.

Endimion is probably Lyly's most elaborate symbolic game. A description might run as follows: Endimion loves Cynthia but cannot
possess her; he is loved by Tellus, the earth, whom he once encouraged.
Tellus enchants him by the aid of Dipsas, a witch, who signifies
'desire' (her name is that of a serpent whose bite causes raging thirst).
He is cast into a deep sleep in which he grows old, and is finally
awakened to chaste and humble love by the kiss of Cynthia. The
predicament of Endimion is the predicament of the courtly lover whose
unfulfilled love of his unobtainable mistress leads him up the ladder
from earth to heaven. Entangled by his lust he is cast into a sleep, just
as the soul, attracted by its reflection in matter takes on the earthly and
impure form of man; but he is finally enabled to triumph by the grace
of his goddess, and is redeemed to the love of the spirit.

This conflict between spirituality and sensuality is echoed on all
levels of the plot. Corsites breaks his word to Cynthia and tries to
obtain his love by trial of physical strength; the fairies pinch him for his
pains, the prescribed punishment for the sensual, and leave him like a
spotted conscience. Eumenides leaves his beloved to rescue his friend,
comes to a fountain, a love image as old as, and older than, the *Romance
of the Rose*, clears the waters with the tears of true love, and is confronted with the need to choose whether to obtain his desire or release
his friend. He chooses Endimion, thus preferring the spiritual over
the fleshly love. The episode at the fountain echoes another platonic
image of the soul's descent to earth: that of Narcissus who fell in
love with his reflection in the water, the element of passion. In his
choice Eumenides is advised by Geron, a morality figure of Good

L

Counsel. But he is more than this—he was once the husband of Dipsas, who procured him to live in a desert, doubtless to expiate in a waste land the sin of lust. Even the comic Sir Tophas falls in love with the witch Bagoa, puts away his arms, such as they are, and falls asleep.

The important thing about this symbolism is its lack of intensity. It forms an important part of the structural pattern of the play, but is quite without the mysticism many of the same images acquire—in Spenser, for instance. It is essentially an ornament. Lyly does not think with it. He does not use it to reconstruct experience. He uses it simply to amuse. It is here we come to the play of memory. He could expect his audience to be familiar with the patterns, so he employs them as a form of wit. His art, like the art of a courtier's conversation, is the art of the commonplace. The pleasure it gives is the pleasure of recognition. He does not aim to startle with something new, but to play with conceptions that were already common property. Lyly handles conventional material and adds little to its significance. The interest is held, not by revelation, but by the delight of seeing old concepts in new contexts. What matters is its exuberance and its inventiveness.

To the rhetoricians invention meant not the discovery of new images, but the accurate recalling of suitable authorities. The authorities, similitudes, and well worn proverbs would be used to 'amplify' the matter. It is a game that has both authority and novelty: it guarantees truth without foregoing surprise. Lyly plays it with expertise on every level of drama. In *Endimion* the matter is amplified in the plot by parallelism (Corsites), by contrary (Eumenides), by similitude (the fable) and enriched by pleasant jest (Tophas). In such a way is the fancy of his audience exercised. The matter is also amplified in two further ways: by allusion, and by words.

One of the chief devices for amplifying matter was by instance. There is not room here for much discussion of Lyly's historical allegory, but it must be mentioned for its place in the play pattern. Wilson Knight remarks that throughout the plays we get the feeling of allusions lost. There is a shimmer of references whose meaning has disappeared. They can probably never be recovered; but one may imagine their effect. They are a necessary extension of the poet's wit.

Wit is that faculty which 'sees similitudes in things apparently different', and topical reference is a particularly entertaining form of similitude. The allusion from idea to contemporary fact always sets up a shower of imaginative sparks. The greed of Midas touches off thoughts about Philip of Spain; Cynthia and Sapho liken the true course of living to the life of the Queen. Many characters, by a word or phrase, suddenly recall a friend or enemy. As with the ideas and images, so are known facts of life suddenly given a new context. In this way allusion goes to satisfy the fancy, the memory, and the reason.

The language of the plays operates on the same basis. Fancy and learning are deployed around a firm frame of logic. Lyly is particularly fond of figures of thought, those tropes that appeal to the mind rather than to the emotion, whose purpose is to explore and define, rather than re-create experience. Exploration and definition are, after all, important exercises of the mind. His use of language incorporates on this level two important elements of play—play of sound, and play of meaning. A return to the speech of Hephaestion already quoted can demonstrate both these points.

The speech is mainly constructed upon the figure of antithesis, balancing the right action against the wrong fact. The antithesis is drawn into the form of a paradox by the image developed from the plot, of Alexander and Campaspe in a master-servant-mistress relationship. The figures of thought, here employed to embody the logic of the argument, are augmented by figures of sound. The main propositions in the argument are connected by alliteration: Son-subject, King-Campaspe-captive. Sometimes the alliteration modulates: swiftest-slowest, shameful-sorrowful. The latter pair are further linked by repeated endings. Sometimes the progress of thought is illustrated in a kind of onomatopoeia by vowel modulation and assonance as in the following: 'Is that mind whose greatness the world could not contain, drawn within the compass of an idle, alluring eye?' The dance of words and the dance of thought accompany one another. Finally the whole is set off by an excursion into pure fantasy with the intrusion of the fish mugil, where reason dissolves into fancy. This curious blend of the rational and the absurd is one of the chief charms of Lyly's work.

Just as the patterns of thought and fancy in the plot are set off by allusion so are they in the language; the handling of commonplace here also is an important part of the game. Much of the dialogue is a treasure house of reference, more or less obscure. Take for instance Alexander's first encounter with Diogenes, where all the cynic's most famous utterances are woven into a dialogue of twenty or so brisk lines; or Apelles countering of Campaspe's comment that Phidias only used five colours with a reference to the demands of contemporary fashion. The delight in the former lies in finding the comments you know so neatly ordered, of the latter in an abrupt collision between learning and fact. Again it is old knowledge in a new context. One of the wittiest examples of this exercise of ingenuity is probably Endimion's long discourse on the constancy of the moon. The whole pleasure of this speech lies in the knowledge that in using the moon in a love story the poet has got himself in a quandary:

> O swear not by the moon, th'inconstant moon,
> That nightly changeth in her circled orb.

Lyly accepts the challenge, laid out by the story, that Cynthia is not merely Diana and chaste, but also the moon and changing, and in a charming exercise in rhetoric proves the constancy of the moon. The speech is long and there is no room to quote it here. Also it is exquisite, and it would be a shame to summarise it. Suffice to say that Lyly takes each accepted disparagement of the moon in turn and overturns it. To an audience versed in wit the speech could never lack tension, long as it is. It is a magnificent *agon* between man and myth.

Through all the plays, then, the emphasis in plot, character and language is on figures of thought, on definition and exploration, thinking not feeling. This is curious in a dramatic writer, for it is just these elements of plot and character that carry in most plays the burden of emotional effect. It is not so here. Not that the emotions are disregarded. They are not. But they are exercised not by plot or character but by mood. It is as we have seen, the rhythm, the involvement in different modes of being, that provides the emotional experience of the play. The body of the play is a game for the mind.

* * *

One aspect of the plays that particularly emphasises this element of play has yet to be discussed—the performance. The plays were all written with their would-be performers, the Children of Paul's, very firmly in mind, and the effect of children on the stage is highly individual. This has nothing to do with the goodness or badness of their performance. Many children are naturally highly skilled actors, and can provide well observed and technically excellent performances of a large range of rôles, including those of women and old people. The point about boys acting women and old men is not that physically they are unable to represent convincingly the tricks and manners of the characters they are playing—in this they often acquit themselves well—it is that they do not suppress themselves to do so. One never loses the awareness of a dual personality. This gives a child performance in an adult rôle a peculiar quality not often observed in adult actors. The quality of self-awareness.

It was this quality the Bertolt Brecht particularly wanted to develop in the company he formed in Berlin—and he found it very difficult. He wanted to do so for two main reasons. He wanted his audience to be aware of what was involved in the actions on the stage, rather than be absorbed in them; and he wanted this so that they would be surprised by the actions and not take them for granted. Brecht's aims in desiring these results were obviously very different from Lyly's, but one can easily perceive how acting of this nature would complete the dramatic texture I have been describing. The self-awareness of the performance, Brecht tells us, does not entirely reject the spectators' sympathy:

> The audience identifies itself with the actor as being an observer, and accordingly develops the attitude of looking on. (p. 93)

One is therefore constantly aware of the characters of the drama as part of the intellectual pattern, and this in turn produces another type of similitude, or playful cross reference: of idea to fact. The characters themselves, and the human characteristics of their rôles, become instances and metaphors—figures of action.

A sense of surprise, too, is automatically involved in making such connections, as it was involved in the recognition of commonplaces of plot and language; and this sense of surprise, at thought, word and deed, finally creates and completes the play world essential to re-creation. All play, Huizinga says:

> is a free activity standing quite consciously outside 'ordinary' life as being 'not serious', but at the same time absorbing the player intensely and utterly (p. 13)

and we can see now the reason for the creation of this extraordinary world; it is not only to exercise the faculties of the soul, but also to liberate them from the limitations of fact. The power of the games of the mind is that they give mind the power over matter. Aesthetic organisation, by releasing physical objects (words, shapes, colours), from the pressures of existence, can reorganise them with freedom. Language allows man:

> to distinguish, to establish, to state things: in short to name them and by naming them to raise them into the domain of spirit. In the making of speech and language the spirit is continually 'sparking' between matter and mind, as it were, playing with this wondrous nominative faculty. Behind every abstract expression there lie the boldest of metaphors, and every metaphor is a play upon words. Thus in giving expression to life man creates a second, poetic, world along side his own. (p. 4)

The play world, the poetic world, is needed so that a man can explore himself fully, more thoroughly than the limitations of life allow. The pleasure of play comes from the sense of extension, the freedom that comes from passing the boundaries of reality.

> The use of this *feigned history* hath been to give some shadow of satisfaction to the mind of man in those points wherein the nature of things doth deny it, the world being in proportion inferior to the soul; by reason whereof, there is agreeable to the spirit of man, a more ample greatness, a more exact goodness, and a more absolute variety than can be found in the nature of things.
>
> (Bacon, *Adv. of Learning*, Bk. II)

Lyly's most poetic virtue is his sense of fantasy. His play world is made welcoming by its extravagance. He reaches to the limits of mind and fancy:

> So much for prophecy, that nothing can prevent: and this for counsel, which thou maist follow. Keep not company with ants that have wings, nor talk with any near the hill of a mole; where thou smellest the sweetness of serpent's breath, beware thou touch no part of the body. Be not merry among those that put bugloss in their wine, and sugar in thine. If any talk of the eclipse of the sun, say thou never sawest it. Nourish no conies in thy vaults, nor swallows in thine eaves. Sow next thy vine *Mandrage*, and ever keep thine ears open, and thy mouth shut, thine eyes upward and thy fingers down: so shalt thou do better than otherwise, but never so well as I wish. (*Sapho and Phao;* II. i. 128)

I doubt if any scholar now could ever gloss that passage fully. I doubt if any of the original audience would have been capable of it.

Or would even have tried to. The exact meaning scarcely matters; what does is the imaginative ability to bring so much so close. One simply gasps at the acrobatics of the mind. Lyly's proverbs, allusions, unnatural natural-history, are all part of that 'more absolute variety than can be found in the nature of things'. They are a demonstration of the cornucopia of the mind:

> Art thou the sacrifice to appease Neptune, and satisfy the custom, the bloody custom, ordained for the safety of thy country? Ah, Haebe, poor Haebe, men will have it so, whose forces command our weak natures; nay the Gods will have it so, whose powers dally with our purposes. The Egyptians never cut their dates from the tree, because they are so fresh and green. It is thought wickedness to pull roses from the stalks in the garden of Palestine, for that they have so lively a red: and whoso cutteth the incense from the tree in Arabia before it fall, committeth sacrilege. (*Gallathea*, V. ii. 11.)

The race of ideas and images is breath-taking. It exploits to the full the great power of the imagination—suggestion. It seems niggardly to stickle for fact.

The effect of Lyly's plays is in the best sense *dilettante*; they exercise the faculties to no other end but their delight. As C. S. Lewis remarked, 'The lightness of Lyly's touch, the delicacy, the blessed unreality, were real advances in civilisation.' And yet his comedies are 'like life' not in the simple, imitative sense; but in the sense that the forces at play in them, intellectual, sensual and imaginative, are the forces at play in life. His writing is a stimulant. It sets the mind playing with possibilities; it activates it; and, like all other good games, gives the players a simple choice: sleep, or work. After all, when the imagination is at white heat the line between work and play becomes indefinable. It is submerged in excitement.

Note

Drama at Court: Documentation. E. K. Chambers, *The Elizabethan Stage* (4 vols., 1923) is indispensable. Mary Steele gives a detailed calendar of *Plays and Masques at Court 1558–1642* (1926). *Documents Relating to the Office of the Revels* for Elizabeth's reign have been edited by A. Feuillerat (1908). H. N. Hillebrand deals with *The Child Actors* (1927). Enid Welsford's *The Court Masque* (1927) and A. Nicoll's *Stuart Masques and the Renaissance Stage* (1937) are valuable.

History and Biography: Modern Works. J. E. Neale's *Queen Elizabeth I* (1934) and A. L. Rowse's *The England of Elizabeth* (1950) give a good picture of the Queen. *England's Eliza* by E. C. Wilson (1939) documents the Virgin Queen cult. The transition from mediaeval to Elizabethan England is fully discussed by G. Wickham in *Early English Stages* (2 vols., 1959 and 1963), and the later transitions by F. P. Wilson, *Elizabethan and Jacobean* (1945). The conditions of Elizabeth's court are documented by L. Stone, *The Crisis of the Aristocracy* (1965). On courtiers, see Eleanor Rosenberg's *Leicester, Patron of Letters* (1955) and J. Buxton's *Sidney and the English Renaissance* (1954).

Sources. Baldassare Castiglione's *Libro del Cortegiano* (1528) was the Elizabethan handbook in Sir Thomas Hoby's translation (1561): it is in the Everyman's Library. Fulke Greville's *Life of Sir Philip Sidney* (1652) has been edited by N. Smith (1907). Sidney's views on *Gorboduc* are taken from his *Apology for Poetry* (1595). The *Letters and Epigrams* of Sir John Harington are edited by N. McClure (1930). The 1625 text of Bacon's 'Of Empire' and 'Of Masks and Triumphs' is quoted in this chapter from E. Arber's edition, *A Harmony of the Essays* (1895). References to poems by Donne are from the first volume of H. Grierson's edition (1912), and to poems by Marvell from the first volume of H. M. Margoliouth's 2nd edition (1952). Milton's *Lycidas* (1637) and *Ready and Easy Way to Establish a Free Commonwealth* (1660) are both quoted from E. H. Visiak's edition of the *Complete Poetry and Selected Prose* (1938): here also are translations of *Epitaphum Damonis* and *Manso*, in which Milton's Arthurian plans are mentioned. Sir John Denham's *Poetical Works* have been edited by T. H. Banks (1928).

Play Texts. *Respublica* is quoted from J. S. Farmer's *'Lost' Tudor Plays* (1907); *Two Noble Kinsmen* from C. F. Tucker Brooke's *Shakespeare Apocrypha* (1908); *Gorboduc* from J. W. Cunliffe's *Early English Classical Tragedies* (1912). Plays quoted from M.S.R. are *King John* (J. Bale), *Patient Grissell*, *Damon and Pythias*, *Susanna*, *Arraignment of Paris*, *Clyomon and Clamydes* and the Gray's Inn 'Masque of Proteus' in *Gesta Grayorum*. *Mucedorus* is quoted from T.F.T. Sidney's pastoral *The Lady of May* is in the second volume of J. Nichol's *Progresses . . . of Q. Elizabeth* (1778), as is a full account of Leicester's Princely Pleasures at Kenilworth in 1575. There is no extant text of 'Palamon and Arcite' but the evidence about it and a discussion of *Damon and Pythias* can be found in

VIII

The Court and the Dramatists

MARION JONES

★

'Princes are like to Heavenly Bodies, which cause good or evil times, and which have much Veneration, but no Rest.' (Sir Francis Bacon, 'Of Empire')

ONE Prince distinctly within Bacon's ken was Elizabeth of England, and his sentence reviews her reign well enough. Essentially unrestful, a dogged luminary, pompous, painted, prickly and purse-proud, she died unvenerable but much venerated, and was considered the cause of the good times her subjects had seen. Though historians over the years have tested and documented this assumption, they have not shown it to be baseless. When the mass of circumstances has been weighed, and the last contributory factor analysed, the uniqueness of the Queen as a person is still shown as the catalyst. Studies of her effect on political and economic developments reveal her as an autocrat, an intriguer, an opportunist, sometimes mistaken, but never by any reckoning negligible.

The regular extension of the phrase 'masterpieces of Elizabethan drama' to cover plays written between the death of Elizabeth and 1616, or 1625, or even 1642, suggests that the reign of Elizabeth was also a good time for drama in England, and that the Queen herself is generally reckoned a cause and benign influence. It is difficult to test and document this assumption without moving outside the date-limits of her reign in the same way. 'Elizabethan' is a mark of general approval, crediting the Queen with some measure of personal responsibility not only for the creative achievements of her subjects during her lifetime

---

'Notes on Richard Edwards' by W. Y. Durand in the *Journal of Germanic Philology* (1902). John Lyly has been edited by R. W. Bond (1902). For Jonson see Note to Chapter X.

but for the establishment of a tradition that took many years to lose its strength.

Where drama is concerned this usage is not specially convenient, for the plays of the Stuart period resemble each other and the rest of early seventeenth-century writing in English, much more than they resemble the plays of Elizabeth's heyday. English culture as a whole shows a more sombre tone and less resilient habit of mind as Elizabeth's reign nears its end. Shakespeare himself made his distinctive contribution to the reign in its last decade, and the accession of James I found him at the height of his powers with a quarter of his life still before him: it certainly cannot be maintained that Shakespeare continued to write in an earlier tradition without reference to the changing patterns and preoccupations of the new reign. The succession of his great plays after 1603 shows a similar modification of sensibility to that discernible in the work of his friends and fellow dramatists; and new writers adopted the new outlook and mood rather than revived the old, or infused a youthful optimism. Nevertheless, there is a sense in which 'Elizabethan' is a more valuable term—even in its extensions and even where drama is concerned—than 'Jacobean' or 'Stuart' strictly applied. 'Elizabethan' really does mean 'partaking of the nature of Queen Elizabeth Tudor'; 'Jacobean' does not mean 'partaking of the nature of King James I'. 'Jacobean' is merely a date-label: 'Elizabethan' is a description by essential characteristics. To outline the view that Elizabeth was indeed and personally the cause of a good time for drama, and that like other stars she continued to exert influence long after her death, is the purpose of this chapter.

It is obvious at a glance that the relationship between Elizabeth and the major dramatists of her reign was not one of straightforward Renaissance patronage. Elizabeth founded no Academy, maintained no playwrights as such, commissioned no play of genius. If indeed, as the story goes, she asked Shakespeare to show Falstaff in love, her direct influence on the greatest playwright within her sphere was not of a kind to elicit his highest gifts: certainly the neat construction, cynical tone and rough country humour of *The Merry Wives of Windsor* are well in line with all the evidence about Her Majesty's personal tastes in drama, but are not the qualities for which Shakespeare's plays in general are most esteemed. In the same way, it was not by direct personal patronage of her reign's characteristic theatrical institution, the public playhouse, that Elizabeth benefited drama: though she let playhouses be built, she did not command or finance their building, and there is no record of her ever attending a performance at any play-house, public or private. If she wished to see a given play, it would be brought to court for her to see: if anyone had a play to show her, he tried to arrange an occasion to present it at court. Rewards and main-tenance from the Queen went to the actors rather than the writers of plays, though some of the schoolmasters who trained the boy players she so admired seem to have written plays for their charges to perform. When Richard Edwards, in her service as Master of the Chapel Child-ren, wrote *Palamon and Arcite* for University actors to perform on her Oxford visit of 1566, the Queen enjoyed the hunting and funeral-pyre scenes immensely, and gave Edwards very great thanks—but no extra money.

To understand this state of affairs it is necessary to set aside the modern standards by which drama as a medium for creative thought and a mode of literary expression is considered the most serious and significant form. Drama as propaganda, drama as a demonstration of wealth and culture, drama as an in-game, drama as a sheer saleable com-modity, were all concepts far more familiar to a Tudor audience. Various degrees of talent and facility can be brought to attempts in each of these fields, and the result be a series of successful shows without any dramatist emerging as a major poet or any text as a literary master-piece. Occasionally, as in Sidney's exquisite propaganda, *The Lady of May*, or Lyly's beautifully finished contributions to the in-game, the excellence of a text does compel admiration; but to the successive Masters of the Revels, whose duty it was to purvey drama to the Queen and court, the elements of spectacle and of competent acting were what needed to be paid for and, so long as the text did not give political or moral offence, its quality as literature was not of much importance. Lavish costumes (however economically refurbished) and adequate rehearsal could bring most shows up to standard. Often the clerk who entered particulars of Revels expenditure did not bother to mention the author nor even to get the title correct. All this is quite in line with mediaeval tradition. The idea that a play-text in the vernacular should aspire to literary distinction was unfamiliar. Up to the end of the fifteenth century nearly every dramatist held his audience and pleased his patron with action and spectacle carried forward in unpretentious verse. There are sometimes passages of greater elaboration, very rarely any traces of the heightened sensibility and love of language that distinguish poet from rhyme-spinner. The Wakefield Master is a lonely figure in his generation, though his work does show that the double inspiration of the poet who works in drama found English a sufficient medium long before the conditions of Elizabeth's reign made the public theatre a place where poets of genius could find fame and make money as popular dramatists.

Though no simple formula will express the influence that Elizabeth exerted on the growth of drama in her reign, there are plainly several factors to be taken into account when attempting the assessment. One is the length of the preliminary period before the London playhouses were opened. In 1576, when James Burbage built The Theatre, Shakespeare was a twelve-year-old at Stratford, but Elizabeth was forty-three, and had been Queen of England for eighteen years. The fact that for most modern readers only *Gorboduc* and Richard Edwards are even comparatively familiar landmarks in the drama of this early period does not make it a less significant seed-time. Another factor is the extension of the Queen's authority and influence to the great personages of her court. Leicester in particular lived like a king, and was a steady supporter of plays and players. In endorsing and furthering the measures of protection that her courtiers were able to offer dramatic activity, the Queen assumed responsibility for a definite policy favourable to the development of drama. A third and important factor is the impact of the Queen as a personality, and of her court as a symbol, upon the imagination of Englishmen in general and playwrights in particular. This was only in part the result of deliberate effort by Elizabeth. Though she took care to preserve the same twofold public image which her father had found so useful—arrogant regality combined with bluff good nature, alternately awe-inspiring and full of charm —it was her unique political and religious position that allowed her to build up a legend in her own lifetime upon the solid foundation of national love and loyalty. There were plenty of rational grounds for believing her to be the main bulwark against foreign domination, and sufficient spiritual as well as material advantages in accepting the Church of which she was Head: but the current of popularity which swept her along was fed from a source concealed deep in the imagination of her subjects. To many Englishmen, perhaps to most, the change of religion meant little more than a translation of faith into a national context. The fate of martyrs on each side served to highlight the points of controversy, but also to emphasise the advisability of settlement.

Though the Anglican compromise met the requirement pretty well, it deliberately left out of account what still seems an attractive feature of mediaeval Christianity, the steady devotion of individual human souls to idealised but less than divine heavenly protectors. The Holy Trinity stood firm and was reverenced, but the relegation of Our Lady and the saints to a secondary importance left much human warmth and interest still in need of an object. So it came about that to many Englishmen both the garden of Paradise and the fortress of Christendom were contracted to the limits of one sceptred island, and the empty niche of the Queen of Heaven was filled by another blessed virgin, Elizabeth.

Much the same transference of emotional energy was responsible for the attitude of the Elizabethan public to the plays of the public theatre when they began to be written. Mediaeval drama is authoritative, didactic, spectacular, relying on traditional responses. Though during Elizabeth's reign the great Guild Cycles were finally suppressed because they enshrined the old faith too effectively, their suppression did not change the popular expectations about drama. The moral plays developed into moral interludes (with whatever theological bias the writer possessed), but people still expected to be instructed and guided by the authority of the writer. The feeling that a dramatist is a mouthpiece for the collectively accepted ideals of his society died very hard in England, and the modern view that a dramatist is a man with something to say who chooses to say it through the medium of drama rather than that of painting or music or any other art was very gradually adopted. The reign of Elizabeth is a watershed in this respect as in many others. When she came to the throne, drama was still affirmative, supporting and entertaining the Establishment. So long as the nation at large had confidence in the Establishment, there was no fundamental difference between drama for the monarch and drama for the people. Greater sophistication and more erudition could be displayed by those who wrote for the court, but the nation aspired to courtliness. For this reason plays about government and plays exhibiting court manners were acceptable to both court and commons. All the resources of mediaeval chivalry and romance were ready to supersede the legends of saints as material for drama. The strength of King Arthur's hold upon Elizabethans, and the easy imaginative alignment of his company with the English court, are familiar enough from Spenser's *Faerie Queene*; and proof that 'the matter of Britain' was still vital in the next generation lies in Milton's plan to use it, rejected in favour of *Paradise Lost*. We now possess only a fraction of the plays which we know from their titles and properties brought knights, ladies, castles, tournaments and magic, Arthurian and otherwise, before the delighted gaze of high and low-born Englishmen during the sixteenth century. Though the mind boggles at the surviving absurdities of *Clyomon and Clamydes* and *Mucedorus*, the first belonged to the Queen's Men, and the second ran to at least seventeen editions as well as being revived for James I and touring Oxfordshire during the Interregnum. Obviously the stock formula pleased everybody except the Puritans. Knights Red, Blue, Solitary and Irish, knights with hobby-horses and knights with burning rocks, good knights and true whose protracted *gestes* never wearied their public, all are lost to us for ever. An extract from the Revels accounts for April 1581 speaks for them all:

> The Mounte, Dragon with the fyer woorkes, Castell with the falling sydes Tree with shyldes, Hermytage & hermytt, Savages, Enchaunter, Charryott, & incidents to theis. CC markes.

The Cinderella view of court life, encouraged by this sort of play, is neatly summarised for the delectation of genuine courtiers in Garter's pot-pourri of a Biblical interlude, *Susanna*, published in 1578 but probably written up to ten years earlier; Ancilla addresses Serva:

> I heard once in my fathers house, a Gentleman declare,
> The worthy customes of the court, and eake the Princely fare,
> The gorgeous Garmentes of eche Dame, their fyne and famous lyfe,
> The noble workes of amorous Knights, their stoute and loving stryfe,
> The pleasure of eche worthy Dame, how they doe hunt and hawke,
> And wearyed with eche pastyme thus, the streates how they did walk;
> The noble maskes that were showed forth in every winters night,
> The Revels and the reveling cheare that did eche harte delight,
> Musitions how they did devyse with songes to please the eare,
> And Musickes arte by instrument that gladded hartes to heare,
> And sometyme the pore mans chylde, that there is plaste to be,
> To honour clymes for vertues sake, and brought to hye degree.
>   (l. 616)

Though the maids agree that this life is not for such as them, they do not question the accuracy of the description. Plainly, however, there was another side to the picture, and as time went on the dramatists began to show it more and more distinctly, harking back to the court-satire tradition of earlier writing. (We remember that Skelton wrote both *Magnificence* and the diatribes in 'Speak, parrot' before we condemn hypocrisy: the visions co-exist.) Donne looked back on the process toward the end of Elizabeth's reign in a verse-letter to Wotton:

> Beleeve mee Sir, in my youths giddiest dayes,
> When to be like the Court, was a playes praise,
> Playes were not so like Courts, as Courts are like playes.
> (Grierson, p. 188)

Later the situation was to get entirely out of hand, but under Elizabeth a delicate balance was held between the real and the ideal. The official platform of the inner group at court and their writers—those schoolmasters, pageanteers and scholars who worked within an established pattern of values and demands, displaying learning and glorifying the Queen—was in fact the genuine and gratified belief of the nation at large about its sovereign and nobility. The dramatists of the London playhouses stood at the centre, close enough to court life to know very well what it was, close enough to popular demand to feel what it must surely be.

To get an idea of the degree of divergence between the image and the reality it transcended, we must look more closely at Elizabeth and her court. What besides the traditional power of *noblesse oblige* persuaded about two thirds of the English peerage to spend at any rate part of their time in personal attendance on their sovereign? Gabriel Harvey's greedy note gives one reason: 'The prynce's Court the only mart of praeferment & honour. A goulfe of gaine.' It was the hope of rewards and offices in the Queen's gift that won her so many gorgeous gifts from her courtiers. Burghley in 1579 urged her to be generous: '. . . gratyfye your nobylyte, and the pryncypall persons of your realme, to binde them faste to you . . . whereby you shall have all men of value in the realme to depend only upon yourselfe.' Elizabeth, however, had not an open hand. One otherwise partisan reporter had to admit that 'amongest her manifold and rare virtues of nature and arte, this was the onlie detraction, that she had not power to geve wher it was merited'. Another merely commented 'she grew to be very covetous in her old days'. The disappointed courtier was heavily out of pocket before he gave up trying, for life at court was expensive in itself. It was also constricting to the soul in more ways than one.

Donne devoted his fourth Satire to a particularly trying specimen of court macaroon, who pries and gossips remorselessly:

> He knowes
> When the Queene frown'd, or smil'd, and he knowes what
> A subtle States-man may gather of that;
> He knowes who loves; whom; and who by poyson
> Hasts to an Offices reversion,
> He knowes who'hath sold his land . . .
> . . . And wiser then all us
> He knowes what Ladie is not painted   (p. 162)

The raw material for both Osric and Polonius lay ready to hand. Another fruitful source of vexation was the Queen's determined flirtatiousness with personable male courtiers and her implacable opposition to their marrying her ladies. This was based partly on policy, because newly-weds tended to leave court for their country estates and she wanted them to stay with her; but partly also on an unlovely quirk of character. Her god-son Harington, who did something to purify court life by inventing the water-closet, reports: 'she did oft aske the ladies around hir chamber, If they lovede to thinke of marriage? And the wise ones did conceal well their liking hereto' (p. 124). Of many disgraced favourites, Raleigh perhaps lost most. It is easy enough to find psychological explanations for Elizabeth's touchiness on this point. The nasty publicity about her relations with Thomas Seymour while she was still a girl, the thwarting of any serious hope to marry Dudley for love by the scandal of Amy Robsart's death, and the political necessity of using her matrimonial plans as bait for suitors from both Spain and France were more than enough to warp Elizabeth, and she seems to have taken unusual pleasure in mystification and whimsy. The Spanish Ambassador, Count de Feria, almost lost patience:

> for my part I believe she will never make up her mind to anything that is good for her. Sometimes she . . . speaks like a woman who will only accept a great prince, and then they say she is in love with Lord Robert and never lets him leave her. If my spies do not lie, which I believe they do not, for a certain reason which they have recently given me I understand that she will not bear children. . . .
> (*Cal. S. P. Span.* 1558–67, p. 63)

On another occasion he notes her favour to Sir John Pickering:

> In London they are giving 25 to 100 that he will be king. They
> tell me Lord Robert is not so friendly with him as he was . . . If
> these things were not of such great importance and so lamentable
> some of them would be very ridiculous. (*ibid.*, p. 67)

We may well agree.

The immediate effect of these conditions on drama at court is easily
noted. Since to present a play to the Queen was an acceptable gift and
bid for favour, courtiers who could afford it did so, and the Inns of
Court and colleges of Oxford and Cambridge went to enormous
trouble and expense to show their paces. Since life at court was an
in-game, some use was made of drama to convey comment on current
events great and small. In *Damon and Pythias*, presented before the
Queen by the Chapel boys in 1564 or thereabouts, the picture of
Dionysius the tyrant is so unfavourable that when the play was published in 1571 its title-page drew attention to an alteration by Edwards
in his Prologue to guard against any misapplication to English affairs:
the revision was intended for the use 'of them that hereafter shall have
occasion to plaie it, either in Private, or open Audience' and read

> Wherein talkyng of Courtly toyes, we doo protest this flat,
> Wee talke of *Dionysius* Courte, wee meane no Court but that.
> (l. 39)

The emphatic disclaimer suggests what was the normal attitude.
Parallels were in fact regularly drawn, with more or less satisfaction,
by those who watched plays. Elizabeth herself detected and decried
several attempts to recommend marriage to her by means of drama.
'This is all against me' she remarked to another Spanish Ambassador,
Guzman de Silva, of the Gray's Inn *Juno and Diana* at Shrovetide 1565.
A blasphemous parody of the Mass that made her enter her chamber
using strong language was got up by some Cambridge students in
August 1564, and this same Spanish Ambassador took the event
seriously enough to write home to his master at length about it. Since
he was not present at the show it is plain that there was comment on
the incident. It was of course no new thing for a play to embody
religious and political polemic. Bale's veteran trouble-maker *King
Johan* seems to have been revived for Elizabeth at Ipswich in 1561, and
she herself was more than once accused of chartering plays that ridiculed

M

the Pope and the King of Spain. Once, however, she flew into a passion
with Dudley, now Earl of Leicester, after an anti-Spanish 'comedy'
which happened to be too strongly pitched for her immediate con-
ciliatory policy toward King Philip, who was busy assembling his
Armada. Personal domestic satire was looked for in plays, but the
prudent dramatist trimmed his sails to the wind: flattering allusions
were at once safer and more profitable. Elizabeth was not in the least
a captive audience. Machyn mentions a play that did not suit, the very
last in 1559: 'the plaers plad shuche matter that they where com-
mondyd to leyff off, and contenent the maske cam in dansyng'.

An excellent example of a play that flattered the Queen by *not*
attempting to influence her views on marriage is John Lyly's *Sapho and
Phao*, presented at Court by a mixed company of Chapel and St. Paul's
boys under Lyly's own direction, probably on Shrove Tuesday 1584.
The man responsible for bringing forward this show and its forerunner
Campaspe was Lyly's patron, the Earl of Oxford, who had just been
received into royal favour again after more than two years of spectacular disgrace and had good reason to gratify Elizabeth with a complimentary display if he could. The Prologue expressly invites the
Queen to enter, for the duration of the play, a fantasy world where
waking judgement is suspended: 'that your Highnesse imagine your self
to be in a deepe dreame, that staying the conclusion, in your rising
your Majestie vouchsafe but to saye, *And so you awakte*'. The central
identification of the play, that of Elizabeth with the heroine, Queen
Sapho, is quickly established. At the centre of a court that resembles
the court of England in containing dissemblers, flatterers and idlers
as well as virtuous statesmen is 'Sapho, fair by nature, by birth royal,
learned by education, by government politic, rich by peace: insomuch
as it is hard to judge, whether she be more beautiful or wise, virtuous
or fortunate' (I. ii. 7). The point of the play is not the conventional,
even formal court-satire, but the victory of Sapho over her passion for
the unhappy ferryman Phao, made divinely beautiful by Venus. At
first sight Sapho falls in love with Phao; but she is shown to be resolved
to die rather than condescend to a suitor of lower rank, however
wildly her affections and his intrinsic merit fight on his behalf. That
Phao too loves at first sight is never allowed to weigh with Sapho:
their encounter is constrained, each resorting to puns and riddles to
express love without responsible declaration. At the end of the play,
when Cupid causes her passion for Phao to die down as suddenly as it

was kindled, Sapho awakes from the enervating dream of love, and can really enjoy her manipulation of sweet-toothed Cupid to humiliate his mother Venus; she can even spare a gracious thought for Phao, left for ever disconsolate and unrequited. This attitude to a disappointed suitor was of course Elizabeth's favourite pose: it is neatly described in a lyric from Dowland's *Third Book of Songs or Aires* (1603) which fits the end of *Sapho and Phao* as if it belongs there:

> Say, Love, if ever thou didst find
> A woman with a constant mind?
> None but one.
> And what should that rare mirror be?
> Some goddess or some queen is she?
> She, she, she, and only she,
> She only Queen of love and beauty.
>
> But could thy fiery poisoned dart
> At no time touch her spotless heart,
> Nor come near?
> She is not subject to Love's bow:
> Her eye commands, her heart saith No.
> No, no, no, and only no!
> One No another still doth follow.
>
> How might I that fair wonder know
> That mocks desire with endless no?
> See the moon
> That ever in one change doth grow
> Yet still the same; and she is so;
> So, so, so, and only so,
> From heaven her virtues she doth borrow.
>
> To her then yield thy shafts and bow
> That can command affections so.
> Love is free;
> So are her thoughts that vanquish thee,
> There is no Queen of Love but she,
> She, she, she and only she,
> She only Queen of love and beauty.

Phao does not stand for any one in particular of Elizabeth's disappointed suitors, though his case is in fact that of Alençon, Oxford himself, and many others who have been suggested by commentators on the play. He is merely the extreme hypothesis, the utterly desirable and in reality desired, whose rejection illustrates the glory of Elizabeth's dedicated self-control. As Lyly put it in *Euphues and his England*:

> such is the grace bestowed upon this earthly Goddess, that having the beauty that might allure all Princes, she hath the chastity also to refuse all, accounting it no less praise to be called a Virgin, than to be esteemed a Venus, thinking it as great honour to be found chaste, as thought amiable. (ii. 209)

Occasionally a play went one step further than figuring Elizabeth by a character on stage, and demanded her personal co-operation by a direct address that involved her in the action. Peele's *Arraignment of Paris*, performed by the Chapel boys in about 1583, was probably the most successful of such devices; the contending goddesses at last gave Elizabeth the mastery, and delivered their golden ball into the Queen's own hands. Sidney's *Lady of May* was unlucky in performance, for Elizabeth, inattentive or arbitrary, gave the wrong decision when called upon and threw the ending out of gear. This seems to have been Sidney's own fault for springing the piece on the Queen like a 'happening' as she walked in the gardens of Wanstead on a visit to his uncle Leicester. As a rule, Elizabeth was long-suffering and intelligent about inoffensive well-intentioned shows: she relished local efforts all the more if they met mishap, but knew how to value elaborately conceived compliment. Her remark to some of her own courtiers who danced a measure immediately after the splendid Gray's Inn masque of Proteus and the Adamantine Rock is significant: 'What! Shall we have Bread and Cheese after a Banquet?' She had of course been hailed in the piece as a universal lode-stone, 'true Adamant of Hearts'. To the end of her life Elizabeth loved masques and dancing, and she never let her own skill grow rusty: she could be tempted into gracing a masque by dancing a part in it herself, in much the same way as the complimentary plays tried to involve her, by direct address. Mary Fitton did this at Lady Anne Russell's wedding masque of Muses in June 1600: Her Majesty became the Ninth Muse.

When we consider the long-term and more far-reaching effects of conditions at court on the development of drama in general, this insistence by the Queen on extravagant tribute, especially in the way of receptions and entertainments with an added fiction as the colour for the presentation of gifts, seems not so much an expedient to raise funds, based on an excess of personal vanity, as a manifesto of her status as monarch, based on a correct sense of what was due to her in that capacity. The people who went on cherishing the Astraea-Cynthia cult of implacable virginity, for ever young and still to be adored, long after Elizabeth had become a difficult old hag, were not all fools and sycophants. Increasingly Elizabeth made good her claims. By devious but unremitting endeavour she set England in order and kept the threats of civil war and foreign domination at bay, thus providing her subjects with that measure of social security which is essential for the increase of the arts, particularly of drama. Within the closed context she created, she worked hard to make her subjects not only contented but as useful as possible to themselves and to her. Though she took a firm line with extremists, she deplored the waste of life and talent when a man preferred martyrdom to conformity. So long as people kept their dissenting views private and went on contributing to the national effort, Elizabeth felt no sort of inner compulsion to martyr them. On public allegiance to her church and government, and on demonstrative loyalty to herself as head of both, she did however very firmly insist. The result of this policy was to put the whole responsibility for fundamental moral decision firmly on the individual conscience, but also to provide every possible inducement to defer any decision, to hesitate before rushing into any opinion out of harmony with the existing order. For many Christians, particularly of the younger generation, there was time to think things out, to grow into new attitudes of faith, to explore the legacy of the past and taste the benefits of the present. Having achieved this much, Elizabeth set herself to maintain the equipoise, to prevent anyone who professed to act on principle from disintegrating her government or church. She prolonged the good moment and kept the wave from toppling. After her the deluge.

Shakespeare and the dramatists of the public playhouses in general were born into the world Elizabeth had created and took over its basic assumptions while they were growing up. They had Elizabeth to thank for the security which gave them time to take in as much as they could of that world's richness and energy. Sooner or later the problems of the individual conscience had to be solved in action, sooner or later the assumptions of Elizabeth's world had to be questioned, and modified, and abandoned. The process took time, both in general and in particular. Donne gives the intellectual justification for delayed action:

> in strange way
> To stand inquiring right, is not to stray;
> To sleepe, or runne wrong, is. On a huge hill,
> Cragged, and steep, Truth stands, and hee that will
> Reach her, about must, and about must goe;
> And what the hills suddennes resists, winne so;
> Yet strive so, that before age, deaths twilight,
> Thy Soule rest, for none can worke in that night.
>   (p. 157)

The best of Elizabethan drama proper, and the darkening tone of drama as the borrowed time began to run out at last, show the effect of this attitude on a whole generation of Englishmen.

The effect of Elizabeth's carefully cultivated image of the court on the drama of the beginning of her reign can be noted in *Gorboduc*, presented at the Inner Temple on Twelfth Night 1562, and at Whitehall for the benefit of the Queen twelve days later. The most respectable of all the attempts to influence Elizabeth's views on marriage, *Gorboduc* is a stiff mixture of Senecan tragedy and Italian dumbshow, 'full of notable moralitie, which it doth most delightfully teach; and so obtayne the very end of Poesie'. The Gentlemen of the Inner Temple were happy to instruct their Queen in the dangers of civil war in a land without an obvious heir to the throne. Sackville and Norton were both on the highroad to State preferment, and in no sense professional dramatists, but their offering to Elizabeth was constructed according to the best precepts and models available to Renaissance scholarship. Sidney was to find fault with its disregard of Aristotle's views on place and time, which Castelvetro elevated into a theory of the Unities some years after *Gorboduc* was written. This freedom has little power to shock the modern reader. *Samson Agonistes* (never intended for the stage) is the kind of thing Sidney could have applauded, and it is a kind utterly distinct from the acknowledged masterpieces of English drama. The real point of interest here is that an unashamedly academic composition like *Gorboduc*, played before a captive audience and not intended to make money, should take over without apology a licence that popular drama in England had always enjoyed, that of telling a story through a succession of scenes ordered chronologically and set wherever indicated by the course of the action. To watch the scene

change from the palace of King Gorboduc to the court of Ferrex or
Porrex and back again can have been no strain to people who had seen
the whole history of the world enacted in consecutive pageants or even
followed the vicissitudes of Patient Grissel or the Nice Wanton.

There was of course no question of talking down, or making con-
cessions to the tastes of an uninformed audience. The court took its
intellectual tone from Elizabeth, who had fairly earned her reputation
for scholarship. Educated in the best Renaissance tradition, she was a
credit to her master, Ascham. The experiment of developing the
intelligence of well-born young women by letting them attempt their
brothers' programme of classical and modern studies had justified itself in England not only with the distinguished circle round Sir Thomas
More, but in the second generation with Mary Tudor, Lady Jane Grey
and Elizabeth. Mary was accomplished without being an intellectual,
but Jane and Elizabeth were brilliant pupils. In 1562 Elizabeth was still
reading Greek and Latin with Ascham every day. Round about this
time she made the translation of a chorus from the Pseudo-Senecan
Hercules Oetaeus that survives in her own hand. When Jasper Heywood
dedicated his version of *Troas* to the Queen as a New Year's gift in
1559, he remarked on her enjoyment of Seneca in Latin. *Gorboduc*
was deliberately constructed to gratify a connoisseur, and its serious
moral purpose was to persuade a serious-minded sovereign.

What is portentous about *Gorboduc* is not the blank verse, nor yet
the use of history to illuminate current political problems. It is the
underlying assumption of the authors that the sovereign who watched
their play was a power for good, and that whether or not she approved
its specific moral she would judge it as a demonstration in a serious context. The entertainment value was a secondary factor—not neglected,
for there is lavish spectacle in the dumbshows, but not the main reason
for putting the play on stage. The public nature of the demonstration is
also significant. The Inns of Court audience and the Court audience
were not vulgar, since they consisted of the nation's upper crust, nobility
and gentry drawn up to London to see and be the world of statesmen-
ship, gallantry and new fashion; but they were popular, in the sense that
there was not a rigid line of demarcation between their culture and
that of the population, gentles and commons, left behind in the shires of
England—not so far as ideals in education and dramatic tradition were
concerned. Wherever a boy happened to start out along the road to
civilisation, he progressed with the same signposts and milestones. And

the same more or less ostensibly moral entertainment was being presented to all comers—the high-born merely got a better view. What the presentation of *Gorboduc* did for the Queen and her courtiers was to emphasise the image of high-minded royalty in a jewelled frame, graciously observing a significant public gesture.

In England this was a mediaeval rather than a Renaissance image. The principle of hierarchy, working even above the King so that God at the top is a rebuke for presumption and a hope for unjustly oppressed subjects, was used by both schools of thought during the English Reformation. *Everyman* had proclaimed it in terms of a Catholic universe; *King Johan* re-stated it at greater length and more clumsily in terms of a reforming Protestant monarchy; *Respublica* neatly invoked it in terms of a Catholic monarch's reaction from bad Protestant rule. The Protestant universe was enshrined in the English Prayer Book:

> O Lord our Heavenly Father, high and mighty, King of kings, Lord of lords, the only Ruler of princes, which dost from thy throne behold all the dwellers upon the earth. . . .

said Elizabethans night and morning as they prayed for their Queen. If the world is a stage, God is the perfect witness:

> As he pronounces lastly on each deed,
> Of so much fame in Heav'n expect thy meed

—the traditional image was still vital for Milton in 1637, though the Anglican hierarchy was intolerable. And from the mediaeval period onwards, both in English society and English drama, the concept of God the All-Seeing was linked with two attitudes of mind which have not survived to our own day. One was the affirmative attitude to the content of plays that has already been discussed as a legacy of liturgical drama. The other was the affirmative attitude toward seeing the King watch a show in his own honour, a legacy from outdoor court spectacles, tournaments and civic receptions, and from performances both religious and secular in the halls of King, nobility, University or Inn of Court. Not to seek entertainment, but to demonstrate allegiance; not to see, but to watch the King see, and to remember that God sees and judges—this was the traditional motivation of the English audience. *Gorboduc* and the greatest Elizabethan plays took its survival for granted.

So of course did those responsible for the seating arrangements in King's College Chapel when Elizabeth visited Cambridge in 1564, and in Christ Church Hall when she visited Oxford in 1566. On both occasions the Queen was placed opposite the acting area in such a way that, while she obtained a perfect view of the play, she was herself fully visible to the public at large, who considered Queen and play as spectacles of equal attraction. This is the grouping that Shakespeare deliberately reconstructed in several of his plays, including *Love's Labour's Lost*, *A Midsummer Night's Dream* and *Hamlet*: and it held his imagination enough to reappear at the end of his life in *The Two Noble Kinsmen*. Shakespeare's audience is invited to watch the courtly audience watching the play-within-the-play, and to relish the double spectacle from a point of double vantage. Each spectator is at once provided with a chance to demonstrate his loyalty as a member of the public at large, affirming the worth and values of the ruler and court shown receiving tribute, and a chance to see the whole situation as God sees it, to judge the ruler and court from outside the action and by the most uncompromising standards.

The way in which Shakespeare chooses to exercise his audience in this double duty throws much light on his view of the court-image at different periods of his life. There is in the first place a clear distinction between the attitude he invites us to share toward the amateur shows, directed by Holofernes, Bottom and Gerrard, and his attitude to the professional show bespoken and managed by Hamlet. The amateur shows are diversions and pastimes for the court, 'abridgements', as Theseus puts it: they can be adapted to the mood of the moment, enhancing gaiety or placing misfortune in a consolatory perspective, but their moral content is conventional and their educational value very slight. It is the relationship between players and audience that secures the effect of these shows, not their intrinsic merit in text or presentation. When the loyal subjects try to propel their ruler before them down the highroad of learning and virtue, he accepts their efforts as tribute, more or less graciously reserving a patron's right to condone inadequacy or find fault as his fancy dictates. Some of the mockery these performances receive from their courtly audiences seems fair enough; but Shakespeare takes pains to maintain the balance of sympathy and to indicate precisely where fun slips into malice. Holofernes is not absurd when he frames the protest 'This is not generous, not gentle, not humble (V. ii. 621). In what sense, however, could the country schoolmaster and his creator legitimately expect the courtiers to be humble? Surely only in the Christian sense of humility before

God, the disposer of all? 'For God resisteth the proud, and giveth grace to the humble' (1 Peter, V. 5). The responsibility of a ruler toward his well-meaning inferiors is a type of God's uncaptious providence, and the thought behind the attitude of Holofernes is that of the parable about the cruel servant who was forgiven ten thousand talents but went on dunning for his hundred pence. None of this is over-stated, and the earthly hierarchy is not severely criticised; but what is interesting (as in the parallel case of Malvolio's sufferings when baited as mad) is Shakespeare's care not to give even the presumptuous and the ridiculous too hard a fall. By taking both the self-destined victims and the self-appointed tormentors quite seriously in their degree as human beings, he manœuvres his audience into a simultaneous awareness of God's patience, man's imperfection, and the ideal of delegated authority against which this imperfection is being judged.

In contrast with this very delicate manipulation of sympathy in plays where authority is on the whole responsibly wielded, the treatment of suspect and divided authority watching a made-to-measure professional show in *Hamlet* leads Shakespeare's audience into a painful moral dilemma. On the surface, *The Mouse-Trap* is just another court abridgement, likely to have a better text and more polished presentation because the players are experts and not volunteers, but still firmly within the 'right-minded patron accepts orthodox moral guidance' tradition. Yet as we watch the King's party settling itself to watch the dumbshow we are uneasily conscious that something is wrong—the familiar double demand on our loyalty and integrity is being made on false pretences. The King is not what he should be: so much has been established for us (though not for Hamlet) by the give-away aside about the harlot's cheek (III. i. 49-53) before the unkingly eavesdropping incident. We are prepared to find the Ghost's charges substantiated by the King's reaction to the mimic murder. This would not be an intolerable situation if we were sure that Hamlet himself were all he should be; but we are not. However much allowance is made for his feigned madness, Hamlet is not in fact fully his own master, let alone the accredited delegate of God. He is in a hideous position, humanly speaking; and though he is geared to good, his perplexities disqualify him from the rôle of right-minded patron. Moreover, we know the players themselves to be on this occasion not a set of people affirming their loyalty to enforcing the correct moral standards, but an extension of Hamlet's personality. *The Mouse-Trap* is synthetic in origin, and worse than this, we learn by the dumbshow that it is more life-like than exemplary—crime is actually shown to pay.

A brief side-glance at another play of the turn of the century, Jonson's *Cynthia's Revels*, shows by contrast how far Shakespeare has moved from the conventional development of the court-image in drama as a means of underlining loyalty to the throne of England. Jonson too is considering a tainted court, and employs the monarch-watches-court-show situation, but his Cynthia is as transcendentally virtuous and clear-sighted as Lyly's Sapho at her most glorious. She disgraces the unworthy courtiers and mischievous gods whose lewd humours profane her court, and incidentally shows a thorough appreciation of the upright Crites, who is as plainly Jonson as Cynthia is Elizabeth. Jonson puts the traditional attitude unambiguously:

> Princes that would their people should do well
> Must at themselves begin, as at the head:
> For men, by their example, pattern out
> Their imitations, and regard of laws:
> A virtuous court a world to virtue draws.
>
> (V. ix. 169)

The bitterness of Jonson's resentment against the 'knot of spiders' who surround the Queen of England is given expression in full detail as he paints the folly and wickedness of Cynthia's erring courtiers, but he retains his faith in Elizabeth as a power for good, who can see through the hypocrites and reward the sincere. This preserves the attitude of Lyly while making allowance for the darker context of life at the end of Elizabeth's reign. The basic assumptions about virtue, sincerity and monarchy remain unchallenged.

In *Hamlet*, Shakespeare lets doubt have a say about all three assumptions. A measure of sympathy and a measure of condemnation must be mixed in any responsible human reaction to the main characters, including the Ghost: only Horatio, Hamlet's own ideal of balance and integrity, remains a constant good, and he is a visitor to the court, a disinterested scholarly observer, whose very love for Hamlet is well this side idolatry. Pandion in *Sapho and Phao* had censured the court from his university standpoint, finding it all too difficult for him: 'Because it is harder to shape a life to dissemble, then to go forward with the liberty of truth'. Lyly lets him be talked out of this position: Trachinus claims that Sapho's court is a miracle by virtue of its mistress. Shakespeare gives Hamlet and Horatio, whose hearts are in Wittenburg, no such excuse for condoning the court of Denmark. Elizabeth is simply not in the picture: Shakespeare is writing a public play about the relationship between private and public virtue, and the topical relevance is not central to his suggested conclusions. The *Mouse-Trap* scene brings home the fact that there is no longer an assurance underlying the action that God is on top.

It is the thoroughness and unpleasantness of the shock to moral values produced by the *Mouse-Trap* incident as a whole that places what Shakespeare usually provides in its true perspective. To have that shock firmly associated with the actor's skill and the playwright's cunning suggests a self-consciousness about the function of drama on an entirely different level from the sententiousness of Hamlet's advice to the players or his topical gossip with Rosencrantz and Guildenstern. At least two entities are brought to trial in *Hamlet*: the court and the theatrical profession, and the crime that connects them is seen to be hypocrisy—that feigning which grows into emotional truth as Claudius plays the politic King and the player changes colour for Hecuba's grief. Yet the play which contains Polonius, Osric, Rosencrantz and Guildenstern, a damaging row of courtiers, also contains Hamlet himself, who would seem to have stepped out of the pages of Castiglione without reference to human possibility if there were not the splendid precedent of Sidney's life and character to underwrite his endowments.

What Hamlet is to drama, Sidney is to history—an embodiment of the courtly ideal, whose glories and limitations provide at once a demonstration of that idea's strength and a criticism of its adequacy. Sidney's impact on the imagination of his contemporaries, at home and abroad, was tremendous: he was quite literally and immediately the glass of fashion and the mould of form to his countrymen, and in his person the ideal image of Elizabeth's court and its actuality most nearly coincided. From the copious evidence about his brief career, and from his own profusion of writing, a clear picture of the man emerges. Beneath his flowing charm and urbanity was a current of passionate pride, and an eddy of no less passionate humility. He is thus the epitome of the Renaissance Englishman, oscillating between two irreconcilable modes of being, under the protection of Elizabeth's grand truce. As a self-acknowledged type, secure in his own rank of a traditional hierarchy, and as a Christian, feeling for God's will and trying to put it before his own, Sidney belongs to the old world: as a magnificent individual glorying in his talents, whose compass wavers from *Noblesse Oblige* to *amour propre*, he belongs to the new. Fulke Greville, his lifelong friend, records two incidents of the field before Zutphen where in 1586 he died: each neatly illustrates one facet of his nature. The chivalrous but impractical gesture of flinging away his leg-armour because a friend had none cost him his life. The draught of water passed on to a dying soldier consolidated his immortality in Christian legend. The real point of interest is that both these actions were completely in character. Though irreconcilable, the elements of his personality were not in active conflict, and he was able to live and die without being forced to decide between them or to work out a compromise. The principle of alternation served him strikingly well. Probably that superb immunity from fundamental misgiving was too good to have lasted Sidney a normal lifetime. If we try to imagine him discussing the problems of Charles I with Fulke Greville in 1628, the year of Greville's death, we can see how rapidly Elizabeth's world fell apart when the long truce came to an end. A man as sensitive and observant as Sidney would have moved with the years to become in history what Hamlet is in drama, a living question-mark.

The true relationship between Elizabeth's court and the dramatists who are called Elizabethan must be stated not in terms of direct patronage, nor even in terms of encouragement and protection within a system which placed financial responsibility on the public at large rather than the court. Both patronage and protection existed, and served to create a context for the development of the theatrical profession, but the masterpieces of Elizabethan drama were not what the patron ordered. Lyly is a great fish in a small pond, and neither the reams of eulogy nor the chips of Seneca for which Leicester and other courtiers paid good gold are of much importance as plays. Perhaps Shakespeare as a boy saw the Princely Pleasures with which Leicester courted Elizabeth in 1575—Stratford is not far from Kenilworth, and Arion on the dolphin's back was a feature of the entertainment. The instance cannot be established, but the general enrichment of the quality of life which men like Leicester and Sidney made in the course of their living can be documented up to the hilt. For an Elizabethan, the greatest of the private moral virtues was Magnificence, and it was this virtue that the court of Elizabeth cultivated to the exclusion of many others. Magnificence is not merely a matter of display and costly pomp, though these are elements which have their share in the development of theatre. Richness of spirit, magnanimity, endowment with all the good gifts of nature and fortune, all belong to the concept of Magnificence. At its best, the court of Elizabeth was an argument for this idea. Its effect on the dramatists was twofold—first to feed their imagination, and then to pose increasingly urgent questions. By what right was this image at the apex of civilisation in England? What lasting validity has the principle of alternation between incompatible modes of being? How much longer could the breathing-space last?

The struggle of the individual conscience, incarnate in a thousand shadows of perplexed humanity, took the English stage for its arena as the reign of Elizabeth came to an end, and made it immortal before the hoarded spiritual capital of that reign at last ran out, at least a generation later. A brief survey of what happened to the image of the court in the years after Elizabeth's death shows clearly what forces she had managed to control or keep at bay. Her personal contribution to the national understanding had been to demonstrate that a woman can be as serious and efficient and interesting as a man: this the dramatists took to heart, as the heroines of Elizabethan drama attest. She had also raised patriotism to a new and positive force. Though she had the body of a weak and feeble woman, she had the heart and stomach of a king, and a king of England too. She told her subjects so herself at a moment of crisis, and their belief in her helped to make the claim true. In her last years she lived to some extent on her own legend, probably unaware that the spirit of extreme Puritan opposition was a snake she had only scotched; but to the end she was a focus for the loyalty and affection that had made England a nation rather than a backward race on an island at the edge of Europe.

To this kind of prestige the mumble-mouthed King of Scots, with his doctrinaire arrogance and notoriously expensive weaknesses, could not hope to succeed. As the incarnation of that long overdue security, the male monarch with heirs male, he was respectfully welcomed: Gunpowder Treason shocked his subjects as an insult to King and Parliament alike; but James had all Mary Stuart's obstinate silliness without her magnetic charm, and his genuine powers as thinker and scholar only made his follies less excusable. When it has been noted that Shakespeare chose the ingredients of *Macbeth*—Scottish history, witchcraft, advice to a monarch—with one eye on the throne, the direct effect of James on the serious drama of his reign has been sufficiently illustrated. References to witches and to the divine right of kings could be relied on to interest James throughout his reign. So could the evils of tobacco, and his own merits. But on the whole there is less flattery than satire in the way James and his parvenu court are treated in plays. *Eastward Ho* and *The Isle of Gulls* brought down the wrath of James and his Queen on the Blackfriars boys and their playwrights. Though Jonson wrote from prison that the first of these plays had been 'so mistaken, so misconstrued, so misapplied', it was instantly published and people went on laughing. In 1597 the comparable satire of *The Isle of Dogs* had been suppressed with the closing of all the playhouses and the censoring of the play itself out of existence. Elizabeth protected her image much more efficiently.

Yet for all this, Shakespeare and his company were the King's Men, playing at the Globe, Blackfriars and the court with prosperous regularity. Though James could not inspire, he could protect and reward. The Henslowe-Alleyn management at the Fortune became Prince Henry's Men, and it seemed for a time that the gallant forwardness of Henry, who was created Prince of Wales in June 1610, would counterbalance his father's ineptitude and provide a new focus for patriotic feeling. But the untimely death of the Prince in November 1612, followed within a few months by the wedding and departure for the Palatinate of the general favourite Princess Elizabeth, left the family of James without a shred of personal glamour. The sickening publicity of the Essex divorce, with the Overbury scandal hard at its heels, substantiated the growing rumours of a corrupted court. Political tension increased as the King was egged on by Buckingham to a series of egregious blunders. He exploited the veteran Raleigh, and then sacrificed him to Spanish vengeance. He threw away England's tactical advantage at the outbreak of the Thirty Years' War. He violently antagonised Parliament without managing to save his own Bacon. Worst of all, he worked to marry England's heir to the Infanta of Spain. In aid of this last fatuity, Jonson, who had loyally provided masques in honour of most public events since the accession of James, was commissioned by Buckingham to prepare *The Gipsies Metamorphosed*. The panegyric on James which Jonson deemed appropriate to this occasion invites his own tart comment on Donne's *First Anniversary*—if it had been written of the Virgin Mary it had been something. That Jonson did not speak for the nation at large is proved by the tumultuous success of Middleton's envenomed political allegory *A*

Game of Chess, which rejoiced in the breakdown of marriage negoti-ations and the discomfiture of Gondomar, the Spanish Ambassador. James himself, Prince Charles and Buckingham were shown as the White King, Knight and Duke, victorious at long last over Black machinations; the White King was an easy dupe, and James took personal offence. How Sir Henry Herbert came to license the play is a minor mystery (Buckingham is said to have arranged it), but on the strength of his licence the King's own Men played for nine profitable days in August 1624, the longest run then on record, before the furious protests of Gondomar closed the Globe and forced the Privy Council to take disciplinary action. That the King's Men survived to mock another day shows the weakness of James rather than his forgiving spirit. Once again the play was rushed into print, more than one edition perpetuating the bitter joke and the failure of the King's cherished plan. The winter of 1624 was not very gay: 'The king kept his chamber all this Christmas, not coming once to the chapel nor to any of the plays'. In March 1625 James died, and left a bankruptcy of credit and goodwill. The Crown and the court were not representative of the noble and puissant nation now beginning to rouse herself like a strong man after sleep. Things had not yet gone too far. Milton was at Cambridge; Cromwell was farming at St Ives: both enjoyed music and (in the family circle) dancing. There was still just room for the new king to step back into Elizabeth's position and make use of the arts to create a new national sympathy. Very few people wanted to risk a head-on collision, nobody positively intended a civil war. Charles had the initia-tive.

But of course Charles was incapable of avoiding the Great Rebellion. He shared his father's political views, and inherited a double portion of Mary Stuart's obstinacy. Though he had also something of her charm, only a blazingly passionate integrity and devotion to duty could have made a lasting personal impression on his serious-minded sub-jects. Charles was simply not a spectacular person. Self-conscious and reserved, a bit of a prig in his quiet way, he made no parade of his small-scale virtues and thought more of his rights than his duties. He made no friends among the common people, whom Elizabeth had taken pains to gratify. When Buckingham was murdered, London broke into celebrations, and the mob cheered across the coffin. Charles had lost his closest and dearest friend, but he did not flash into a public demonstration of grief and anger—the mob was given no chance to see him moved and soften its ugly mood. He pressed on with the unpopular policies that were steadily widening the gap between king and responsible subject on issues of religion and government. The extravagance of his young French bride, brought up on the principle of conspicuous expenditure for kings, and the effeminate affectations of their court, were additional grievances. It is ironic that the unparalleled glories of the Caroline masque reflected no lustre on the throne, but were counted as shameful evidence of wanton prodigality. The term 'Caroline drama' is normally used for the satirical London comedies of the period rather than its magnificently melancholy tragedies. Yet the resignation and self-command with which Calantha in *The Broken Heart* dances out her measured defiance to fate's repeated blows is closer to the true nature of Charles himself than anything 'Jacobean' had been to his father. When total defeat left Charles isolated in body as he had always been in mind, he grew toward his destiny. His gestures were on the right royal scale. Nothing became his life like the leaving of it, and in remote villages men fell dead with horror at the news. To understand, to interpret, to prefigure—the most devoted dramatist could do no more for the only begetter of his genius. In this very limited sense, Ford is Caroline. In the wider sense he is still Elizabethan—not because he was born before 1603, but because his image of what befits a ruler did not derive from secretive Charles and bumbling James. Personal panache was what had counted at the court of the Virgin Queen.

The link between the institution of kingship and the survival of drama was obvious to seventeenth century writers:

> They that would have no KING, would have no Play:
> The *Laurel* and the *Crown* together went,
> Had the same *Foes*, and the same *Banishment*:   (p. 94)

Denham was greeting Charles II, who promptly reopened the theatres at his Restoration. Certainly the closing of the theatres in 1642 was more than a sudden spiteful blow at the Cavalier party's main source of amusement, and an opportune move to suppress anti-Puritan propaganda. It represented the triumph of a principle and a policy which had been steadily and vociferously opposed to the very essence of drama since the English Reformation, and is not dead today. God is a Spirit, and they that worship Him must worship Him in spirit and in truth. To play, to personate, to pretend, may well offend the in-dwell-

N

ing Spirit of God by violating the soul's self-conscious integrity and blurring the perception of things as they are. A suspension of disbelief, in any other context than that of Bible studies, shows a will most incorrect to heaven. At best, plays can be no more than an expense of time, energy and money better dedicated to the service of God. At worst, they are the very pomps of the devil, pulling down the heavy judgement of God on the idle generation that maintains them with their concomitants of scandal and abuse. Against this attitude no reform of playhouse conditions or censoring of material to be played can prevail. 'Dost thou think, because thou art virtuous, there shall be no more cakes and ale?' Implacably, yes. But the unregenerate enjoys plays, and the sovereigns of England are often culpably unregenerate.

> No other care they bear of things above
> But with Astrologers divine, and *Jove*,
> To know how long their Planet yet Reprives
> From the deserved Fate their guilty lives:
> Thus (Image-like) an useless time they tell,
> And with vain Scepter, strike the hourly Bell;
> Nor more contribute to the state of Things
> Than wooden Heads unto the Viols strings.
>   (p. 104)

Marvell, here deploring Charles I and his father, had already expressed his view of their relation to Elizabeth. He pointed out how Oliver Cromwell was able to ruin the great work of Time,

> Though Justice against Fate complain,
>   And plead the antient Rights in vain:
>   But those do hold or break
>   As Men are strong or weak.
> Nature that hateth emptiness,
> Allows of penetration less:
>   And therefore must make room
>   Where greater Spirits come.   (p. 98)

The indefatigable Cromwell exercised every power that was proper to a ruler of England, and was a brilliant success. But when offered the Crown itself he drew back sharply: 'I cannot undertake this government with the title of King'. The title was not empty, though the throne was vacant and the authority transferred. To the Regicides monarchy was indissolubly and fatally wedded to the court and to court entertainment—as Milton fulminated,

> . . . a King must be ador'd like a Demigod, with a dissolute and haughty court about him, of vast expence and luxury, Masks and Revels, to the debauching of our prime Gentry both Male and Female; not in their pastimes only, but in earnest, by the loose imployments of Court-service . . .

This was not the way in which the majority of the Elizabethans had looked at their monarch's pomp.

From this brief survey of the relationship between ruler and drama in the years after Elizabeth's death, several points of interest emerge. The first is that the personal protection of the monarch went on being extended to the acting companies of the public playhouses as well as to the devisers of court revels, in spite of occasional signs of disaffection and in the face of Puritan opposition. The second is that the essentially courtly pastimes with some dramatic content, masques and triumphs, showed a rapid elaboration of spectacle and expense under the Stuart kings. ('These things are but Toyes. . . . But yet, since Princes will have such Things, it is better, they should be Graced with Elegancy then Daubed with Cost': Bacon's remark passed unheeded.) The third is that even though respect for the court as such declined with its contamination, the ideal of kingship and courtesy proved to be indestructible. It took a Regicide to inveigh against kings in 1660, and the crowds who cheered Charles II from Rochester to Whitehall were welcoming back not only a king but an order of life which included cakes and ale.

Note

Biography. Anthony Mundy was born the son of a London draper in 1560. His occasional career as an actor seems to have begun before his seventeenth year, but was interrupted for a time while he served as an apprentice to the printer and stationer John Aldee, as a spy among English Catholics on the continent, and as a versifier and pamphleteer. He resumed his acting around 1581, but continued to write not only pamphlets and verse but romances as well—his own *Zelauto* (1580) was succeeded by his translations of thousands of pages on the adventures of Palmerin, Palladine, Palmendos, Gerileon, Primaleon, and Amadis over the next eighteen years. Sometime in the early 1580's he also took up the writing of plays, and his earliest known play, *Fedele and Fortunio* (an adaptation of Pasqualigo's *Il Fedele*) was entered in the Stationers' Register in 1584. He apparently continued as an active playwright thereafter, although only two extant plays from the next dozen years can be safely ascribed to him, *John a Kent and John a Cumber* (c. 1589) and *Sir Thomas More* (c. 1593). He wrote plays regularly for the Admiral's Men between 1597 and 1602, but except for one, *Sir John Oldcastle* (1600) which he co-authored along with Drayton, Hathway and Wilson, his only known surviving plays from this period are *The Downfall of Robert Earl of Huntingdon* and *The Death of Robert Earl of Huntingdon*, both printed in 1601. After 1602 he left the stage for the dignity of the draper's trade bequeathed him by his father; over the next twenty years he produced a few translations, additions to Stow's *Survey of London*, a chronicle, and nine civic pageants; after that, he laboured quietly on more additions to Stow's *Survey* until his death in 1633.

Texts. All the surviving plays are included in the *Malone Society Reprints*; and all but *Fidele and Fortunio* in J. S. Farmer's *Tudor Fascimile Texts*. In this chapter quotation is from the M.S.R. and T.F.T.; signature references are given, in lower case letters for *The Downfall* and in capitals for *The Death*.

Scholarships and Criticism. The standard work on Mundy is still Celeste Turner, *Anthony Mundy* (1928), but this should be used in conjunction with her revisions in the light of recent scholarship ('Young Anthony Mundy Again', *Studies in Philology* (1959), pp. 150–68). See, also, I. A. Shapiro, 'Shakespeare and Mundy', *Shakespeare Survey*, 14 (1961).

The only satisfactory general discussion of the Huntingdon plays yet available is in H. Jenkins, *The Life and Work of Henry Chettle* (1934). The indispensable sourcebook for all study of Elizabethan hackwriting is Henslowe's *Diary* (1961), ed. R. A. Foakes and R. T. Rickert; the commentary on the *Diary* by W. W. Greg in his edition (1904–8) has still not been replaced. In default of specific studies on the techniques of dramatic hackwriting, one may consult R. A. Foakes, 'The Profession of Playwright', in *Early Shakespeare* (Stratford-upon-Avon Studies 3, 1961), Mary Hyde, *Playwriting for Elizabethans* (1949),

IX

Hackwriting and the Huntingdon Plays

JOHN C. MEAGHER

By the late 1590's, the theatrical entertainment of the London populace had become a substantial business, and most of the trade was divided between two dramatic companies, the Chamberlain's Men and the Admiral's Men. We know little about whatever pressure the public might have exerted for quality in the plays they presented, but the survival of the diary of Philip Henslowe, the financier of the Admiral's Men, reveals a decided pressure for variety; in a typical fortnight in 1597 the Admiral's Men gave twelve performances which presented eight to ten different plays, of which one might be new and another might be appearing for the last time, its receipts having fallen off badly after eight or a dozen showings. Such a pace demanded a constant supply of new plays, and the Admiral's Men accordingly kept in touch with a group of playwrights who worked sometimes separately and sometimes in conjunction with one another to keep up the production of dramatic texts. Some of them—Ben Jonson and George Chapman, for instance—were writers of some genuine distinction; but the care which such men usually invested in their plays made it impossible for them to fill the constant demand of the active stage of the Rose theatre. That task accordingly fell to the others. In 1598 Henslowe laid out payments for work on more than thirty plays, almost all of them the individual or combined efforts of his five most faithful hacks—Anthony Mundy, Henry Chettle, Michael Drayton, Thomas Dekker and Robert Wilson.

Modern taste in Elizabethan drama is formed in the image of artistic

---

and a variety of works on the general literary and theatrical ambiance; besides works by Doran, Bradbrook and Chambers cited in the prefatory notes to Chapters I and II above, the following are relevant here: A. Harbage, *Shakespeare's Audience* (1941) and *Shakespeare and the Rival Traditions* (1952), and I. Ribner, *The English History Play in the Age of Shakespeare* (1957).

standards which had not yet triumphed in the heyday of Henslowe's hacks. The standard fare of the late Elizabethan stage was not the plays of Jonson and Chapman, but the work of men who made a living by turning out plays in two or three weeks' time. The surviving examples of their plays are probably a better key to the basic dramatic standards of the time than the work of their more distinguished contemporaries. For not only did their work dominate the stage by sheer volume— their reputations were by no means inferior to those of playwrights who are now taken much more seriously. In 1598, Francis Meres singled out the English writers who best bore comparison with the greatest comic dramatists of the ancient world in his *Palladis Tamia or Wit's Treasury*, and his selection from Henlowe's contributors reserves a special commendation not for one of the immortals but for one of the more methodical hacks: 'the best for Comedy among us bee ... Anthony Mundye our best plotter, Chapman, Porter, Wilson, Hathway, and Henry Chettle'. Meres's testimony is instructive even if we may wish to question his taste. If we are to understand Elizabethan plays in an Elizabethan perspective, we must include in our point of departure an understanding and at least a hypothetical appreciation of the basic standards and methods of Henslowe's hacks.

The texts upon which such a study can be based are unfortunately few. In the year in which Meres registered his opinions on the Elizabethan dramatic scene, Henslowe paid for more than thirty plays: yet only two have survived. Those two are the focus of this chapter, and as far as we can tell from Henslowe's records, their case seems typical. The first of them makes its initial appearance on the fifteenth of February, 1597/8, when Henslowe purchased from Anthony Mundy 'a playe boocke called the firste parte of Robyne Hoode'. Five days later, Henslowe made an initial payment for a sequel to it; and by the middle of March, the two parts of 'the downefall of earlle huntyngton surnamed Roben Hoode' were duly licensed by the Master of the Revels and launched upon their brief career on the boards of the Rose. They appear to have been at least modestly successful—one or both played at Court during the festivities of the following Christmas season. But they were typical of the dramatic ephemerality of the time. There is no evidence of their having appeared on any stage since the 1590's.

If the Huntingdon plays have subsequently been neglected by producers—and even by scholars—it is understandable. They are not artistically distinguished. They represent neither new departures in the theatre nor unusually late survivals of old departures. They do not excel in stage-craft, nor use source materials ingeniously, nor exhibit touches of great poetry, nor even anticipate better plays. Their interest for the historian of drama lies especially in their representativeness rather than their dis-tinction: they are *le drame moyen sensuel*, examples of the sturdy hack-work that formed the staple diet of the late Elizabethan stage and then, for the most part, quietly disappeared. As such, they provide a satis-factory opportunity for investigating the probably typical approach of a relatively unambitious playwright addressing himself to the task of writing a respectable and entertaining play rather quickly, without running the risk of artistic distinction.

It is impossible for the critic to be totally fair to the merits of the Huntingdon plays, because we do not have them in their finished form. The only text is that published by William Leake in 1601, and the manuscript used by the printer was apparently a set of 'foul papers', the author's late but not quite final draft. For the investigation of the techniques of Elizabethan hack-work, however, the irregularity of that manuscript is an additional advantage, since its incompleteness pre-serves in fossil form evidence of several important decisions and changes of mind made by the playwright during composition. Such decisions and revisions usefully supplement the inferences that can be drawn from the overall character of the plays; indications of the process of growth are keys to the playwright's dramaturgical values and techniques.

To begin with, it is clear that the play delivered to Henslowe in the middle of February was not exactly the one which Mundy originally sat down to write. He appears at first to have designed a single play to cover the story of the betrayal and exile of Robert, Earl of Huntingdon, with his subsequent life as Robin Hood, probably ending with his death; to this, he also joined an historical plot, dealing with the political struggles between Prince John and the Bishop of Ely during the absence of the crusading King Richard I. Earlier drafts may possibly have pre-ceded the version printed in 1601; but the draft from which Leake pub-lished was written essentially in the order presented by the printed text, and begins with a fairly finished version of the scenes which cover the exile of Robert and the beginnings of the struggle between Ely and John. It was apparently after these scenes were written that an im-portant inflection of the plot occurred to Mundy.

In order to provide Robin Hood's traditional Maid Marian with a courtly history paralleling that of Robin Hood himself, the opening scenes of *The Downfall* present her as the daughter of Lord Lacy and the betrothed of Robert, Earl of Huntingdon. Mundy also makes her the object of Prince John's amorous attentions; he may have got the idea from Michael Drayton's poem, *Matilda* (1594), which deals with the relentless pursuit by King John of Matilda, daughter of Lord Fitzwater, or it may be that Mundy thought explicitly of Drayton's poem only after he had created the parallel. At any rate, after writing the first few scenes, Mundy saw the advantages of exploiting the established literary history of Matilda: from this point on, Marian and Lord Lacy appear exclusively under the names of Matilda and Lord Fitzwater.

This metamorphosis was to become importantly influential later on, but at first it does not seem to have affected the original plot of *The Downfall* very deeply beyond the mere change of names. The play continues to develop rather as one might have anticipated from the opening scenes. Mundy still intended a single play, and as he neared the end of *The Downfall* he wrote evidence of this intention into an aside by Skelton, the master of ceremonies in the play's induction-epilogue framework:

> The Abbots malice, rak't in cinders long,
> Breakes out at last with Robins Tragedie. . . .
> Wherefore still sit you, doth Skelton intreat you,
>   While he *facete* wil breefely repeate you, the history al,
> And tale tragical, by whose treachery, and base injury,
> Robin the good, calde Robin Hood, died in Sherewodde . . .
> (i2–2v)

It is not clear when he changed his mind. It may be that he finished the play as he had originally intended before recognising that a more full and faithful dramatic version of Drayton's *Matilda* could be joined with the representation of Robin's death and some of King Richard's glories as the foundation of another play. In any event, he discovered that he had plot enough for five pounds' worth of sequel. He then rounded off *The Downfall* with a happy restoration and transferred either a completed or an intended version of the death of Robin Hood to the beginning of a sequel play, whose projected content be outlined in an epilogue appended to *The Downfall*:

> The second part shall presently be pend:
> There shall you see, as late my friend did note,
> King Richards revels at earle Roberts bower,

The purpos'd mirth, and the performed mone,
The death of Robin, and his murderers.
For interest of your stay, this will I adde,
King Richards voyage backe to Austria:
The swift returned tydings of his death,
The manner of his royall funerall.
Then John shall be a lawfull crowned king,
But to Matilda beare unlawfull love.
Aged Fitzwaters finall banishment:
His pitious end, of power teares to move
From marble pillers. The Catastrophe
Shall shewe you faire Matildas Tragedy,
Who (shunning Johns pursute) became a Nunne,
At Dumwod [sic] Abbey, where she constantly
Chose death to save her spotlesse chastitie.   (l2v)

But this plan too was short-lived. On 15 February, Mundy delivered *The Downfall* to Henslowe and entered into negotiations for its sequel. Five days later, perhaps after the Company had examined *The Downfall* through a reading at their favourite tavern in Fish Street, Henslowe issued an initial payment to Dowton to give to Mundy for 'his seconde parte of the downefall of earlle huntyngton surnamed Roben Hoode',[1] and on 25 February twenty shillings more followed for Henry Chettle to help with its composition—possibly to write the section dealing with King Richard.[2] But it was soon realised that the story of King John and

---

[1] Henslowe's *Diary*, ff. 44-44v. The conjectured tavern reading is not merely fanciful: the *Diary* records the purchase of 'The Famous Wars of Henry I and the Prince of Wales' in the middle of March, 1597/8, and adds immediately afterward an entry for five shillings 'lent at that tyme unto the company for to spend at the Readynge of that boocke at the sonne in new fyshstreate' (f. 45). Another payment for 'good cheare' on Fish Street is recorded on 25 March, on the occasion of the purchase of 'Earl Godwin and His Three Sons' (f. 45).

[2] Chettle's rôle in the composition of *The Death* is an important but regrettably elusive question. After an extensive study of the problem, I am satisfied that no argument purporting to identify his work in the extant text has yet been built upon adequate evidence (some are demonstrably improbable); that in fact there is evidence for a basic homogeneity of authorship throughout the Huntingdon plays; and that it is even possible that Chettle's contribution does not appear in the extant text at all. The question will be taken up at greater length in the introduction to the M.S.R. of *The Death*; in the meantime, the most responsible position on the authorship of *The Death* seems to me to be that Chettle's work, if present in the extant text, is either very limited in extent

Matilda was rich enough by itself, and that there were independent possibilities in Richard's adventures in Austria and his funeral. The latter plot was therefore spun off for a separate play, written by Chettle, Mundy, Wilson, and Drayton the following June as 'The Funeral of Richard Coeur de Lion', and the former became the basis of *The Death*. This change probably took place before Mundy had gone very far; just after the extant version of *The Death* represents the tragic end of Robin Hood in precisely the manner promised in the epilogue to *The Downfall*, and makes the initial arrangements for Richard's return to Austria, the revised plans for the rest of the play are revealed in an abrupt transition which dismisses the fate of Richard and looks exclusively to the tale of King John and Matilda:

> Yet knowe full well, to please this company,
> We meane to end Matildaes Tragedie. . . .
> You must suppose king Richard now is deade,
> And John (resistlesse) is faire Englands Lord . . .
>   (D2v-3)

Hereafter, the composition proceeds according to plan: Drayton's story of King John and Matilda, loosely imitated in *The Downfall* and conformed there to a prior plot of John and Marian, proved sufficient for a more faithful dramatic redaction as well. On 8 March, Henslowe laid out the final payment for *The Death*, and it is likely that plans for a now lost 'The Funeral of Richard Coeur de Lion' were also afoot by that time. The original *Downfall* had been fruitfully conceived: each of its plots had begotten dramatic offspring.

The original conception had probably derived its first form from a passage in Grafton's *Chronicle*. After treating King Richard's commission of Ely and his departure for the crusade, Grafton digresses into an account of Robin Hood, taking note of his original nobility and of the

---

or very like Mundy's in manner. But since the properly conservative circumlocutions would be improperly awkward, I shall speak of *The Death* in this chapter as if it were Mundy's; the reader is therefore asked to remember that this is intended qualifiedly, and that references to Mundy in my remarks on *The Death* should be taken as meaning 'Mundy (and/or perhaps Chettle)'. This qualification does not apply to *The Downfall*. There is no evidence for Chettle's participation in the extant text of that play; his additions of November, 1598 (*Diary*, f. 52) would have been made to a copy more finished than the foul papers from which Leake published *The Downfall* in 1601.

prodigality which eventually caused his bankruptcy and outlawry.[3] Neither the nobility and bankruptcy of Robin Hood nor his historical association with the period of Richard's crusade was traditional. Grafton's notice seems to provide the germ of both plots of *The Downfall*.

Grafton has little more about Robin Hood, but Mundy had plenty of other material to use in amplifying his treatment of that story. Some of this has not survived, which makes it risky to assert the originality of the Huntingdon plays' treatment of Robin Hood; but there is evidence both that Mundy used Robin Hood literature extensively, and that he could be independent of it. He accepts without substantial changes standard characters such as Little John, Friar Tuck and Maid Marian; but the prehistory given each of them in *The Downfall* seems to be his own invention. Some specific adventures of Mundy's Robin Hood are thoroughly indebted to earlier literature (Robin's rescue of Scarlet and Scathlock from the gallows is based on a conflation of several popular ballads),[4] while others, such as the manner of Robin's death, are unprecedented in extant writings. It is clear that Mundy deliberately deviated from the traditional fare of stage Robin Hoodery, and it seems that he regarded his deviation as a well-calculated risk. When one of the characters of the induction framework suspends *The Downfall* near the end to express concern over the play's omission of traditional 'jeasts of Robin Hoode' and 'merry Morices of Frier Tuck' (i2),[5]

[3] *Grafton's Chronicle*, I (1809), p. 221. (This reproduces the original edition, *A Chronicle at large*, printed in 1569.)

[4] See ballads numbered 133, 134, 140 A–C, and 141 in F. J. Child, *The English and Scottish Popular Ballads* (1882–98). The very existence of Scarlet and Scathlock is a conflation: in earlier Robin Hood literature, there is in their place only one character, variously named. The conflations could of course have been made in lost ballads. But then, Mundy wrote ballads too.

[5] These would have been known through playlets attached to the May games—e.g., those printed with *A Merry Jest of Robin Hood*, ca. 1560 (later reprinted by White, n.d.). There are sections of *The Downfall* that break into a jingling tetrameter, and the reason may be merely a diverting attempt to imitate the style of such playlets. But some of these merry jests and morrises would undoubtedly have appeared also in the lost 'pastorall plesant Commedie of Robin Hood and little John', entered on the *Stationers' Register* in 1594. This may even have played at the Rose, which would help explain the extent of the collection of Robin Hood properties in Henslowe's inventory on 10 March, 1597/8; see *Henslowe's Diary* (1961), p. 317 ff., especially the suggestive entry 'i hatte for Robin Hoode, i hobihorse' (p. 318).

Skelton's reply is redolent of the experienced confidence of the Henslo-
vian hack:

> His Majestie himselfe survaid the plat,
> And bad me boldly write it, it was good.
> For merry jeasts, they have bene showne before,
> As how the Frier fell into the Well,
> For love of Jinny that faire bonny bell:
> How Greeneleafe robd the Shrieve of Notingham,
> And other mirthfull matter, full of game.
> Our play expresses noble Roberts wrong,
> His milde forgetting trecherous injurie: . . .
> If these that heare the historie rehearst,
> Condemne my Play when it begins to spring,
> Ile let it wither while it is a budde,
> And never shewe the flower to the King.   (12)

The flower survived, and certainly part of the reason was the dramatic (and commercial) attractiveness of Mundy's new design for Robin
Hood, with an unprecedented emphasis on Robin's generous charity
that reaches almost hagiographical dimensions. The playwright was no
slave to sources. But some of his treatments of Robin Hood material
are only qualifiedly original—new to the Robin Hood tradition, but
not to the stage. Mundy totally reshaped Much, the miller's son, from
the way he found him in the Robin Hood literature, where he is a
standard Merry Man, almost indistinguishable from Scarlet or Little
John. But although Mundy's reshaping of Much is almost total, it is
neither gratuitous nor imaginative: his motive and his model for the
change can be found throughout the drama of the 1590's in the form
of the stock stage clown, whose absence would have been a distinct
disappointment to the audience at the Rose. Mundy merely includes a
character who performs with the expected silliness, incongruity, bawdi-
ness, and verbal malapropisms, and gives him Much's name. However
revolutionary it may be for Much's reputation, from the theatrical
point of view it is neither new bottle nor new wine.

Theatrical tradition exerted an enormous shaping pressure on the
Huntingdon plays. Even the co-ordination of Robin Hood material with
a plot drawn from political history, though it may have been suggested
by Grafton's *Chronicle*, was more likely a principle which Mundy
took straight from the stage. *Edward I* and *George a Greene* had both
been played successfully at the Rose within the four years prior to the

composition of *The Downfall*. The combination of Robin Hoodery with historical drama was accordingly well-established. Grafton provided the particular historical plot, but probably not the idea.

In fact, Grafton did not provide even all the particular historical plot. The need for material soon drove Mundy beyond Grafton to other sources. Raphael Holinshed's *Chronicles* (1587) provided considerably more detail, an obvious advantage to an eclectic dramatist; Mundy accordingly shows a much greater debt to Holinshed's information than to Grafton's. Indeed, his search for good dramatic hints seems to have taken him as far as John Bale's *Acts of the English Votaries*, where the description of Ely's capture is closer than either Grafton or Holinshed to the representation in *The Downfall*.[6] We cannot be sure where Mundy got his chronicles—they would have been a considerable investment for an Elizabethan dramatic hack, though a prudent one during the vogue of the history play.[7] But he clearly did have access to them, and used them for an ample and unsystematic cribbing whose range and carelessness are nicely embodied in a remark in *The Downfall*: 'Richard is a king,' says Prince John, 'In Cyprus, Acon, Acres, and rich Palestine' (g4v). *Acon* is simply the name by which Grafton designates the town known to Holinshed as *Acres*.

Mundy used the chronicles, but it would not be quite accurate to say that he learned his history from them. He gleaned to serve his independent purposes, and the resulting representations in the Huntingdon plays are frequently quite innocent of historical accuracy. *The Death* shows Chester, Winchester, and Mowbray among the defenders of King John; Holinshed clearly states that they were on the other side. The first part of *The Downfall* emphasises the tyrannical ambitions of Prince John, aided by his scheming mother; Holinshed agrees with the other chronicles that the tyranny was rather on Ely's part, and shows us a responsible Queen Eleanor who carefully keeps King Richard informed about political developments during his absence. These divergences are typical: the plays see history neither steadily nor whole.

If history generally appears with its spectra rearranged, it is frequently

---

[6] *The first two parts of the Acts or Unchaste Examples of the English Votaries* (1550), o3–3v; cf. *The Downfall*, e2–2v.

[7] The existence of Mundy's earlier nondramatic historical publications (e.g., *A Watchword to England*, 1584) and the quality of his later ones (e.g., *A Brief Chronicle of the Success of Times*, 1611) lend strength to the hypothesis that the necessary books were in Mundy's own library in 1598.

by a passage through previous literature rather than through the playwright's imagination. Mundy frequently had a choice between chronicle and literary versions of the same material, and he usually opted for the latter. The wars of King John with his barons arose, according to the chronicles, over the King's refusal to honour the ancient laws of the land; in Drayton's poem, *Matilda*, the wars arise over the King's lustful pursuit of chaste Matilda. *The Death* follows Drayton. King Richard, according to the chronicles, had a relatively uneventful imprisonment in Germany, never got beyond Jerusalem on his crusade, and spent his last months warring in France; *The Downfall*, following romances and ballads,[8] tells the story of Richard's heroic deeds during his imprisonment in Austria, refers to his siege of Babylon, and sends him back to Austria to meet his end.

In short, the Huntingdon plays were built on a literary bias that reminds us how clearly they owe their allegiance to drama, not to history —and in the less obvious sense as well as the more, for their representation of a wicked Prince John and a scheming Queen Eleanor (which is one of their sharpest divergences from the chronicles) flouts history mainly because such plays as *The Troublesome Reign* and *King John* had done so before them. John and Eleanor came to Mundy dramatically ready-made; there was no good reason to let mere history modify his preconceptions about such established characters.

It is not only history that the Huntingdon plays bend so freely to the shape of the stage. The same phenomena appear in their handling of even so literarily well-digested a source as *Matilda*. *The Death* follows the main lines of Drayton's story, but freely transposes, alters, omits, and invents. The reasons are almost always specifically theatrical. Matilda's Amazonian participation in the Barons' Wars keeps her actively present in *The Death*, but is the child of dramatic expediency, not to be found in Drayton's poem. The majority of Drayton's elegant monologues are ignored or contradicted by the play, their slow-paced sophistication being dramatically unsuitable even for extensive imitation in all but a very few cases. Drayton's King John is a well-drawn regal and courtly figure who speaks with a smooth and graceful eloquence, and his messenger is a sophisticated 'devill, walking in a humane shape',[9] an atheistic Machiavel, skilful in persuasion. But

[8] See the examples in George Henry Needler, *Richard Coeur de Lion in Literature* (1890), and in Thomas Evans' *Old Ballads*, ii (1810), 81–7.

[9] *Matilda* (ed. 1596), stanza 117.

despite the opportunities created by Drayton, Mundy adjusts his King to a condition of blunt and irascible crudity, true to the legacy of *The Troublesome Reign*, and throws over Drayton's messenger to imitate the sturdy and old-fashioned devil of the Tudor morality plays: coarse, gloatingly immoral and slightly bawdy. Even the Fitzwater and Matilda of *The Death* seem to betray by their shallow simplicity Drayton's poetic achievement. But it is not because of the playwright's incapacity to translate his source faithfully into drama: it is more precisely the result of the hackwriter's prudent sense of economy. Drayton was primarily interested in the poetic reactions of his characters; Mundy was interested in the dramatic actions of his, and where the two do not coincide, the stage is the touchstone.

Having assembled a considerable body of historical, literary and theatrical material, Mundy selected from it and shaped it in accordance with his considerable experience of what worked on the public stage. He exploited the audience's acquaintance with popular literature, heeded their taste for both the novel and the familiar, and accordingly organised his play according to the proven—if sometimes ruthless— principles of theatrical efficiency by which he had built his reputation. These principles required the minimising of unnecessary sophistication in plot, in character, in language. But the main law of dramaturgical economy operative in the construction of these plays is as positive as it is simple and obvious: maximise the dramatic uses of characters, places, and actions, by means of whatever selection, distortion or invention of material may be necessary. This principle is applied extensively and imaginatively enough in the Huntingdon plays to make Mundy's reputed skill as a plotter at least credible.

The character named Warman provides a particularly good example. He begins as the unjust steward of the Earl of Huntingdon, and might easily have been forgotten once his primary task, the outlawry of the earl, was accomplished. But Mundy observed that he could double as the indispensable Sheriff of Nottingham, and accordingly has Ely present him with a commission to that office (c1v), thus extending his usefulness to the greenwood scenes. Then (with rather less plausibility) after John usurps the throne, he commands that Ely be sent to Warman's jail in Nottingham (e2v); Warman can therefore be involved in Ely's subsequent escape and so combine the dramatic necessities of getting Ely free and bringing himself (through John's wrath) to deserved grief. It is, albeit somewhat improbably, a fairly successful piece of dramaturgical economy: by doing the work of three characters, Warman's employment heightens the interest in the traditional confrontation between Robin Hood and the Sheriff, allows his established untrustworthiness to make Ely's escape more plausible, and incurs the punishment merited by his initial misbehaviour as Robert's steward. But even that is not all. Being a handy tool, Warman is made the source of John's information concerning the treachery of Sir Hugh Lacy (c4-4v) and the agent of the Prior's disgrace (g3-3v).

These economies obviously make a play somewhat easier to follow, since they reduce the number of characters to be kept straight by the audience while permitting the remainder to contrive maximum action. Mundy knew this, and also appreciated the contribution of minor connective devices to the tidiness of the action and the flow of information, and therefore invented connections to serve a variety of other ends—to effect transitions, to clarify attitudes, and generally to promote an illusion of coherence that helps knit more closely the disparate and sometimes rather improbable actions of the play. Warman's rôle in the persecution of Scarlet and Scathlock could have been derived quite adequately from his office as Sheriff of Nottingham, but to this the playwright poignantly adds a list of the kindnesses of Scarlet's family to Warman (and to Warman's father!), including the original preferment of Warman to his lord (i.e., the Earl of Huntingdon) and, with deliberate irony, a rescue from the gallows (d3v).

So the small connections multiply. Warman gloats just before the rescue that Scarlet and Scathlock had hoped to be aided by the Earl of Huntingdon, whose bankruptcy (Warman thinks) puts such aid out of the question (d4); a casual line from Little John reveals Robin's earlier benevolence to the widow Scarlet (d1v); Friar Tuck, not yet of Robin's company, is brought into the scene as confessor to the prisoners, and when Robin wishes to learn something about Tuck's background, he asks Scarlet, who just happens to know (d4v); Tuck turns out to be of the same abbey as Robin's wicked uncle, the Prior, and happens to be acquainted with Jinny (f2v), who in turn is not only the sweetheart of Much but the daughter of the widow Scarlet as well (e4v). Few of these minor revelations have any significance at all beyond the moment of their occurrence—they contribute not to the plot, but to the general dramatic illusion of the coherence of events.

The same tendency is evident in *The Death*. Lord Bruce is kinsman not only to Hugh le Brun, whose activities are bothering King John toward the beginning of the play (E2v), but to Fitzwater too (E3v)—unhistorically, in both cases. Hubert, later in the play, happens to know (and, of course, to mention casually to King John) that the Abbess of Dunmow is carrying on with a monk of Bury (I1); it later transpires (as soon as it is dramatically indispensable) that this same monk has long pestered John for his infallible preferment to the office of Abbot, and can therefore be induced to levy some helpful pressure on Matilda through the Abbess (I2v). When Matilda is to be wooed by one Wigmore, it is done by proxy: one of the Bruces appears with the mission of excusing the proxy suit, and the chosen vicar turns out to be Leicester (E3v). The same scene reveals an even more notable economy in the process of being instituted: it originally included both Fitzwater and his son, but Mundy apparently discovered that Young Bruce, already designed into other actions of the play, could profitably absorb the functions of Fitzwater's son. He therefore altered his plans for Young Bruce and moved him into this scene to replace the now supererogatory Young Fitzwater, who was then put completely out of existence. The extant text has arrested the process of composition just before the full realisation of the change.

The spirit of economy (occasionally bordering, like some of the examples already cited, on absurd coincidence) is operative in matters of place as well. When Robert and Matilda first meet with Little John and Much in Sherwood Forest, the forthcoming execution of Scarlet and Scathlock chances to be mentioned, whereupon Little John observes that they happen to be within sight of both the appointed gallows-tree and the widow Scarlet's house (d1v). When Fitzwater is exiled in *The Death*, he requests permission to visit Matilda once more and is warned that he has only until sunset; he promptly catches sight of Dunmow Abbey, and the transition to the next scene does not demand the clearing of the stage (H4–4v).

The well-known conventional flexibility of the Elizabethan stage is not often glaringly abused in the Huntingdon plays, but Mundy often does exploit its resources to effect a simple shift of location where another writer might have cleared the stage first. The Huntingdon plays manage to include more dialogue in their scenes than is the average for the extant plays of the time, and they achieve this not through a diminution of action and diversity but by bringing stage conventions to the aid of continuity. *The Downfall* moves from Little John's struggle with the Sheriff through Robert's tryst and escape to Prince John's uprising against Ely, without ever clearing the stage (b4–d1); and *The Death* plays without a break a sequence that goes from the last valiant stand of Fitzwater and his allies through their defeat and capture, through Fitzwater's last interview with Matilda at Dunmow, through King John's plotting with the monk and with the messenger Brand, to Hubert's soliloquy on loyalty (H2v–13v). This is not to say that Mundy never wrote two scenes when they could be reduced to one, nor that he handled the stage with remarkable subtlety, but merely that he had adequately learned his lessons at the theatres: he knew the tricks of stagecraft and was sensible of the dramatic value of on-stage transitions, occasionally taking some trouble to avoid clearing the stage unnecessarily.

Such strategies as these reveal the playwright's concern for the coherence of his play, and the more ambitious of them achieve enhanced coherence at a fairly deep level of organisation. But the majority are superficial and localised, adequate to promote the illusion of order where it is temporarily needed but careless of long-range effects.

The Huntingdon plays therefore move constantly but not consistently, balanced precariously on the edge of the events of the moment and the devices required to justify them. For minor movements, this causes little difficulty. Mundy is fairly careful to motivate entrances and exits, and can usually do so on the spot without egregious awkwardness (a notable exception being his sudden invention of an illness for the absent Archbishop of York (g2v) in order that the Prior might be temporarily free to soliloquise and receive some bad news from messengers). But this kind of management is less satisfactory when the playwright must organise a more complex action or order a substantial reversal. Attempts to handle such problems only when they occur, without adequate prior planning, are bound to produce cumbersome results, especially if the playwright tends to work on the level of dramatic illusion rather than in deeper plot-organisation.

For instance: before he reforms and joins Robin's band, Friar Tuck proposes to help the Prior by trapping Robin. He forms a plan involving the unwitting assistance of Jinny. Jinny, says Friar Tuck,

> Loves, and is belov'd of Much the millers sonne,
> If I can get the girle to goe with mee,
> Disguis'd in habit, like a Pedlers mort,
> Ile serve this Execution, on my life.   (f2v)

The point of the disguise is obviously that they might avoid the suspicion of the outlaws. But what is the point of his mentioning the mutual love of Jinny and Much? Presumably, it is that her visit would therefore not be suspicious, an advantage that is plainly cancelled by the proposed disguise—and in any event a factor which must inevitably (except in such a play as this) make a disguised visit to the greenwood a most curious proposition from Jinny's point of view. What seems to have happened is that Mundy, faced with the problem of getting Tuck and Jinny to the greenwood, thought of two ways of solving it and used them both, not noticing that they were incompatible. To be safe, when he brings Jinny on a few lines later, he has her soliloquising an already formed intention to go to the greenwood. A similar overcompensation occurs in *The Death* when Mundy takes on the considerable job of repairing the character of King John after his cruelties have taken their final toll. The time has now come for the reconciliation required to present a united England against the threat of French invasion, and to resolve the play. But John's reputation is at its nadir: Matilda has been poisoned, and Bruce has just shown to the assembled company the bodies of his mother and brother, starved by the King's command. This is quite a gap for an on-the-spot bridging, but the absence of long-range planning left Mundy no choice. John now reveals, for the first time, that he had had second thoughts about the famishment of the Bruces, had ordered his agent Brand to take them food, and had been assured by Brand that he had already, out of pity, left food for them. Sir William Blunt, warden of the castle, supports John's story,

> Which argues in that point his innocence:
> Brand did beare in a months provision;
> But lockt it like a villaine, farre from them:
> And lockt them in a place where no mans eare
> Might heare their lamentable wofull mones:
> For all the issue both of vent and light,
> Came from a loover at the towers toppe,
> Till now Lord Bruse made open this wide gappe.
>   (L3)

The entire speech is a multiple rationalisation. Brand must bear the blame that John might be forgivable; Blunt must be provided with an excuse for not having aided the captives; and his excuse (the inaccessibility of the Bruces' prison) must be clarified to explain its apparent incompatibility with the victims' very obvious accessibility on the upper stage. The dramatist is not for a moment daunted by the patent absurdity of an argument which supposes that Brand, under orders to lock up the Bruces without food, carried along a month's supply anyway (even though he had not the least intention of giving it to them) and then relieved the King with an unnecessary lie that would undoubtedly have cost him his head as soon as the King discovered the truth. Nor does Mundy seem to notice that Blunt's innocent awareness of the Bruces' imprisonment makes his subsequent ignorance the more culpable, or that his testimony about the month's food half-substantiates Brand's story but has nothing at all to do with the support of John's. The speech is a specimen of expedient ingenuity, designed to excuse John by villifying Brand, while keeping Blunt unstained. The playwright is not concerned with piecing together an airtight argument but rather with piling on enough testimony to convince the audience. It would probably serve its purpose to the drowsy ear in the late afternoon at the Rose, and that was enough.

Such accidental inconsistency is a characteristic feature of the Huntingdon plays. Mundy often turned his attention so exclusively to the exigencies of the present action that he failed to retain that general sense of tact required for a consistently intelligible unity of design. It is hard to avoid the conclusion that he cared little for such unity. The Huntingdon plays are designed to provide a continuity of interesting action, which is not the most aesthetically ambitious form of design but adequate for dramatic entertainment—and certainly easier to put together in two or three weeks[10] than loftier conceptions.

It is in this regard that the modern reader's natural sympathy with Elizabethan drama most clearly falters. The strong contemporary bias for aesthetic unity and against 'contrivance' is deeply inbred, and the satisfaction of these canons still largely determines our ranking of early dramatists. It is difficult for us to see that these were not characteristic Elizabethan prejudices, that in fact many playwrights do not seem to have particularly valued them—and that even those who satisfy them

[10] Few of the plays recorded in Henslowe's *Diary* during this period seem to have taken longer than three weeks between their initial approval and their final delivery. Henslowe occasionally sets a deadline. Mundy was given two weeks to produce a comedy for which he contracted on 9 August 1598 (*Diary*, f. 49: cf. deadlines given to other playwrights on folios 43v, 45, 46, and 47v, ranging between one and three weeks).

did not necessarily consider this their most notable achievement. To the extent that we feel driven to explain all Elizabethan stage foolery by pointing patronisingly at the groundlings or by invoking a hidden thematic relevance; to the extent that we feel obliged to adjust our interpretations of characters and of speeches in order to preserve psychological truth; to the extent that we permit ourselves to be disappointed by structural imbalances, mystified (or impressed) by inconsistencies in time, and embarrassed by possible improbabilities, we shall find it hard to understand why *The Downfall* was selected to play at Court and how its author acquired his reputation. Indeed, we shall find it hard to accept in the greatest Elizabethan dramatists many things for which we now frequently feel obliged to find excuses. I do not mean to imply, of course, that the order in Jonson's plots or in Shakespeare's patterns of imagery is merely accidental; but I do wish to suggest that it would be critically fruitful to consider the Huntingdon plays as dramaturgical paradigms rather than as examples of theatrical inadequacy. It is true that Mundy falls short of Jonson and Shakespeare. But it is more accurate to say that Shakespeare and Jonson go beyond Mundy. The evidence suggests that it is not in the great plays but in the products of successful standard hackwriting that the basic principles of late Elizabethan dramatic composition are to be most clearly exemplified and the relevant critical standards most clearly revealed.

Accordingly, the handling of character in the Huntingdon plays is superficial, rather crude, but eminently practical. Main characters are organised, as one would expect, according to their functions in the action and their moral dispositions (excluding comic characters, who are typically excused both from affecting the plot and from having an ethical dimension). Characters are usually quite good or quite nasty. Occasionally a moral middle-ground emerges, but this is a highly unstable state, and usually seems to be due to the playwright's carelessness rather than to his design: normally, the middle-ground is crossed in a single leap. Conversions and lapses are both ordinarily complete, at least temporarily.

The moral positions of characters are of course intimately connected with their functions in the plot, and both of these are rather arbitrary and unpredictable in the Huntingdon plays. Consequently, each major change of circumstances redefines those characters who cause it, but can (and occasionally does) threaten the intelligibility of those who are less directly involved. Mundy frequently provides the necessary information by resorting to the expedient of having them redefine themselves by stating their reactions to what has transpired, either in group discussions or in asides. The device is crude, but it preserves order.

Not surprisingly, there is a tendency to a certain extravagance in the way characters represent their positions. There was no point in taxing the Rose's patrons with finesse. Robin Hood not only treats his betrayers with kindness when they repent—he releases the unrepentant Doncaster from a just captivity and sends him off with a hundred pounds to comfort him (B1). When Queen Eleanor and Prince John are thwarted in their attempt to prevent the escape of Earl Robert and his sweetheart, the Queen resolves to 'turne love, to never changing hate', while John vows to follow Robert 'with revengefull murdrous hate' (c3v), though neither's animus is put to any further dramatic purpose. Warman's despair (i4–4v) and Young Bruce's angry grief (L1–1v) are uttered at length, in the most superlative terms, and Lady Bruce's gratitude for a trifling gesture of mercy from King John is hardly less extreme (G2). Brand chokes when he accidentally pronounces the word 'honest' (K2), and Doncaster, accused of raping a nun, modestly acknowledges a thousand other victims (C3).

The same kind of extravagance is sometimes applied to events. The Prior must not only be banished, but have his barns accidentally destroyed to reinforce the point (g3); and Warman, once fallen, encounters and is abused by three persons to whom he once was kind (i2v–4)— no kindness of his having been mentioned anywhere in the play until it could be put to this use. King John is likewise confronted simultaneously with the famished Bruces, poisoned Matilda, a French invasion, and the threatened defection of his most valiant peers (L4v).

Plays constructed with such heavy-handedness cannot be expected to be inhabited by flexible characters, and flexibility is unnecessary when action can be contrived without it. Hearts can be changed in a twinkling by an encounter with catastrophe or a stroke of good fortune. There is therefore no need for gradual awakening or for the complexities of character by which substantial changes can be dramatically anticipated. Abrupt reversals of character have their own conventional logic on the Elizabethan stage. But, more usefully still, that logic is not inexorable. The dramatist may arbitrarily make his characters react to any event in whatever way best suits the requirements of the plot. Warman and the Prior both lose everything, escape to the greenwood, and are charitably received by Robin Hood. They react differently, but only because it is convenient to have them do so. The significance of any event is entirely up to the playwright if, instead of building laws of behaviour into his characters, he rather metes out decisions, as he goes along, from the general law that action must be sustained. Such a method has its price, for coherence is easily sacrificed to expediency; but it does sustain the action.

Action is not, of course, Mundy's exclusive concern in the Huntingdon plays. The ethical bias of the Elizabethan stage was strong (note its importance in Mundy's handling of character), and the Huntingdon plays frequently pause to reflect on their own action in order to press home, at least temporarily, a general moral conclusion. Both plays, for instance, deal with types of rebellion and thus call dramatically into question important principles of civil order; each accordingly seizes a critical moment to put into the mouth of a sympathetic character an eloquent defence of the universal and inviolable duty of obedience.[11] But in themes as well as actions, these are largely piecemeal plays.

Nothing could make clearer Mundy's failure to achieve thematic coherence than his almost total disregard of the best opportunities to fix the theme of obedience as a necessary implication of the action. Toward the end of *The Downfall*, the reconciliation is secured through the submission to Richard of those who had opposed him in his absence, concluding with the usurping Prince John. Any one of these characters would provide a splendid opportunity for clinching the principle of obedience: in a speech of penitent submission all the truths voiced earlier by the indignant Leicester could be finally affirmed. Mundy lets the opportunity pass. The rebels submit, and are reinstated, offstage, and nothing is said again about their temporary defection. Prince John never utters a remorseful word to the King whom he betrayed— despite the example given the dramatist in Holinshed's account. A similar opportunity arises at the end of *The Death*, with a similar result. Leicester proposes to escape the tyranny of King John by accepting the rule of the Dauphin. The principle of dutiful obedience to a legitimate king, the theme of Hubert's earlier soliloquy, is the obvious argument for the loyalists to use; instead, they plead that Frenchmen (and particularly King Louis) cannot be trusted, that the Dauphin Louis could be worse than John for all they know, and that John is deeply remorseful (M1–1v). The reconciliation is secured on the strength of these

[11] Leicester in *The Downfall*, h2–2v; Hubert in *The Death*, I3–3v.

arguments, and the best chance for clinching the duty of obedience is allowed to pass.

These are missed opportunities certainly, but probably not missed simply through carelessness. Leicester's outrage at usurpation and Hubert's sense of duty serve dramatic purposes in their respective places. It may never have occurred to our playwright that those purposes might be thought sufficiently relevant to later scenes and situations to dictate the way in which they should be handled, when a resolution could be found for the plot without arguments from political philosophy. The duty of obedience was not a thematic preoccupation for the author of the Huntingdon plays, but an incidental general reflection. This is the case with the majority of the general reflections in these plays: they are occasioned by circumstances and cannot be considered any more universal than the scenes in which they fall.

The closest the Huntingdon plays get to an essential theme is through their recurrent emphasis upon the virtue and power of charitable forgiveness. The central figures, Robin Hood and Matilda, are both paragons of generosity, and both succeed in thawing the vices of others merely by pardoning them. But even this lacks the contagion necessary for the establishment of a theme. This kind of charity is a property of Robin and Matilda, not of the plays. The dying Robin asks the repentant Prior to take advantage of the legal loophole allowed to clerics and live on, a better man, and begs King Richard to spare his life: 'Let sweete forgivenesse be my passing bell' (C4). Richard promptly sentences the Prior to death. King John's final reformation, which might appropriately have been occasioned by Matilda's dying forgiveness, arises simply from the horror of his deeds. His victim's charity is not even reported to him. Thus even the most pervasive thematic idea is only a particular effect that never acquires the proportions by which the plays might be drawn to assume its shape. Thoughts and principles are presented as the reactions of specific characters to specific circumstances, not as the general truths discovered by life in action. This was apparently enough to satisfy not only critical standards but even the Elizabethan appetite for moralising. If a play generally encouraged the audience to do good and avoid evil, the dramatist could fully discharge his moral obligations merely by occasionally letting his characters toss off a weighty precept. It was not necessary to let this interfere with his main dramatic business. Indeed, it might be wasted effort to blend the two more closely—a book published in 1596 recommends the plays of

Sophocles and Euripides as examples of the sort of tragedy most fit for our reading: 'honest and full of grave sentences, interlaced with pleasaunt talke'.[12]

There is yet another correlative to the general organisation of the Huntingdon plays to be found in the medium of expression. These are verse-plays, reserving prose almost exclusively for the use of comic characters, in accordance with the common practice of the time. But they are written in verse probably only because verse had become the conventional dramatic medium. They rely primarily on a direct and unambitious style, using it as an essentially transparent medium through which events, character-traits, and the connections of the plot may be easily viewed. Metaphor and simile are allotted sparingly and are more often ornamental than functional when used. The prosody is also simple: a straight end-stopped iambic pentameter is the rule throughout both plays, but just carelessly enough to permit the frequent occurrence of the rawest sort of padding to achieve regularisation (e.g., 'Let him, let him, let him make thee as sad' [b1]), as well as both hypersyllabic and hyposyllabic lines.

This is not to say that the Huntingdon plays are deliberately unpoetic, or even that Mundy declined to concern himself with poetic effects. Nearly a third of the lines are rhymed (and sometimes cross-rhymed); this, together with the frequent displacements of normal word-order made to secure the rhymes, can even give the reader an impression of a certain self-consciousness about poetry. If such an impression is seriously damaged by the occurrence of

> O Honourable Awbery de Vere,
> Let sorrow in a sable sute appeare (L4),

it is nevertheless reinforced by a passage like this, in which the parenthetical betrays just such a self-consciousness:

> Now are yee, worthy and resolved men,
> Come to the cage where the uncleane birds bide,
> That tyre on all the faire flight in the Realme.
> Summon this Castle, or (to keepe my words)
> This cage of night-hid owles, light-flying birds.   (G2)

But that is, of course, precisely the point. Passages like this, like Prince John's sonnet-like address to Matilda (k3v), like Hubert's defence of

---

12 *Delectable Demands and Pleasant Questions, with their Several Answers.*

poetry (E2), stand out somewhat awkwardly from the surrounding lines, because the Huntingdon plays use two different styles which are never successfully blended. There is a static and adorned style, highly metaphorical and well suited for the elaboration of a mood or the vivid narration of an event; and there is a kinetic and plain style, direct and well suited for carrying the flow of dramatic action. The former usually appears at a pause in the action: a reflective soliloquy, a lament, a digression, a narration. When the action picks up again, the more 'poetical' style yields to the more plain. It is a practical solution. Each style is nicely adapted to the kind of dramatic job for which it is employed; stylistic homogeneity would unnecessarily compromise both of them—and, in addition, would diminish the variety valued on the Elizabethan stage.

For anyone attached to general consistency, bathos and anticlimax occur frequently in the Huntingdon plays, as a result of the abruptness with which they move from one event or mood into another. Our playwright either had no gift for graceful transition, or simply considered grace an unnecessary and dispensable dramatic luxury. After their rescue from the hangman, Scarlet and Scathlock entertain their audience with a lively narration of their past outlaw history; when they are done, Mundy puts into the mouth of their new master the words which will serve to shift the conversation to the next topic: 'Of that enough' (f1). Similarly, Mundy has no scruple about leaving a flurry of heroics stranded in mid-air. Leicester works himself into a peak of fervour with a long speech to his troops, ending with 'Courage, upon them, till wee cannot stand' (h2v), only to discover that his seeming opponent is a dear friend who is quite nonplussed at the sight. The emotion or diversion is itself satisfying, and may be abandoned abruptly once it had served its purpose.

Again and again the artistic blemishes of the Huntingdon plays seem to point this same neglect of the larger effects in favour of the smaller and more immediate. Mundy was usually careful to see that what happens at a particular moment is intelligible and appropriate, but he demanded an intelligibility only of the most practical and limited kind (often confined to explaining away evident difficulties) and his criteria of appropriateness were essentially those of dramatic expediency, with arbitrariness usually dominating over the inner logic of character and situation. If a certain turn of events can arrange the plot more tidily or vary it entertainingly, the circumstances and information necessary for its minimum justification can be provided. To make things happen and resolve them in the end, to garnish scenes with moments of poetry and flights of emotion, to fill the stage with a continuity of interesting action—to do all this is to build an entertaining play, which is none the less entertaining for being irregular in the texture of its moods and verse and events and characters.

There were some pains taken with the overall construction of the Huntingdon plays, and there is abundant evidence to demonstrate that their author was not always careless of the coherence and total effect of his work. But his primary concern was with the immediate require-ments of the action, moment to moment, and often at the cost of those gradual transitions and overall strategies that are indispensable for the achievement of a totally satisfying artistry. This may be a considerable failing from the aesthetic point of view; yet the Huntingdon plays nevertheless remain interesting and perhaps even exciting from moment to moment—and surely their author would have asked no higher praise than this. This was enough for the professional hack. It apparently satisfied the patrons of the Rose. It wasn't until November that the prospect of a more discriminating audience drove the Admiral's Men to hire Henry Chettle 'for mendinge of Roben hood for the corte' (*Diary*, f. 52). He was an appropriate choice for putting the finishing touches on Mundy's hackwork. Not only had he been involved, at least temporarily (and perhaps substantially), in the composition of *The Death*—he had also kept in condition through the intervening eight months by contributing to more than a dozen other plays.

Note

Biography. Ben Jonson was the posthumous son of a 'grave minister of the gospel'; he was born in or near London in 1573 and educated at Westminster School under the antiquary, William Camden. He was probably taken from school and put to his step-father's trade of bricklayer in 1588. He seems to have left this uncongenial trade in 1591–2 to serve as a soldier in the Low Countries and, later, to join a company of actors. He married in November, 1594. By 1597 he was writing plays for Henslowe. In 1598 he killed an actor in a duel (for which he was imprisoned and branded as a felon), became a Roman Catholic in prison (and remained one for twelve years), and saw his *Every Man in His Humour* performed by the Lord Chamberlain's Men. On the accession of James I, he was commissioned to write court masques and wrote thirty masques and entertainments during James's reign. In 1616 James granted him a pension of 100 marks a year for life; he was then at the height of his fortunes, having friends, patrons, and followers among the nobility, men of affairs, scholars, and poets. In July, 1619, he was granted an honorary M.A. degree at Oxford— an act without parallel in the career of any Jacobean dramatist. In 1623 he may have been lecturing on rhetoric at Gresham College in London. In 1628 he had a stroke which rendered him an invalid until he died in 1637.

Works. His greatest comedies are *Volpone* (1606), *Epicoene* (1609), *The Alchemist* (1610), and *Bartholomew Fair* (1614). Seven comedies, masques, non-dramatic poems, and his two tragedies, *Sejanus* (1603) and *Catiline* (1611), were published under Jonson's close supervision, as his *Works*, in a folio of 1616. This was reprinted in 1640, and a second volume published containing five further comedies, as *Bartholomew Fair, The Devil is an Ass* (1616), and *The Magnetic Lady* (1632), and masques, two dramatic fragments, poems, a translation of Horace's *Art of Poetry*, a grammar, and 'Observations on Poetry and Eloquence', called *Timber*.

Modern Editions. The *Works* are edited by C. H. Herford and P. and E. M. Simpson (11 vols., 1925–52); quotations in the following chapter are from this edition. There is an edition in the Everyman Library (2 vols., 1910).

Scholarship and Criticism. The best biography is still that of Herford in *The Works* cited above. This edition also contains generally sound introductions to each of the plays, and commentaries which are rich in analogues, though often disappointing in critical comment. Recent general studies of the plays have been written by J. Enck, C. Thayer, and R. Knoll. L. C. Knights has a concise chapter in *The Age of Shakespeare*, ed. B. Ford (1955). Studies especially concerned with the early plays are C. R. Baskervill, *English Elements in Jonson's Early Comedy* (1911); O. J. Campbell, *Comicall Satyre and Shakespeare's 'Troilus and Cressida'* (1938); A. H. King, *The Language of Satirized Characters in Poetaster: a Socio-Stylistic Analysis* (1941); J. Barish, *Ben Jonson and the Language*

X

Ben Jonson: The Makings of the Dramatist (1596–1602)

EDWARD B. PARTRIDGE

★

IF one were to judge Jonson's development as a dramatist simply on the evidence of the authoritative Folio of 1616, one might be badly deceived. It makes Jonson look like a dramatist who sprang, fully armed, out of the Apollo chamber, ready to compose a series of maturely conceived, carefully written, and scrupulously edited plays. The Folio, to be sure, contains early work—the two *Every Man* plays, *Cynthia's Revels*, and *Poetaster*. Yet the *Every Man In* printed in the Folio is a fully revised version, possibly finished as late as 1610–12 and not the play as first performed in 1598 or as first published in the Quarto of 1601. And most of the other early plays are carefully revised texts, some including matter never heard or printed before (such as the satire on the court in Acts III and V of *Cynthia's Revels*) or heard once and printed for the first time (the 'Apologetical Dialogue' of *Poetaster*). Furthermore, the Folio deliberately excluded at least three kinds of plays:

1. A play like *The Case is Altered* which was published as his, but which he seems to have regarded as too crudely experimental to be given a place in his canon.

2. Plays like *Eastward Ho*, of which he was only part-author.

3. Plays which he had written, but had not published and refused

---

of Prose Comedy (1960); J. Penniman, *The War of the Theatres* (1897); R. Small, *The Stage-Quarrel between Ben Jonson and the So-called Poetasters* (1899). The books by Campbell, King, and Barish are particularly valuable. The editions of the early plays in the Yale Studies of English are still helpful for their annotations.

to put in his published works. One of these may have been *A Tale of a Tub*, perhaps first produced in 1596, but later revised and produced again in 1633. Another may have been the lost *Richard Crookback*, a history play for which he was paid by Henslowe in 1602.

In other words, by such revisions and exclusions, the Folio shows us a mature craftsman rather than an apprentice.

To gain a sense of Jonson as apprentice or even journeyman is not easy. Some of his early work was suppressed. *The Isle of Dogs* (1597), which he worked on with Thomas Nashe, was so completely suppressed that only its title and its reputation for seditiousness remain. Some has been lost. His supposed collaborations with Dekker such as *The Page of Plymouth* (1599) and with Dekker and Chettle, *Robert, King of Scots* (1599), were generally the kind of history or romantic tragedy that Jonson would have felt well lost. Any young man learning his craft as a playwright in the 1590's, even one as independent as Jonson, almost inevitably would have collaborated with others as 'co-adjutor, / Novice, journey-man' (*Volpone*, Pro., 17). Trying to track down such collaboration at any time is difficult, but it is especially difficult in the four middle years of the 1590's when, according to A. Harbage and S. Schoenbaum, many anonymous plays are known of but are presumably lost. Since even conjecturing how much hand Jonson had in these lost or fragmentary plays would be profitless, we are finally thrown back on the Folio, with such help from the Quartos as we can get, and on an early play, *The Case is Altered* (published in 1609, but apparently produced in 1597) which was not in the Folio. We ought to rule out *A Tale of a Tub*, I think, because, though a first version may have been written in the 1590's, the text we have was so thoroughly reworked for its 1633 production that it ought not be admitted as evidence of Jonson's early craftmanship.

*   *   *

We might begin by asking what abilities a dramatist must have. First of all, he must be able to conceive and render a series of coherently related events, an 'action', which he can credibly resolve. Since such an action involves agents, he must be able to conceive characters and render them at least temporarily believable. Good drama requires agents whose ethos is significant and an action whose imitation is itself a pleasure to see and hear. Then agents who act, to some degree, as human beings are involved in two processes—thinking and speaking—which a dramatist must learn how to represent economically and decorously to make his imitation credible, significant, and beautiful. Speech, whether arranged colloquially or metrically or melodically, involves the dramatist in something like a score which he must orchestrate. Since such agents are impersonated by actors who perform on a stage, even if only in the mind's eye, the dramatist must learn how to use the theatrical conventions of his time or to transform them for his own benefit. All of these abilities finally must unite in one: the ability to arouse and control the requisite emotional states of an audience.

How such emotions are aroused is hard to say; that they *are* seems evident. Let us simply say here that a spectator at a play receives a continual rain of ideas and of visual and auditory images from the spoken words, the represented action, and the spectacle of the play; that his imagination, controlled by the developing action, fuses these ideas and images into an experience that prolongs and intensifies their sensory effect; and that this psychic prolonging and intensifying produce the spectator's emotional reaction to the play. The quality and intensity of an audience's emotions, though highly variable and rarely easy for the dramatist to calculate, can be modified, if not controlled, by the kind of action he represents and the social and moral nature of the agents he chooses, by the words he gives them to say and the syntactic and prosodic art he brings to their dialogue (and, finally, of course, by the kind of production the whole play receives).

While he is acquiring such necessary abilities, the dramatist must work out at least provisional answers to three questions: what does he conceive his function to be? what kind of audience does he want to judge his work? what, in the whole universe of the past and the present, is he going to draw on for his subject matter and how is he going to use it in his imitation? In the following discussion we shall see how Jonson, one of the most self-conscious of English writers, deliberately worked out answers to the first two of these questions in his early plays—answers which he generously shared with his contemporaries. Like any good artist, he spent most of his life seeking different answers to the third question; even in his earliest extant plays we find radically different solutions to the problem of what raw materials he should use and how he should use them decorously.

Since I shall not specifically deal with the sources of Jonson's plays later, I make a brief comment on them here. Earlier critics, such as

Dryden, Upton, and Gifford, emphasised the classical sources for the situations, the characters, the ideas, and the images of his plays; more recent critics, such as C. R. Baskervill and L. C. Knights, the medieval English or contemporary sources. Each emphasis is, to some extent, right. In truth, as the commentaries of Herford and Simpson indicate, Jonson, like Shakespeare, drew materials from any available source— ancient or modern, English or foreign. But, eclectic as his borrowing was, his values and his point of view were distinctly his own: neither simply 'classical' (though he drew freely on Latin culture), nor simply 'contemporary' (though he always gave life to what was ancient and domesticated what was foreign).

So much has been made of Jonson's use of the classics, and made so competently by Herford, for example, in his introduction to *Poetaster*, that I do not wish to consider it here. Nor do I wish to go over the ground that Baskervill—to counteract the notion of Jonson as borrowing chiefly from the classics—fully explored, except to say that necessary as his emphasis on the English and medieval roots of Jonson's work is, it can lead one to some dubious conclusions. I can not really believe that 'the whole mood of middle-class England' enters into Jonson's work or that Jonson was 'in accord with the democratic spirit of the average Englishman' (pp. 21-2). Even if I could admit that there was a middle-class sentiment in Tudor England (and J. Hexter argues cogently against it[1]), I find it hard to accept a chief satirist of London citizens as its exemplar. 'Democratic', too, seems scarcely the word to apply to a dramatist whose severest criticism was given to the very men—the newly rich and the ignorantly powerful—who, in his view, were intent on destroying the social hierarchy of England. More convincing than these conclusions is Baskervill's discussion of Jonson's debts to medieval allegorising and to contemporary dramatists, though even here one must be wary of seeing an influence where there is only a similarity. Obviously, dramatists learn from each other. Jonson may have learned more what he did not want to do, than what he did want to do, from seeing what others had done. He did not want his diction to be so grotesque as Marston's. He did not want to handle eccentrics so affectionately as Dekker handled them. So great is his reaction from some of the practices of his contemporaries that I am tempted to use Herford's statement about *Every Man In*—'Few Elizabethan plays owe less, in fact, to the stimulus or guidance of previous literature' (i. 345)—

[1] *Reappraisals in History* (1962), pp. 78 ff.

as an estimate of how much he borrowed from the dramatic work of his contemporaries. This poet who, as Dryden said, 'invades authors like a monarch' on the principle that to imitate is to convert the substance or riches of another to one's own use, rarely found the dramatic technique of his contemporaries either substantial or rich enough to convert to his own use. The crucial word, of course, is 'convert'—to transform. The whole world was there to be transformed, but the form Jonson finally created was so thoroughly his own that its derivations are much harder to discover than are the sources of the subject matter they are instrumental in converting. At any rate, I shall concern myself neither with the sources of his subject matter nor with the few debts he must have owed to the technique even of contemporaries he often criticised, but with the evidence in the plays themselves of his growing ability as a dramatist.

*   *   *

The Case is Altered (1597) and the first version of *Every Man in His Humour* (1598) show a young dramatist feeling his way, working out a set of characters, and learning how to conduct an action and control a point of view. In neither play does he work out the method that he worked out, or reach the control that he reached, in the plays after 1605. In fact, as early as *Every Man out of His Humour* (1599), he discarded the pattern which he had worked out in *Every Man In*. In both the earlier plays he sets his action in Italy, goes to classical sources for some of the situations he dramatises, and joins—in *The Case is Altered*, lightly; in *Every Man In*, more closely—two distinct actions. Both plays reveal a playwright who was still derivative in his situations and characterisations; both, but especially *Every Man In*, foreshadow a greater dramatist with an observant eye, a remarkable architectonic skill, and a unique attitude.

In its sources, its setting, and its art *The Case is Altered* reveals an Elizabethan which the Jacobean Jonson clearly repudiated. The sources of the plot are Plautus' *Captivi* and *Aulularia*, and the fusion of them shows Jonson doing to Plautus what Plautus had done to Menander. He tries to combine comic and latently melodramatic elements in the Shakespearean pattern without being able to follow the analogical method or attain the mood of Shakespeare's comedy. Thus, in the main plot appears a father with two daughters and two sons, one lost in infancy and saved from his father's rage only by a last minute revelation;

P

and, in the minor plot, a father with one daughter who has a host of admirers. Throughout the play are evidences of inexperience. I. iv and v, though comic enough, betray the hand of an apprentice who has not learned how to handle exposition economically. The satire on Antony Balladino, which may have been interpolated after an early production, is neither closely related to the action nor adequately exploited after the first act. The erotic entanglements of two daughters and four suitors scarcely seem worth the effort comically. And the discoveries at the end of the play turn out to be more melodramatic than comic. Never again would Jonson, later the master of comic dénouements, resolve his play so irresolutely. All in all, the whole play starts more hares than it runs down. The brain which creates but does not sufficiently exploit five different lovers for Rachel, and four different comic servants, may have an Elizabethan richness, but it does not have a Jonsonian economy. Still, with all its weaknesses, it everywhere suggests that the dramatist who can do this much can do a great deal more. Already there are signs of the unique signature of Jonson. One of these is the imaginative use of the motif of the altered case (where 'case' means a change in love, a loss of gold, a new suit of clothes, a rise in status, and an ironic reversal). Another is the language of Juniper, a first sketch of the grandiloquent speech which Jonson was to exploit, in different ways, in his later plays. A third is, as Herford puts it, 'his extraordinary gift of inventing characteristic traits', a gift already mature (i. 313). There are two scenes in particular which show his early grasp of complex comic techniques: one, V. viii, is a scene of overhearing, though it is more melodramatic than strictly comic; the other, V. xi, involves a nearly symmetrical cross questioning. Both techniques indicate an early interest in the elaborate plot construction which his major plays illustrate.[2]

In *Every Man In*, even in its Quarto version, we are on more secure ground.[3] The first two Acts develop the two main lines of comic

[2] J. Enck has written a suggestive interpretation of *The Case is Altered* in *Jonson and the Comic Truth* (1957), pp. 21-34.

[3] A striking proof of Jonson's maturity is his careful revision of *Every Man In* for inclusion in the 1616 Folio. Since three thorough discussions of this revision have been made, I shall not even summarise it here. The most systematic comparison of the two texts is that of C. Grabau in *Shakespeare Jahrbuch* (1902). H. H. Carter's edition of both texts in parallel columns is helpful. Herford's summary of what the changes reveal about Jonson is illuminating (i. 358-370).

action—Knowell Senior's concern for his wild young son, and Kitely's jealousy of his attractive young wife—and Jonson connects them skilfully by having Knowell Junior a close friend of Wellbred, Dame Kitely's brother. The coherence of these early scenes is strengthened by parallels, contrasts, and variations characteristic of the later Jonson, but new to the Jonson of 1598. In Act I the country gull, Stephen, helps us to get into proper focus both the town gull, Matthew, and the young gentleman, Edward Knowell. In Act II the balance and variation become pleasingly symmetrical: Downright, the country squire, puts down the town gull, while Wellbred, the city-bred half-brother of Downright, sets out to show up the country gull. A new grasp of comic character is clearly revealed by three minor figures, all traditional, yet each freshly drawn: Cob the waterman; Brainworm the wily servant; and Bobadill the braggart.

Having introduced, in the first two Acts, all his characters except Judge Clement, Jonson proceeds to show every man luxuriating in his humour in Act III. Stephen is melancholy because being melancholy is fashionable. Bobadill proves himself to be that most startling of braggarts—the braggart as melancholy pedant. Kitely exhibits his jealousy when he sees his pretty wife surrounded by gallants, but insists he is not worried at all. Brainworm adopts the disguise of Fitzsword to enjoy his trickery of everyone, but especially of his master, Knowell Senior. The fools make fools of themselves, and the gentlemen enjoy laughing at them. In this world enters a comically arbitrary judge, Clement, who immediately arrests Cob for speaking against tobacco.

But the real maturity of the play most strikingly appears in the way Jonson resolves his plot. He exploits the talents of two mischief-makers, Brainworm and Wellbred, to draw the actions more coherently together. Brainworm tells Knowell Senior that Junior has made an assignation with a citizen's wife at Cob's house; Wellbred manages to send both Dame Kitely and Kitely himself separately to the same house on the same errand—to retrieve an erring mate. By the end of the fourth Act the plot has wound itself into a series of false accusations: Dame Kitely accuses her husband of whoring; Kitely accuses his wife of lechery and his servant of pandering; Cob beats his wife for being a bawd; Brainworm arrests Stephen for stealing Downright's cloak and is himself caught by his own latest disguise. The world turns out to be an exhilaratingly ridiculous world to watch when all its immortals are in their humours. The final resolution takes place in a court of law whose judge is like a god with a sense of humour. He burns Matthew's bad poetry, welcomes Brainworm as a myth-maker, purges jealousy from Kitely, excludes such confirmed asses as Matthew and Bobadill, banishes discontent, anger, care, and jealousy, and dedicates the night to friendship, love, and laughter. Nowhere was Jonson later to reach so genial a conclusion, not even in *Bartholomew Fair*, which ends with another feast at the home of the scarcely god-like Justice Overdo. Even in this early play, though, we see a comedy of exclusion in which fools banish themselves from the society of sometimes rational men by their invincible folly. If comedy is a mimesis of the nature of things, as Jonson seems growingly aware it must be, then it can only show that, while all may be called, not all will come or, coming, be chosen.

Not even in *Every Man In* had Jonson worked out the kind of comic action which is central to his major plays—the plot in which a deceiver or baiter works on the follies of fools and, by the very process of fooling them, makes a fool of himself. His intriguers are in intrigue for the sport of it, and depend more on comic tricks than on the ridiculous weakness of others to succeed. Only Brainworm is caught by the extravagance of his own trickery. Only tentatively, too, do we find Jonson edging toward the theory that 'humour' is a ridiculous imbalance which needs to be purged before a man can be wiser. Thus when Wellbred, in a baiting mood, speculates on the possibility of a wife's poisoning her unwanted husband and is startled to see Kitely sicken at even the thought of it, he says, 'O, strange humour! my verie breath ha's poyson'd him', and advises Kitely, 'For shame, bee wiser' (IV. viii. 29). Closer to the concept of humour that Jonson describes in his next play is Piso's definition of it for Cob: 'as tis generally received in these daies, it is a monster bred in a man by selfe love, and affectation, and fed by folly' (Q, III. i. 156). This definition is sharpened in the Folio to Cash's 'It is a gentleman-like monster, bred, in the special gallantrie of our time, by affectation; and fed by folly' (III. iv. 20). In both passages Piso-Cash emphasises, as Jonson characteristically does in his later comedies, affectation as the source of the humours; in the Folio, Cash defines the source even more strictly: humour is bred in a man when he affects to be something in the society of men that he is not.

Jonson's next play reveals that, like Shakespeare, he was not content to do again what he had already done once successfully. Except for these two, almost no Elizabethan or Jacobean comic dramatist dared to adventure once he found his particular style and form. Dekker, Middleton, Beaumont and Fletcher, Chapman, and Massinger were generally content to keep on doing what they did well—for which we ought to be grateful. Each of Jonson's four greatest comedies, though uniquely his, reveals extraordinary differences in tone and style. His plays before 1603 reveal a comparable diversity in comic effect. At first sight *Every Man out of His Humour* (1599) might make one regret that Jonson so frequently followed the Senecan motto he appropriated—*Tanquam explorator*—and that he gave us this at times jarring play rather than another *Every Man In*. On the printed page *Every Man Out* begins as formidably as a Brahms symphony whose opening bars let you know you're in for it. The title-pages of the three Quarto editions with the words, 'as it was first composed by the author B. J. containing more than hath been publickely spoken or acted', indicate that Jonson was interested, as perhaps only Lyly had been before, in restoring or keeping the integrity of his play, which he conceived as a work distinct from, though not unrelated to, the performance it received. That he added short sketches of the characters indicates his interest in his plays being read. (To use such sketches as evidence that, as Una Ellis-Fermor argues, Jonson's nature was 'originally non-dramatic' or that, as Meredith charged, his humour is 'a scholar's excogitation of the comic' seems to me wrong, and demonstrably wrong as soon as we turn to the play itself.[4])

Nothing that Jonson had written up to this time, nothing, indeed, in the history of Elizabethan drama, quite prepares one for *Every Man Out*.[5] Its opening scene, called a Grex, is choral in function, though a dialogue in structure. Asper, the bitter satirist, rendered comic by his extravagant diction and extreme attitude, draws the attention of two commentators, Mitis and Cordatus, to the monstrousness of the time, especially of its wits and poets. All three emerge as genuine dramatic creations: Asper as a castigator so ridiculously intense in his harangue that he twice loses his train of discourse in his fury at fools; Mitis as a

[4] Ellis-Fermor, *The Jacobean Drama* (1958), p. 100; G. Meredith, 'Essay on the Idea of Comedy', *Works* (1911), xxiii, p. 11. Ellis-Fermor's criticism of Jonson seems to me uneven: brilliant on the structure of *The Alchemist;* quite wrong on the early plays.

[5] See O. Campbell, pp. 54–81 and G. Hibbard, *Thomas Nashe* (1962), pp. 74–5 for different theories of the play's derivations. Campbell thinks that Jonson deliberately tried to make the play 'a recognisable dramatic equivalent' of the formal verse satire prohibited by the bishops in 1599; Hibbard considers Nashe's prose satires a possible influence.

critic who reads plays by the rule book and who can be dragooned by a classical citation; Cordatus as that most difficult of voices to dramatise—a moderate and judicious gentleman who does not always avoid both dullness and pomposity.

This opening chorus reveals Jonson working out dramatically several things which neither of his previous plays deliberately concerns itself with. First, he is moving toward a conception of comic types and, at least provisionally, finding it not so much in the psychology of humours as in the affected use of such a psychology, chiefly by social climbers. When Asper summarises the basic physiology of the humours and metaphorically applies them to the general disposition of men (ll. 88–109), he is only expressing one conventional way of classifying people in the Renaissance, as we can now use Sheldon's terms to speak of somatypes. The original Jonsonian note is touched when Asper speaks of the abuses of the word 'humour', especially by those who affect a humour in 'an apish, or phantasticke straine' (l. 116). In other words, Jonson is not—at least here—using the faculty psychology for much more than a springboard into what later came to be his dominant concern: the comedy of affectation and imposture.

A second concern grows out of this first one: if the ridiculous characters are those who affect a humour, a satirist like Asper will then:

> scourge those apes;
> And to these courteous eyes oppose a mirrour
> As large as is the stage, whereon we act:
> Where we shall see the times deformitie
> Anatomis'd in every nerve, and sinnew,
> With constant courage, and contempt of feare.

No doubt Jonson is here stating what he conceives the purpose of any satirist to be. But we should not identify Asper with Jonson. Certainly no one as conscious of the dignity of a poet as Jonson was would want to be identified with the extreme Asper, whose principles are excellent, but whose behaviour is at times silly. We are forced to disengage the two even further at the end of the play when we hear that Asper has been acting the part of Macilente, certainly a thoroughly unpleasant mask. Jonson, we must remember, was writing a play and not advertisements of himself. Thus, while Asper the scourger and anatomiser of the time's deformity belongs to the long tradition of Aristophanes the *kathartes*, Asper the self-appointed squeezer of humours out of 'such spongie natures, / As licke up every idle vanitie' (ll. 145–6) is too closely associated with Macilente, whom Buffone pictures as 'soaking' in the humours of others like a dry crust (V. iv. 26), to be anything but comic. In other words, Jonson is unfailingly dramatic here (and elsewhere in these early plays) and sees, and wants us to see, even characters like Asper (with whose function as a satirist he might agree) still as much an object of ridicule as an ass like Fastidious Brisk (whose values he could only revile).

Finally, in this opening Grex, Jonson uses Asper and Cordatus to help educate his audience—in a way that not even a more tactful playwright than he could have made palatable. This educating takes three forms. One is Asper's sharp distinction between the all too vocal critics who spoil the play for others by their jests, and the 'attentive auditors' who 'come to feed their understanding parts'. Another is Cordatus' insistence, after he has given a short history of drama, that every age should enjoy the same free power to invent that Menander and Plautus had. A third, and the subtlest, is the use of Cordatus and, with qualifications, Mitis as judges throughout the play: as they are, so should judicious listeners be—sympathetic, understanding, and perhaps (unlike them) silent.

After this long opening scene, the play unfolds in a series of layers. The Prologue enters to bandy words impudently with Cordatus, and their exchange is interrupted by Carlo Buffone, who drinks a health to the audience, and introduces the play, which opens only on further experiments in perspective. First to appear is Macilente, the envious one who feels himself caught up in an ironic cure for his wounded soul:

> For every cordiall that my thoughts apply,
> Turnes to a cor'sive, and doth eate it farder.

Macilente lies down when he sees the next two characters coming. One of these, Buffone, comments on the other, Sogliardo, in an aside. By this introduction of his characters in three separate groups Jonson makes possible a complicated scene of reciprocal commenting. Buffone, seeing a good meal, plays up to Sogliardo, who wants desperately to be a gentleman, and seeing a fool, Buffone jeers sardonically at Sogliardo's stupidity. Intermittently, the hidden Macilente scoffs at 'mushrompe gentlemen' like Sogliardo and prostitutes like Buffone. Outside both of these groups and evaluating their actions are Cordatus and Mitis, who can act as the classical chorus in introducing a character, shifting a scene, emphasising a point, suggesting an attitude.[6] Thus, when Sordido, Sogliardo's almanac-reading brother, enters, Macilente demonstrates both how much he enjoys the strange humour of Sordido and how gnawingly envious he is of Sordido's wealth. Then, at the end of the Act, Cordatus points out that Macilente does not envy Sordido for being a wolf in the commonwealth, but for being rich and fortunate. Such a distinction leads naturally to the ethical distinction, important for the whole play, between envy or grief at another's happiness, and hatred or grief at another's monstrous actions.

The second Act carries on much that the first had begun. We see examples of those who affect such humours as a bright suit of clothes, a fastidious word, and unnatural behaviour. Two humours in particular are satirised. One is that of Puntarvolo, the knight whose mechanical posturing is exactly contrary to the ease of the true courtier. The other is the fashionable dress of Fastidious Brisk and of Fungoso, who wants to translate himself from a son of Sordido to a gallant like Fastidious by buying the latest apparel. Again two sets of observers are used to complicate the dramatic perspective. Again Macilente rails at chance and blind Fortune, but with such increasing venom that by the end of the Act he wants to drown the world and himself. Again, too, in the chorus at the end of the Act Cordatus continues to discuss the aesthetics of drama with Mitis.

In the third Act the anatomising of the time's deformity is shown in another mirror of England—the middle aisle of St. Paul's. (The other chief mirrors chosen are the country, the court, an inn, and a debtor's prison.) In the third Act new characters are brought in to illustrate new kinds of affected humours—Shift the pimp affecting courage and skill with a rapier; Clove and Orange, two coxcombs who pretend to be scholarly. For the first time some of the characters begin to be out of their humours: Orange and Clove dropping their affected erudition when they fail to impress Buffone and Puntarvolo; and Sordido giving up his wretched humour, which he feels has made him monstrous, when he is cut down before he can successfully hang himself. Still directing our attention during these and other actions are the three sets

[6] Critics differ radically on the success of such scenes within scenes and groups commenting on each other. R. Knoll, *Ben Jonson's Plays* (1964), p. 47, thinks them unsuccessful; W. Armstrong, 'Ben Jonson and Jacobean Stagecraft', *Stratford-upon-Avon Studies* 1: *Jacobean Theatre* (1960), pp. 54-5, finds them resourceful.

of commentators, placed in various points of view: Buffone fully within the action, Macilente on the edge of it, Cordatus and Mitis completely outside it.

Technically, one of Jonson's problems must have been that of retaining dramatic movement in a play whose plot has almost completely given up a story which rushes forward into its own future. He solves this problem in several ways. He initiates new conflicts, such as that between Deliro, the husband besotted on his wife, Fallace, and Fastidious Brisk, the courtier whom Fallace dotes on. He shows the established jibers still jibing when the action moves into the court. He brings in new courtly affectations—for example, the 'complements' by which Sogliardo and Shift address each other. He even shows Macilente in a temporarily more sociable humour, and suggests that, since envy lives on what it feeds on, it would die if society itself were better. A subtler dramatic movement comes from the increasingly harsher world of abrasive vanities and stabbing egos that the scenes create. Macilente's humour proves only briefly more sociable, his envy and malice storing up to break out first in his poisoning of Puntarvolo's dog, then in his ecstatic feeding on the discomfiture of others. Buffone, another eater, thinks man an even more nourishing food for man than pork is, but settles for pork because pig is closest of all animals to man's nature. Exposure follows exposure in a crescendo of exploded humours— Saviolina revealed as a bad judge of gentlemen, Shift exposed as a coward, Buffone silenced only by having his mouth sealed by the enraged Puntarvolo, Fastidious Brisk put in a debtor's prison where Fallace's visit to him drives Deliro out of his doting humour. Macilente, having no one to envy in a society shown to be empty of merit, is finally at peace, like the others, out of his humour. Perhaps here, in this reciprocal scourging of the humours, we can see the first intuition of what later came to be Jonson's recurrent comic pattern: monstrous behaviour, whether affected for reasons of vanity or adopted for reasons of hypocrisy, blows itself up. 'Mischiefes feed / Like beasts, till they be fat, and then they bleed'. But the feeding and the self-destruction come only in a society whose harmony depends on putting people out of the humours which its life as a society of contending egos inevitably creates and intensifies. Since affected humours endlessly arise in human society, they need constantly to be scourged by courageous satirists like Asper, and their scourging must be understood by judicious auditors—such auditors as Jonson hoped were in the audience for this extraordinary play.

Q

Cynthia's Revels (1600) gives one a sense more of a dramatist luxuriating in newly won power than of one exploring new worlds. Indeed,
after *Every Man Out*'s daring experiments in structure and perspective,
it seems more a pause than a step forward. True, Jonson moves more
confidently—some would say presumptuously—into the court which
he had ventured into more humbly in *Every Man Out*. (To say that he
presumes to dramatise even the Queen seems to me wrong; Cynthia is
the idea of queenliness, not Queen Elizabeth, however much Elizabeth
wanted to confuse the two.) And in this world of the court, which,
city-bred and only twenty-seven years old, he could scarcely claim to
know with the intimacy that his satire might suggest, Jonson moves
with an assurance that could only irritate both those who were unmistakably in the court and those who were unmistakably not in, but
wanted to be. Jonson's answer—and it is a good one—might have been
that he is writing a play, not a report, and that plays imitate nature, not
'reality'. True, again, he explores this world in a style new to his work:
that of mythological allegory derived in part from the plays of Lyly.

Still, the real charge against *Cynthia's Revels* is not that its author is
presumptuous or its method derivative. The real charge is that the play
is dull, boring, ponderous, tedious, undramatic, incoherent, formless—
to sample a few of the opinions. Even the usually sympathetic Herford
came to the summary conclusion that 'satire, moralising, and allegory
entirely overpower and extinguish dramatic action' (i. 397). Let me
admit that no play of Jonson's taxes a reader's patience so heavily as
this one. But, to say something obvious, let me add that a dramatist
can be judged only on the basis of a performance of his work, either
actual or vividly imagined. No one would conclude that an early
symphony of Haydn was tedious simply by looking at its score, yet
thousands judge the early Jonson or the late Aristophanes tedious because he is 'unreadable'.

The Induction begins in a lively manner: three of the boy actors
struggle for the right to speak the prologue, and one of those who lose
this privilege tells the argument of the play to get revenge on the playwright. Once again we see Jonson moving his auditors gradually into
a complex action, and here even exposing the whole argument so that
they can then watch the action unroll in detachment. In this Induction,
too, we find Jonson continuing to school his audience. That he explicitly and repeatedly calls them 'auditors' or 'auditorie' reveals his
emphasis: they come to hear a play, and not merely to see it; they come

to hear and not be heard. Here as before Jonson is deliberately trying to create his own audience, apparently not feeling the fullest confidence in the gentlemen at Blackfriars. The qualities he wants them to have are succinctly expressed in the Prologue which one of the boys finally speaks:

> If gracious silence, sweet attention,
> Quicke sight, and quicker apprehension,
> (The lights of judgements throne) shine any where;
> Our doubtfull authour hopes this is their sphere.

Silence, attention, and quick apprehension are certainly required if one is to see and remember the design of this play that develops so slowly and so elaborately. Three commentators, Cupid, Mercury, and Crites, are worked into the action more conventionally (and less interestingly in terms of perspective) than the commentators in *Every Man Out*. The double title—*Cynthia's Revels or the Fountain of Self Love*—suggests the double focus of the play. The relation between the fountain, which we see in the first Act, and the two courts, one ideal, the other actual, which we see in the later Acts, only gradually becomes clear: self-love produces the defective court which the image of Cynthia and her ideal court burns away. The dedication of the play in the Folio —'To the Speciall Fountaine of Manners, the Court'—distinguishes the two courts and relates self-love to the corruption of the actual court. The fundamental connection between the fountain of self-love and the egotistic action of the characters appears most sharply in IV. v where, just after the water from the fountain is brought in, Amorphus, Hedon, and Asotus demonstrate different aspects of the same self-love.

The clear design of the action appears both in the repetitive scenic pattern and in the characterisation. Each of the first four Acts involves three related groups: the self-lovers; the divine pages, Cupid and Mercury who hit them off (Cupid naturally satirising the women; Mercury the men); and the mature castigator of fools, Crites, with some occasional help from Arete, his feminine counterpart. In these Acts Jonson demonstrates the ease with which he can handle large groups of characters by the simple device of pairing them: Hedon the voluptuous and Anaides the impudent; Amorphus the deformed and Asotus the prodigal; or to change the standards, Asotus the citizen's heir and Anaides the country boy newly come to town. Furthermore, each gallant is given a mistress and an attendant, both of whom emphasise something about him. These various pairings are done for ethical reasons as part of the allegory and for linguistic and vocal reasons as part of the orchestration of modes and discourse, kinds of diction, and 'voices' (see Barish, pp. 113-21). This pairing is given another twist in the final masque when the light ladies and the fops disguise themselves by assuming 'the most neighboring vertues as their masking habites' (Ind., 101-2). So clear a design is a clear gain, though it may have been bought at a certain price. For instance, the characterisation repeats *Every Man Out*, but less intensely: Crites and Asper; Amorphus and Puntarvolo; Asotus and Fungoso; Hedon and Fastidious Brisk; Anaides and Carlo Buffone. Then, too, as Barish points out (p. 116), the voices of these feather-weights, except for that of Amorphus, are not sufficiently distinguished.

Jonson's growing control over the form of his play may come from his growing awareness of his aim. Though the aim itself may not have much changed since his writing of *Every Man Out*, it is expressed more precisely than before and from more than one point of view. We must infer it, of course, from the speeches of the derisive and judicial characters. Crites ends his first long soliloquy with a justification of his censorious attitude: 'While fools are pittied, they waxe fat, and proud' (I. v. 65). Mercury later expresses a similar attitude when he asks Crites 'to inflict just paines / On their prodigious follies'. Their purpose should be to 'correct' and 'punish' with laughter the follies of men who fall beneath the dignity of man (V. i. 10-22). Then, when Cynthia discovers that the masquers who have assumed the rôles of the virgins of Perfection and of the sons of Eutaxia are really the butterflies who flit around the court, she pictures them as 'impostumes' which grow in the palace and declares, 'We must lance these sores / Or all will putrifie' (V. xi. 67). By this final scene Crites himself has arrived at a view of folly which does not at first seem to agree with any of their previous statements. He now recognises what might be called the peripety of vice:

> But there's not one of these who are unpain'd,
> Or by themselves unpunished: for vice
> Is like a furie to the vicious minde,
> And turnes delight it selfe to punishment.

A similar awareness of how self-destructive vice is appears, as I have said, in *Every Man Out* and was to reappear in the Apologetical Dialogue spoken at the end of *Poetaster*. These two apparently disparate views—the one that vice must be actively castigated and the other that it defeats itself—can be reconciled if one remembers that Jonson always pictured man in a society. The vicious person punishes himself and turns delight itself to punishment because he lives in a society whose other members ridicule or censure foolish or immoral behaviour. Hell, Jonson saw long before Sartre—though not quite in the Sartrean way— is other people. A satirist lives to be the sinner's Hell.

Cynthia's Revels marks a road down which Jonson was to move only in the masques—the road of mythological allegory with a burlesque antimasque. In it the antimasque so completely takes over the play that not even a long-winded Cynthia can quite blow it away. A more just, though less comic equipoise between virtue and vice, sense and folly, is kept in the masque that more pleasingly covers the same ethical ground—*The Masque of Queens* (1609). In this masque 'True Fame bred out of Virtue' is heroically celebrated. In the *Revels* notoriety bred out of folly is mock-heroically satirised. The masque seems much the more enjoyable because in it Jonson called on the arts of music, dance, costuming, and scenery more imaginatively than he called on them in *Cynthia's Revels*, where he relies too much on satirical castigation of word games, a little of which can go a long way.

With *Poetaster* (1601) we reach that point in Jonson's development about which an enormous amount of historical criticism has been gathered: that is, his part in the war of the theatres.[7] Too often Jonson has suffered that disengagement of his ideas from his art, of his characters from the plot they move in, and even of his plays from the theatre they were written for which seems particularly to plague Elizabethan dramatists. Thus the characters of *Poetaster* are extracted from the seamless fabric of the plot where they live the only lives they can be said to live and are absolutely identified with Londoners who were known to have had actual existence. When one sees a play being so racked, one feels one's self sinking dismally into the platitudinous preacher who lurks not far below the surface of most of us: the preacher who says patiently, 'But a play is only a play, not a transcript of life. And a character is a set of conventional signs, not a human being. And a dramatist cannot really be identified with any of his characters, not even

[7] Brief treatments of this war can be found in Ellis-Fermor, *The Jacobean Drama*, App. I, and M. C. Bradbrook, *The Growth and Structure of English Comedy* (1955), chap. 7.

when he claims to be talking about himself. And the meaning of a play is the play itself, and not some reduction of it.' Such preaching is all so dreary, and perhaps no longer necessary now that we can distinguish the 'voices' created by the poet from the poet himself. In the past, especially with Fleay and Penniman, too much time was misspent trying to decide whom Jonson, Dekker, and Marston meant by the characters in *Poetaster*, *Satiromastix*, and *What You Will*. Some weight should be placed on the personal references in these plays—some, but not much. A play is never simply what its creator intended it to be. The objective form of *Poetaster* makes Horace only Horace and not Jonson even if Jonson meant Horace as an idealised portrait of himself. Surely A. King is right when he claims that Crispinus is the type of a poetaster, and not a lampoon of Marston, though a number of details are drawn from Marston's work as a dramatist.[8] The dramatic form changes what would have been, in conversation, a personal attack into an aesthetic and, thereby, impersonal structure.

If one persists in seeing these plays as parts of a quarrel, the quarrel itself may be seen as another example of late sixteenth century flyting rather than the desperately serious 'war' it is usually described as having been. For its participants flyting had a number of obvious virtues: it was a way of gaining an audience since everyone loves a good fight, a way of getting rid of one's spleen since everyone has spleen, a way of finding and exercising one's style, and, above all, a way of making a name for one's self—all at the same time that one got paid for it. Though I do not want to argue that the tradition of flyting completely explains the quarrel, flyting can account for much of it that seems purely personal.[9]

Concentrating on *Poetaster* simply as an offensive in the war of the theatre usually obscures its real merit as a play. In it one can see the hand of the dramatist who, within two years, was to write *Sejanus* and within four, *Volpone*. The action opens authoritatively with the Gorgon-like figure of Envy arising out of the centre of the stage, as out of Hell, saluting the light that she wishes were darkness and wishing, vainly, to blast the pleasure of the audience by misinterpreting the meaning of the author. Receiving no help from the actors and 'poetapes' she calls on, she begins to sink. Then an armed Prologue appears

---

[8] King, pp. 59–60. See also p. 2, n. 8 and xxii–xxiii.

[9] G. Hibbard discusses both flyting and Nashe's influence on the early Jonson in *Thomas Nashe* (1962), pp. 75–6, 180.

to tread her malice down into the earth and to declare that the poet, who knows the strength of his own muse, seeks a mean between base dejection and the vanity of arrogance. Having thus focused our attention and marked out the emotional range the play is to move in, Jonson distances the whole subject by finding in Augustan Rome an ideal type for the endless struggle between knowledge and ignorance, culture and barbarism, poet and poetaster: Crispinus, the versifier who challenged Horace to see which one of them could write faster, becomes the type of a poetaster, and Horace, the type of the poet. In the mature style he had been gradually evolving Jonson arranges around this central contrast a series of motifs and characters which supply different perspectives on it. The action opens 'off-centre' in the study of the first of several poets we meet—Ovid, a minor but genuine poet —and reveals that like Horace later, he has to face two persistent problems: the envy of poetasters and the criticism of practical people. To show that, as he says in the Apologetical Dialogue, even the 'great master-spirits' of the Augustan Age 'When wit, and artes were at their height in Rome' had detractors, Jonson had Ovid speak an elegy in which the mortality of envy is contrasted with the eternal fame of true worth. The other problem—what practical people think of poets who muse and dream their time away while others get on in the world— is represented by a conflict that the gentlemen of the Inns of Court must have found especially pertinent: Ovid Senior reviles his son, who he thought was studying the law, as 'Ovid the play-maker'. When Ovid denies having written a play, he is cursed for having written a poem. Joining in this criticism of the life of a poet is Captain Tucca, who complicates the whole comic perspective of the scene by cursing everything—poetry, the law, and life. Ovid draws together both of these problems by praising 'sacred poesie' in a soliloquy whose idealistic fervour and poetic power have rarely been properly acknowledged.

Act II, still off-centre, offers another view of the society in which the poet lives, the relevance of which is made clear only in the last Act. We see the fashionable group of the court gathering at the home of a citizen, Albius, to carry on its love affairs in privacy. Here we first meet Crispinus, the poetaster, whose chief design seems to be to seduce Albius' pretentious wife, Chloe, with the help of a poet's gown. In Act III poet and poetaster are brought together in a fine comic scene in which Crispinus tortures Horace by prattling on about verse. Also introduced as foils to Horace are a player, Histrio, and Demetrius, a 'dresser' of plays who has been hired by the players to abuse Horace. Abusing them all is Tucca, whose pungent, colloquial style authenticates and tests the whole scene. Rare is the scene in any subsequent play of Jonson which is not tested by one or more Tuccas.

The final two Acts place in ironic contrast a number of the motifs already introduced: the home of Albius and the court of Caesar Augustus; the trifling careers of poetasters and the grave lives of real poets like Virgil and Horace; the empty adulation of a Chloe ('what a prettie foolish thing it is to be a *poet!*') and the weighty judgement of a Caesar who considers poetry 'the most abstract, and perfect' of faculties 'if shee bee / True borne, and nurst with all the sciences' (V. i. 17–20). Three scenes in particular make clear how great Jonson's power had come to be. In one of them, the banquet of the gods (IV. v.), we hear Jonson, later to prove one of England's greatest mock-heroic poets, mingle tones and levels of discourse which, now lightly, now heavily, jostle against each other. The domestic wrangling on Mount Olympus achieves the double movement of burlesque: Roman aristocrats pretend to be gods and goddesses, and celestial affairs are rendered in colloquial language. The trivial is inflated, and the great are demeaned. A lover's quarrel between Ovid and Julia appears as a contention between Jupiter and Juno; and Juno addresses Jupiter as 'King cuckold-maker'. Since the masquers are aware of this double incongruity, they act, too, as witty commentators on the scene they are the chief participants in.[10]

The second of these scenes comes after Caesar, breaking in on what he judges to be an impious travesty of the gods, separates the lovers by exiling Ovid. (Even the best of kings, we see, can go so far wrong as to banish a poet for harmless fun.) Ovid and Julia bid good-bye in a love scene which Gifford dismissed, wrongly, I think, as 'ridiculous'. Since it follows directly after Ovid's soliloquy praising the court of Augustus as the abstract of all Rome's virtue and a sacred sphere in whose circle the chief end of life is circumscribed, and praising Julia as the abstract of the court, it must be meant as a rendering of an heroic love in an heroic style, the kind of scene that Jonson later rendered straightforwardly only in his masques. It prepares us, by the tone it establishes and the heroic style it exemplifies, for the final Act. There the ideal court is revealed in its ideal action—praising knowledge and

10 E. Talbert, 'The Purpose and Technique of Jonson's *Poetaster*', *Studies in Philology* (1945); this whole essay is one of the best on the play.

poetry, elevating the type of heroic poet, Virgil, to the chair of the Emperor, condemning the player who misinterpreted Horace's poetry, indicting, trying, judging, and punishing the poetaster and the play dresser both for their artistic sins and their envious maligning of the true poet. Few scenes reveal more emblematically Jonson's conception of the poet and of the audience the true poet deserves.

One last proof of Jonson's maturing power in *Poetaster*, and perhaps its most convincing one, is its mastery of dramatic speech. More clearly than any previous play, except possibly *Every Man Out*, it demonstrates not only that Jonson had an extraordinarily sensitive ear for the texture and the rhythms, the norms and the distortions of human speech, but also that he could use this sensitivity to speech imaginatively to suit the words of his characters to their part in the action of the play. Excellent stylistic studies which best reveal this mastery in *Poetaster* have been written by A. King and J. Barish. After marshalling convincing evidence, King concludes that, in what he considers the most linguistically varied of all Jonson plays, pedantic expressions are ridiculed for their inkhornism or Latinity, courtly expressions for their fashionable affectation, and new figurative expressions for their neologistic indecorum. He sees the satire on Crispinus as no mere episode in the stage quarrel, but as 'one of the important steps toward the establishment of standard literary English' (pp. 60-2, 216-18). Barish, whose studies of the language of all these early plays are rewarding, analyses with especially fine insight the speech of Tucca, whom he considers, as King does, the greatest characterisation in Jonson's early period (pp. 121-30).

*　*　*

Jonson notes in his *Discoveries* that of all the poets the comic comes nearest to the orator because

> in moving the minds of men, and stirring of affections (in which Oratory shewes, and especially approves her eminence) hee chiefly excells. What figure of a Body was *Lysippus* ever able to forme with his Graver, or *Apelles* to paint with his Pencill, as the Comedy to life expresseth so many, and various affections of the minde? There shall the Spectator see some, insulting with Joy; others, fretting with Melancholy; raging with Anger; mad with Love; boiling with Avarice; undone with Riot; tortur'd with expectation; consum'd with feare: no perturbation in common life, but the Orator findes an example of it in the Scene. (viii. 640)

Here the mature critic reveals what the mature dramatist seems to have discovered by his own practice. One could wish that the critic had not slipped quite so simply from the 'affections of the minde' which are expressed by the characters in the plot ('raging with Anger; mad with Love') to the emotions which are aroused in the spectator, whose minds are moved, and whose affections are stirred. Still, the passage makes clear that Jonson, like most Renaissance critics, emphasised the extraordinary emotional power of comedy, from which grow its ethical and educative powers.

This passage emphasises two principles which we have seen him working out almost from the beginning of his career. One is that comedy represents perturbations or agitations which upset the desired harmony of life. The examples he gives—raging, mad, boiling, tortured—illustrate the extravagant emotions which an imbalance of humours creates. Second, though he claims that the comic plot renders all the perturbations of common life, he emphasises here, and usually exemplifies in his plays, the harsh emotions whose excesses can only be derided rather than the gentle ones whose excesses are often admired. Very early Jonson gave up trying to induce, or at least exhibit, certain emotions, partly, perhaps, because he realised that Shakespeare could arouse them more skilfully, but mostly because they could have no place in the comedy that he thought should be written: such emotions as pity, longing, romantic love, idealisation, parental tenderness, filial devotion, benignity, mercy. Certainly a great deal to give up. But consider what he did with the emotional states he did try to render: mockery, quarrelsomeness, reproach, envy, anger, scorn, menace, desire for power and prestige, anticipation of triumph over others, glorying in the defeat of enemies. A comic poet stirs up 'gentle affections', as he says in the Dedicatory Epistle to the Universities for *Volpone* (l. 123), but only by deriding the harsh emotions whose excesses prevent the stirring up of the gentle ones.

Conceiving of comedy as derisive, not comforting, and as bracing, not relaxing, he gradually created out of what T. S. Eliot called his 'large and unique view of life' a special comic world which ironically caricatures much of the real world. Early in his creative life he discovered the principles governing this comic world:

1. Few men are judicious; most are foolish. The foolish are of two sorts—the impostors and the gulls.

2. Most men are in disguise.

3. Most men desire ridiculously to become something they are not and try futilely to transform themselves or lift themselves to a scale of being other than the one their natures placed them in.

4. Life is inevitably ridiculous, being so full of imposture and folly.

5. Vice and folly are their own worst enemies, the evil and the foolish defeating themselves, the one by their own over-reaching, the other by their imperviousness to experience. Good men could therefore take joy in the radical, if sometimes well-masked, health of human society.

Since humours arise from man's foolish affectation of another self and since perhaps, as Barish argues (pp. 217–18), vapours represent perversity inseparable from flesh and blood, the function of the comic artist is periodically to purge the humours or to blow away the vapours which incessantly gather in society.

The plots that Jonson invented to represent such a comic world normally do not emphasise the cause-and-effect relationships common to the naturalistic drama since Ibsen. Nor are they, except for *The Case is Altered* and, to some extent, *Every Man In*, similar to the highly stylised pattern of motivated actions and psychologically true relationships characteristic of Shakespeare. From *Every Man out of His Humour* on, Jonson spent most of his dramatic life working out variations on a plot which had as its 'core' or 'thread' a relatively simple, coherent story. For example: a morose hater of noise marries to disinherit a hated nephew, but the nephew outwits him. Around this thread he arranged characters, episodes, and recurrent motifs which are connected to it and to each other not necessarily according to human motivation (though Jonson freely drew on such motivation when he wanted to), but primarily according to the total design of the play. Nothing in a Jonson play, as A. Sale says, 'has any reality *apart from its position in the play*'.[11] As the play evolves, its design, though composed of many parts, 'beginnes to be one, as these parts grow, or are wrought together' (viii. 647). And as it gathers its unity, it gathers its power to move the mind and stir the affections. Thus, in *Epicoene*, the derisive exposure of Daw and La Foole is not logically connected to the story

[11] *Every Man in His Humour*, ed. A. Sale (1949), xii. Sale's whole discussion of 'pattern' is penetrating.

of Morose and Dauphine; the two are connected to each other and to other incidents as parts of a series of baitings, exposures, and ironic reversals, the sum of which comprises the plot. Such an artificial design might best be described in the musical terms that E. E. Stoll used some years ago—theme and variations, repetition of motifs, inversion, and transposition.[12] (Analogies are dangerous, I know, but only if one thinks they offer literal truth rather than correspondences.) Any of Jonson's comedies after *Every Man In* creates its effect by balances, contrasts, and combinations of episodes, characters, and motifs, as a musical work balances, contrasts, and contrapuntally combines voices, phrases, and melodic lines.

By 1602, then, after a scant half dozen years of deliberate and self-conscious development, Jonson appeared ready for the mature work of his career. He had early determined that, as he later phrased it, he was to '*raise the despis'd head of poetrie again . . . and restore her to her primitive habit, feature, and majesty*' (v. 21). Assuming the civilising rôle of a seventeenth-century Matthew Arnold, he had tried, not very successfully, to form an audience for the plays he was writing. He had come to the first intuitions of the dramatic structure he was later to vary so richly, and had searched out the cast of characters who gathered vivacity, as Herford points out (i. 439), as he retraced them. He had gained an early mastery of two kinds: one over the modes of dramatic speech which individualises and vivifies its speaker; the other over the resources of various Elizabethan stages, public and private. After 1602, moving with his customary deliberateness, he turned to tragedy and wrote *Sejanus* (at first with a collaborator, then, in 1605, alone), and next began to produce those royal entertainments and masques which consumed so much of his mature energy. Then, after having slowly gathered his powers, he finally wrote *Volpone* in 1606. Not even in *Volpone* did he quite find the precise English focus that he found in his later plays and in the Folio *Every Man in His Humour*: London for a setting, and, for a cast of characters, the full English social scale below the peerage (the peerage itself being a main source for the characters of his masques). Only in *Volpone*, and not fully before, did he create the highly allusive speech by which he could bring in metaphorically the perspectives he had brought in by choral commentators in his earlier plays.

[12] *Poets and Playwrights* (1933), p. 149.

Index

[This index excludes information, systematically arranged for reference purposes, given in the notes before each chapter]

245